MW00345797

So You Want to Work in Sports

So You Want to Work in Sports

Advice and Insights from Respected Sports Industry Leaders

K. P. WEE

ROWMAN & LITTLEFIELD
Lanham • Boulder • New York • London

Published by Rowman & Littlefield
An imprint of The Rowman & Littlefield Publishing Group, Inc.
4501 Forbes Boulevard, Suite 200, Lanham, Maryland 20706
www.rowman.com

86-90 Paul Street, London EC2A 4NE, United Kingdom

Copyright © 2022 by The Rowman & Littlefield Publishing Group, Inc.

All rights reserved. No part of this book may be reproduced in any form or by
any electronic or mechanical means, including information storage and retrieval
systems, without written permission from the publisher, except by a reviewer who
may quote passages in a review.

British Library Cataloguing in Publication Information Available

Library of Congress Cataloging-in-Publication Data

Names: Wee, K. P., 1977– author.
Title: So you want to work in sports : advice and insights from respected
    sports industry leaders / K. P. Wee.
Description: Lanham, MD : Rowman & Littlefield, [2022] | Includes
    bibliographical references and index. | Summary: "In this book,
    such industry-leading sports professionals as Ted Sobel, Fred Claire,
    Ari Kaplan, Debbie Antonelli, and Ann Meyers Drysdale offer practical
    advice and tips for those wanting to pursue a career in sports,
    including marketing, publicity, broadcasting, journalism, management,
    scouting, analytics, and more"—Provided by publisher.
Identifiers: LCCN 2022002849 (print) | LCCN 2022002850 (ebook) | ISBN
    9781538153192 (cloth) | ISBN 9781538153208 (epub)
Subjects: LCSH: Sports—Vocational guidance. | Sports
    administration—Vocational guidance.
Classification: LCC GV734.3 .W42 2022 (print) | LCC GV734.3 (ebook) | DDC
    796.02/3—dc23
LC record available at https://lccn.loc.gov/2022002849
LC ebook record available at https://lccn.loc.gov/2022002850

For Nahyun, my muse

Contents

Foreword

I first connected with K. P. Wee when he was writing a book about former pitcher Tom Candiotti, who I had signed as a free agent during my days as the general manager of the Los Angeles Dodgers. The book on Candiotti was aptly titled *Tom Candiotti: A Life of Knuckleballs*, covering the career of a pitcher who threw an unusual and unpredictable pitch.

In retrospect, K. P.'s successful career as an author and sports media personality has taken its own unusual and unpredictable path. Candiotti discovered the knuckleball pitch because he wanted to stay in the game he loved. K. P. discovered writing because he wanted to follow his passion for sports.

After the Candiotti book, my connection with K. P. drew stronger as I saw his passion and dedication. Our connection and friendship led to K. P.'s book *The 1988 Dodgers: Reliving the Championship Season*. This book features many of the players who were a key part of a championship but were not always in the headlines.

The passion and determination of K. P. is evident in everything he does, and in *So You Want to Work in Sports*, K. P. connects with an all-star cast of sports professionals who followed their passion to find a place in the sporting world.

There are several books that come from the academic world that cover the subject of the business of sports, but what elevates K. P.'s work is that this book provides real-life stories of careers and insights that are both informative and inspirational. K. P. connects with not only well-known personalities in the sports business world, but also those who have found great satisfaction and success in roles outside of the limelight.

Almost every area of the sports business world is covered here with personal insights and guidelines for achieving goals. K. P. covers a wide range of personalities, from team owners to agents, photographers to famous sports personalities, and minor-league operators to major stadium managers. The wide world of the business of sports can be found here.

K. P. comes from the academic world as a self-motivated, dedicated, and accomplished educator with experience working with students to achieve their goals and ambitions. As both a writer and educator, K. P. opens the door to learning about the business world of sports, and he does so with his typical passion and dedication to students.

Fred Claire
Former Los Angeles Dodgers executive VP and general manager

Introduction

Imagine having some of the most experienced sports industry leaders in the same room sharing tips and advice with people interested in sports jobs or looking to further their sports careers. In one corner of the room, you are talking to a radio sportscaster who has been in the business for decades and is willing to answer every question you have about breaking into sports radio. Next to him are several play-by-play broadcasters who have called games in multiple sports willing to share tips about the world of announcing with you. Perhaps you're into sports management. Well, move along further and you'll get a chance to pick the brain of a sports executive who has worked for franchises in all the major professional sports. You can talk to a highly respected basketball executive about running a franchise and about broadcasting in hoops. Walk along to another part of the room and you'll find a pair of league presidents in baseball who are eager to share their words of wisdom with you. Then, there is also a co-owner of a Major League Baseball franchise waiting to field your questions. The CEO of the Rose Bowl is there to answer your questions. A sports photographer is eager to share his thoughts with you, as is a sportswriter who covers baseball for a living. As if that's not enough, there are individuals with experience and background in analytics, digital media, sports agency, scouting, international sports, and other areas in the sports business, all willing to guide you and answer your questions.

That, in a nutshell, is what this book contains: insights from those who know what it takes to not only break into, but also succeed in the sports industry, ready to answer the questions you might have about a career in sports.

Sit back, go through the pages, and learn from these sports industry leaders. Put the ideas most relevant to you to use, follow some of the tips provided, and land that dream job in sports that you have always wanted.

Instructor's Note

This book has been written to be a valuable reference book for aspiring sports professionals and an engaging read for anybody interested in listening to insiders within the sports industry discuss how they do what they do in the competitive world of sports. If you are an instructor in secondary and higher education, you will find much in the pages of *So You Want to Work in Sports* to help you prepare for your courses. With insights from sports industry leaders from different fields—whether it is broadcasting, journalism, marketing, management, ownership, analytics, or many others—this book can be used by readers for a variety of purposes and the perspectives and advice provided are intended to help readers on their way to an exciting and successful career in sports.

Acknowledgments

I would like to thank everyone who agreed to be interviewed for this book. First and foremost, I want to thank Fred Claire, former general manager of the Los Angeles Dodgers, for giving me the idea to write *So You Want to Work in Sports*, with the goal of helping students and others interested in working in the sports industry. As an educator and instructor, I found a great sense of satisfaction in completing the interviews and compiling the valuable insights for this book so that those aspiring to work in sports can benefit from the advice and words of wisdom provided by these sports industry leaders—and actually put those ideas to use and someday achieve their goals. So, thank you, Fred, for encouraging the project. Thanks also to the team at the *Life in the Front Office* podcast for allowing some content from their shows to be used. My thanks, too, to sportscaster Alex Feuz for his help with one of the interviews.

Thank you Chris King, Barry Turbow, J. P. Hoornstra, Steve Granado, Neil Stratton, Ted Sobel, Marsha Collier, Ben Hwang, Jeff Pearlman, Ronald Shapiro, Richard Kee, Andy Dolich, Ari Kaplan, and Pat Gallagher, in particular, for taking the time to grant additional interviews or providing follow-ups.

Some friends provided encouragement and pep talks throughout this process, and I would like to single out Rick Tanton and Rick Ambrozic, in particular. Thanks also to fellow educators Roger Chong and Stan Markotich. Thank you for your friendship.

I

BROADCASTING/ PLAY-BY-PLAY

1

WNBA and College Basketball Play-by-Play

Debbie Antonelli, ESPN College Basketball Analyst

Job title: College basketball and WNBA analyst, ESPN

Education/training: Master's degree in sports administration (Ohio University); college basketball playing career

Key pieces of advice: For young women pursuing a career in the sports business industry—no job is too big or small. Don't assume anything. Ask questions and work your way up the ladder. For players dealing with media and other types of interviews—body language. Brag on a teammate. No BS in your social media. Branding.

Debbie Antonelli, who covers games for ESPN and CBS Sports Network, is a national basketball analyst averaging eighty college games per season. With more than thirty years in sports broadcasting—which includes her work as a WNBA broadcaster since the league's inception in 1996—she's considered an expert on women's basketball at both the collegiate and professional levels.

Named one of the top one hundred most influential figures in women's basketball in the summer of 2020 for her contributions to the sport, Antonelli discussed her career on the mic—including how she prepares for her broadcasts and the four Bs she recommends for interviews of any kind—and offered insights gleaned from her years on the road covering women's sports.

Antonelli, who played forward at North Carolina State University for coach Kay Yow, could've taken different paths within the sports realm. She was on track to become an athletic director and also received offers to coach. But she ultimately took the broadcasting path. "I played for Kay Yow at NC State," said Antonelli. "She's a Naismith [Memorial] Basketball Hall of Famer. I had an incredible relationship with my coach as a middle schooler to a camper to being recruited and playing for her. Then, of course, my career as a broadcaster—she had an influence on all those areas. I got my master's degree [in sports administration] at Ohio University. I left there to fulfill an internship at Kentucky. So I got the chance to work at the University of Kentucky as the director of marketing, where I learned about how to help market and promote the greatest brand in basketball, arguably—Kentucky men's hoops. Then I worked at Ohio State University as well, working with Ohio State football. So I learned a lot about marketing and branding and licensing and all those things in the eight years that I was working in college athletics.

"And in the process of working in college athletics, I had—and still have—a love affair with the game. I love playing. I love talking the game. And I had the chance to work some games on television and radio. When I did that, I felt like those were really fun. It kept me in the game. It kept me preparing for broadcasting games, very similar to the way a coach would approach a game. It just worked out that I got very fortunate to get in the right situation at the right time, back when, on the women's side, there weren't many games at all on TV. So I feel like I'm one of those chapters from Malcolm Gladwell's book *Outliers*, where you get lucky, get your start, and put your ten thousand hours in, and here I am, sitting at my home in Mount Pleasant, South Carolina, getting ready to call a WNBA game. Because of COVID and the changes in our industry, I've been calling games from home in my in-home studio, and it's pretty cool."

Like an athlete or a coach, Antonelli does a large amount of preparation to be successful. As a basketball analyst, preparation adds insight, perspective, and value to a broadcast. "I love to watch film, and so I like to not just watch a game but try to break it down," she said of her preparation routine. "Hit the pause button. Look where help is coming from. Think about why a screen is set at a particular angle and a particular spot on the floor. I like to be a really strong student of the X's and O's part of it."

To give an example of her preparation for a broadcast, she discussed how she gets ready for a Las Vegas Aces–Dallas Wings WNBA contest, which was set to begin two hours after her conversation with me. "For my game today, for example, I've got Las Vegas playing against Dallas. Dallas has the top scorer in the league, a woman named Arike Ogunbowale, who has over 21 points a game. She's an MVP candidate in terms of her numbers, but Las Vegas is the number-one team right now. They have a player named A'ja Wilson, whom I watched play through college at the University of South Carolina. I watch film, I read game notes, and I have a resource called Synergy, where I can go dive in. [Synergy is a company that partners with the NBA, WNBA, NCAA, FIBA, and international pro basketball leagues and creates web-based, on-demand video-supported basketball analytics for the purposes of scouting, development, and entertainment.] So I dove in last night on some particular detail about those two players, trying to come up with a number or a nugget or something that would maybe describe how they score effectively or maybe a way you'd want to consider defending them. So watching film [is a big part of my preparation]. Because we're doing everything remotely and virtually, the WNBA provides all these Zoom calls with players and coaches, so I have access to them. I already know most of the coaches in the league, so I can call their cell phone and speak to them before the game. Reading game notes, taking down some stats, and then having a general understanding of some of the tendencies and some of the things that a team might like to run inside a game or in an offensive situation. I just study the game that way, and then I try to give the viewer something that they can watch for or something that they can learn from listening to me explain a player's story or a 'how' and a 'why' a coach decides to do something inside a game."

And although she's been in sports broadcasting for more than three decades, Antonelli still strives to improve her game each and every night out. "I think I'm constantly trying to work harder and work smarter," she related. "I've been doing this for thirty-three years, so I've had a long career in the business. I still have an incredible passion to be able to do it. But I'm not going into situations where I'm trying to prove something. I'm going into a situation where I'm trying to improve. That's what my attitude needs to be. I don't ever think that I'm smarter than any coach or player in the gym. I'm certainly not at practice every day. So I want to make sure that I'm providing a fair and balanced broadcast and that I'm having a lot of fun doing it. If I've done my homework and I'm really prepared, and I'm fair and balanced in the way I deliver a game—and if you've listened to me, you know I'm going to have fun because I really enjoy what I get to do—then I think I don't have to prove anything. I think I need to go in with the attitude to try to improve, and I try to do that in every situation inside the game."

Working in sports—particularly before COVID-19—means being on the road all the time. How does Antonelli, who's also raising three children, maintain a healthy work–life balance? The simple answer is that her family is supportive of her career, which allows her to be the best analyst she can be. "I sometimes refer to it as basketball deployment, with no disrespect to the military," she said, referring to life as a sports broadcaster. "But that's certainly the way it feels around here. I do have three boys. My husband is a terrific supporter of everything that I do. There is an incredible balance to having a career on the air and on the road, with three boys to raise. I've been a creature of habit, a lot of early morning flights to get to the next place, or the last flight out to get to the next place, especially if I'm coming from home. But my general preparation when I'm traveling and on the road is, I watch a lot of film on airplanes. I go to practices and shootarounds when I can. If I can get into the film room with a coach, I'm desperately trying to do that, just because I think listening to their vernacular and some of the concepts that they're trying to teach helps me do a better job of teaching those things on the air as well, and trying to share the story and the message of what they're trying to do with their team. But a lot of game notes, a lot of stats, a lot of film work. When I'm traveling, I'm in the gym. My life on the road is pretty much airport, gym, and hotel. And that's about it."

When she's not on the road and not with her family, Antonelli is busy mentoring young players aspiring to reach the pros. One of the things she preaches: the four Bs. "I tried to come up with something that would be easy and simple to help players in their media interviews, whether it's on camera or in a postgame situation," she said. "I thought, what would be the best way for me to try to help share a message about how to handle the media? What I ended up doing was turning it into, not just dealing with the media, but how to handle an interview when you get a job or how to handle that public speaking class, or give them some tools that will be easy for them to remember. So I came up with what I call the four Bs."

Antonelli's four Bs are as follows:

Body language: "We all know the cliché: 'You only get one chance to make a first impression.' People say that a lot, but it's so true. Your body language and how you approach a situation—What's your body language in the classroom? What's your body language in a media setting?—certainly dictates the tone in the viewers' eyes."

Brag on a teammate: "In a team sport, it's not about you. It's about the team. Even when you're not playing a sport, you're always going to be on a team, whether it's a team made up of your family or a team made up of your coworkers. So bragging on your teammate and thinking about the situation being bigger than yourself and how you go about constructing a conversation or how you handle certain questions in the media or job interview questions about bragging on teammates."

No BS in your social media: "I have a few rules that I lay out for them about their voice and what it can mean, and how it matters, so you don't have a bunch of BS."

Branding: "If you have good body language, if you brag on a teammate, if you're a good teammate, if you don't have any BS in your social media, you're setting yourself up for who you want to be. And you control that. You control the narrative for your brand. I also like to make that brand sound like team ego. What do you want people to see when they see your team play? What do they want to know about you? Are you guys going to be a team that always spreads back on defense? Or only a couple of players spread back on defense? Are you a team that communicates? Or are you a team that just goes through things halfway?"

Antonelli continued: "Those are my four Bs, and that's the short version of it. But I love delivering that to teams because I think it resonates with them. So if you're a player that might be nervous in a postgame situation and you're going to come over and do a postgame interview, if you think about the four Bs, it will help you answer the question."

As for advice for young women looking to work in the sports industry, Antonelli provided three tips: No job is too big or too small. Don't assume anything. Ask questions and work your way up the ladder. "Number one is, no job is too big or too small," she said. "No market is too big or too small. If you get an opportunity to find out about the business from the ground up, I think you need to learn it. It will definitely pay off later when you get into a higher-level position, about why all those jobs behind the camera, in my instance, are so important. There are two people that are in front of a broadcast, but you might see thirty people behind the broadcast that you never see or hear from. But we know as teammates that are in front of the camera that all thirty of those people matter as much as—or more than—you matter for what you say on the air.

"And I think you don't assume anything. If you really want to give it a try and you're interested in the business, then try to be intentional about finding out and asking questions and sticking your nose in and volunteering. Working your way up the ladder, if you will. Not everyone gets to start at ESPN. My first twenty-eight years of my career were without any security, as I did not have a full-time contract. I had contracts with lots of different networks but no minimum number of games that they were required to hire me for. That's not job security. It took me my first twenty-eight years to finally land that contract with ESPN, so it took a while. There were a lot of games that I did early on where I had to drive through the night. Or I didn't get paid very much to do. But I knew if I kept working hard enough that my work ethic, my preparation, and my passion for the game would eventually come through. Thankfully, thirty-three years into this, I still love what I get to do every day."

Finally, Antonelli offered up three words she lives by daily: Build. Serve. Empower. "Those are my three words that I use as my power words for all decisions in my life," she said. "As a mom with three boys, as a wife with a husband, as a person with a full-time career, and having responsibility as a stakeholder inside our game, I want to be somebody who builds. I want to be constructive with my time and with my words. I want to help. I want to make choices around, 'Is this something that's going to be constructive? Am I going to be a good builder around this idea or topic? Is it a good decision for my family?'

"'Serve' is a quality that my coach Kay Yow thought was the most important quality for a really good leader. When I asked her that one day, she said, 'Serve and leadership.' Although that was a long time ago, 'build' and 'serve' are two words that I think about every day. If I build and serve and I share my story, I think I'll empower others to do the same thing and empower others to come up with what their three words are. As we all know, not everything goes as planned. We all have adversity and obstacles and challenges in our lives. But I want to have the right attitude about attacking and going on offense about all of those situations that may arise. I think about 'build' and 'serve' and how I've been able to do something for someone else. And usually when I think about building and serving and doing something for someone else, I feel like I can get through whatever that adverse situation is because I know it won't last long."

An example of her applying "Build, serve, and empower" is her annual fundraiser for the Special Olympics. Antonelli and her son Frankie—who's a multisport, multi-gold-winning, Special Olympic athlete—have held a free-throw marathon event every year in May since 2019, and their efforts have helped raise more than $200,000 for the Special Olympics. For this event, she makes one hundred free throws at the top of each hour for twenty-four consecutive hours, meaning she will have scored twenty-four hundred free throws at the conclusion of an entire day in trying to raise funds for a worthy cause. (To learn more about this fundraiser, visit http://24hoursnbn.com/.)

2

Baseball Radio Play-by-Play

Jeff Levering, Sports Broadcaster

Job title: Radio play-by-play broadcaster, Milwaukee Brewers

Education/training: Degree in broadcast journalism (Chapman University)

Key piece of advice: Just keep showing up.

Milwaukee Brewers radio play-by-play broadcaster Jeff Levering, the 2020 recipient of the National Sports Media Association Wisconsin Sportscaster of the Year award, has learned from some of the best in the business.

Levering, who played Division III college baseball at Chapman University in Southern California, did public address announcing for different sports in college. Asked at what point he realized he wanted to do play-by-play, Levering had the following to say: "If you asked my old teammates when I was in high school or even in college, when I was sitting on the bench, they'd tell you that I was always doing play-by-play. If I was waiting for my turn to hit, I was always just kind of calling play-by-play. The public address was a great way for me to work on my enunciations and pronunciations of different names of people that would come in in different sports.

"But I didn't realize that the play-by-play was going to be my route until I actually did a game. That would've been my junior year of college, and it was a softball game that my multicamera video production class was putting on together. Nobody wanted to do play-by-play. Everybody wanted to stay in the [production] truck, and I said, 'Well, this is my opportunity to do it, see if this is something I want to do.' That was the game that really gave me the itch to continue it. I did the softball game, one basketball game, and one football game. That was it for my collegiate career in terms of play-by-play. I didn't do a full baseball game until the summer of 2006, which was a year and a half after I'd graduated. Someone needed me to fill in, I knew the right people at the right time, I did a game, and the rest is history."

After Levering's college career finished, he decided to go all in with pursuing a broadcasting career, starting as an intern at Fox Sports West and then scoring his first paid play-by-play gig with the Class A Advanced Rancho Cucamonga Quakes, a Minor League Baseball (MiLB) team in Southern California. He then spent two years as the radio voice and manager of public relations for the Double-A Springfield Cardinals in Springfield, Missouri, before landing the role of lead broadcaster for the Triple-A Pawtucket Red Sox. In 2015, he made his way to Milwaukee, where he took the role as the Brewers' third broadcaster, covering the road games that veteran play-by-play announcer Bob Uecker didn't make. Today, Levering is calling games on the Brewers Radio Network, now the number-two broadcaster behind Uecker. During the off-season, Levering calls college football on Fox and serves as a play-by-play announcer for college hoops on Fox Sports 1 and the Big Ten Network.

In terms of education, Levering advises aspiring broadcasters, "The journalism degree is a really, really important part. It doesn't have to be television broadcast journalism. But a communications degree. I'd say get a nice base in writing, so a lot of journalism and print writing would be very smart, and how to write copy for news or sports on television. I think those are very, very important things.

"In terms of play-by-play, there aren't a lot of classes—unless you go to Syracuse. Even Chapman didn't have a lot of actual play-by-play classes. It's just kind of, 'Okay, here's a microphone. Here's the sport. Go do it!' That's the best way to learn if you want to do play-by-play. If you're thinking about being more behind the desk and things of that nature, there are a lot of different classes you can do. Production level—different classes that are there, too. But for the kids that are just getting into it and are going to college, the biggest thing would be to hone your writing skills. Make sure you know how to be concise. And then try and put those things into play when you're actually on camera. That's the biggest part of any part of journalism. And making sure you have a strong base, too."

In terms of calling games on TV versus radio, Levering, like virtually any broadcaster you ask, said there's a big difference. "On the radio side, you're the artist," he said. "You're describing everything. You have to put everything on the canvas in describing what's happening on the field. If you're doing television play-by-play, you're just doing the edges. You're supplying a little bit of highlights here and there—because everybody sees what's happening on the canvas. You can use your eyes and see what's happening, and all you're doing is providing a little bit of extra. That's all you're doing on the television side—and making sure you're having good banter with your color commentator and making sure you get your sponsorship reads in there. In terms of the differences in styles of broadcasting, you are the eyes and the ears on a radio broadcast.

"And the way that Vin Scully used to teach it, you have your little egg timer and you flip it over, and when the sand is down, make sure you give the score and you give the inning. That way, if someone's driving in their car and they just happen to turn the game on, they know exactly what's happening. You give the score, and you flip the egg timer over again, and then you just move on. So you're always cognizant of making sure that you're catering to the people that just turned the game on. Maybe for the people who are there from the first inning until the ninth inning, they might get annoyed when you say the score too much. But, in my opinion, you can't say it enough because that's why people are listening. They want to know how we got there. You're giving the broad strokes of the painting. People don't know what's happening until you tell them. That's one of the beauties of the radio broadcast. You are the eyes. You are the ears. You are *the* descriptor of providing that game. You can be so creative.

"You could do that without even talking, too. When in [postpandemic] times where there are fans at the ballpark, fans in the arena, or fans in the stadium, where when you don't talk and the crowd talks for you, that says a lot more than anything you could ever say—and that's a really important lesson that I learned a long time ago. Sometimes, saying nothing is saying way, way, way more than you need to. And that's a beautiful thing, letting the game breathe. And you can let the game breathe a lot more on the television side than you can on the radio side. But by saying nothing sometimes, you say a lot. I appreciate the creativity of the radio side a little bit more than on the television side. Both are outstanding mediums, but two totally different styles."

In terms of calling a game for the Brewers—the team that pays him—versus calling a game for a national audience, Levering said of course he caters to the home team on the Milwaukee broadcasts. "I'm on salary from the Brewers," he said. "So, I'm always going to slant my broadcast out toward the Brewers. When you're embedded with the team and you're traveling with that team, and you know those players inside and out because you're on the planes, you're on the buses, you get to know these guys more than you'd think, you're obviously going to slant your broadcasts that way. And I'm fine with being a homer. And there's a difference between just bashing the other team and just really being positive for your team. You can be really positive for your team and then be also very positive for the other team when something else good happens. You don't have to be all negative about the other team just because they're playing the team that you happen to work for.

"Even the national basketball games that I do for college, while I don't have any stake in the game, if it's a Big Ten game and they're playing a nonconference opponent, I'm going to play it like the Big Ten is the conference and is the 'home team' because that's the network that I'm working for—that's the entity that I'm working for. And the fans want to know more about, say, a Wisconsin Badgers team as opposed to Arkansas-Pine Bluff, just to give an example. When they're watching the game, they're watching Wisconsin as opposed to watching the opponent. So you can do your job and do it very well and not necessarily be a homer, but you can be very positive for both teams and not go down a negative route whatsoever."

It's important for students to understand that when you first start out in broadcasting, you don't immediately get a job in the big leagues upon college graduation. You have to pay your dues in the minor leagues, so to speak, beginning your journey in obscure towns where you might be handling media relations, negotiating radio contracts, selling corporate sponsorships, and taking on other responsibilities. "The best way that I can describe that," Levering said, "is just be ready to do anything. I did corporate sales. I did group sales. I had to negotiate a radio station contract in my first year. It was, 'Okay. You got your job. Here it is on a Monday. We don't have a radio station. Good luck. Opening Day is three months away. Have fun. And here's your budget.' Those were all things that I had to learn on the fly. When I first started, social media was just starting. So I had to learn what that was all about and what mediums we needed to be a part of. I had no technical savvy on how to run a website. But it was, 'Hey, listen, not only are you going to broadcast and do media relations, you're also going to have to run our website for us, so you'd better learn that!'"

Levering pointed out that it's like that in other industries outside of sports, too: "You learn a lot of the stuff on the fly. Nobody's telling you how to do it. You've just got to figure it out. And it's that way a lot in life. You don't have that training necessarily for everything, but you've just gotta get out there and you gotta do it. And you don't know until you do it. Going back to what we'd discussed earlier, there might not be classes for play-by-play, but you just have to get out there and you just gotta do it. You gotta feel it. You have to listen back to it and see how good it was or how bad it was, and not just have your mom and dad listen to it. But you have to have objective people listen to it, too. It's that way with every job that you're going to have. But you have to wear a lot of hats. For me, when I was first starting, it was, 'Okay, I've got all these other duties. I need to do all these different things.' And then, the icing on the cake—and the fun part at the end of the day—was, 'Okay, now I get to call a baseball game.' So that was the reward at the end of the day from everything else.

"And it goes back to when I first got out of college and I was an intern at Fox, I learned every job in the production truck and every job behind the scenes. Because I have that knowledge now, I feel like I'm a better broadcaster, because I know what everybody else is doing on the other side behind the scenes, [from] the graphics department and the producers and the directors and the technical directors [to the crew] running the cameras and the FoxBox. It makes me a better broadcaster because I know all of those different roles. That's a very important thing."

Having mentors in the industry is important, and when you're in college, you should begin developing relationships with guest speakers who come and give talks in your classes. "Steve Physioc has been my mentor in this business," Levering said. "He's now the voice of the Kansas City Royals on television and on the radio. But he was in Anaheim when I was going to school. Chapman, where I went to school, is on the same street as the Angels' ballpark—Angel Stadium—about a mile away. He came and spoke to one of my classes. His daughter was actually looking at Chapman, and I knew that I was one of the only people in my class that wanted to do play-by-play. When he came and spoke to one of my classes, I was front and center. I was listening to everything he was talking about. I was just so thrilled to meet him. Once the class was over, I offered to take him and his daughter for a tour, just so I could keep talking to him and develop that relationship. Lo and behold, I get that internship with Fox [now rebranded as Bally Sports West], which was the rights holder—and still is the rights holder—to the Angels broadcast, and they decided to send me down to Anaheim to fill in as a production assistant, basically 'water boy.' Just go take waters to all the camera guys. Get stats or get coffee. Just be the 'gofer' for the day. I had a chance that day to not only sit in the production truck for most of the time—and run tape and figure out what the day-to-day is down in a Major League Baseball broadcast—but in the middle innings, I had an opportunity to sit in the booth. And I sat behind Steve Physioc and Rex Hudler, and their statistician and their stage manager. I just got to take it in, and—other than the other times when I did play-by-play myself—those were the moments where I went, 'Man, this is the best seat in the house. This is what I want to do.'"

As for where a lot of his demo tapes came from for his first job, it was thanks to Physioc: "Steve told me, 'Get a little recorder. And if you're down here for a homestand, grab that recorder and go into the booth next to us—where the high home camera is set up—and call a couple of innings. Give me the tape at the end of the night. I'll listen to it on my way home and give you some pointers when I come back to the ballpark tomorrow.' That's where I started doing baseball. I was always *playing* baseball—all the way through college. I hadn't had a chance to call baseball when I was in college. That was my indoctrination into baseball, learning the tempo of it, the rhythm of it, what I can get away with saying, and what I can't get away with saying. It was all because of Steve. He's been an integral part of my career all the way through the minor leagues, every single stop. He's always put a phone call on my behalf to my potential employer without me asking him to do that."

To emphasize his point about the importance of developing relationships in the industry, Levering recapped his journey from his first radio job to his current stop in Milwaukee. "It is about the relationships and the contacts that you have because I wouldn't be where I am without the contacts or even those relationships," he said. "Everywhere I've been, it's because—not necessarily in Milwaukee but everywhere leading up to it—I knew somebody at that other place. Getting my job in Rancho Cucamonga was because I knew the public address announcer that I went to college with. When I went to Double-A Springfield, it was because the guy that was their radio announcer took my job in Rancho Cucamonga, and I ended up taking his job in Springfield. When I got to Triple-A in Pawtucket, I previously had worked in the same league with their former radio broadcaster, so I had some ins there in Pawtucket. So it's not without the connections. They're so important."

Because having connections is vital in the industry and because he's benefited from these relationships along the way, Levering helps out when aspiring broadcasters reach out for advice: "I take it to heart, like Steve Physioc has been my mentor. When young broadcasters e-mail me or send me demo tapes, I always take it to heart to try and help them out—because it's not without help that you get to where you want to get in this business. So it's really important to cultivate those relationships."

Still, Levering offered a small piece of advice in that regard: "There's a big difference between being persistent and then being over the top, too. You can be persistent and think, 'I want to talk to this person about possible job [opportunities] or even just mentorships,' but maybe don't e-mail them every single day if they don't respond because that can be on that edge of, 'Hey, listen, that's kind of like badgering.' You want to be persistent but not annoying because then your relationship can go sour in a hurry. It's that way with potential employers, too. But once you get your constructive criticism, if there's a conversation, you go out and you go do it, you respond, try and get better. Those are how those relationships continue."

Although different broadcasts have their own styles, Levering shared a tip he learned from Brewers TV play-by-play announcer Brian Anderson: the three Ss. "That's the combination of 'silence, stories, and statistics,'" he said. "You think about juggling a little bit. If you've got three plates that are spinning on those sticks, it's a nice balance of having those three. It mostly goes for the television side—and a little bit on the radio side—where you want a balance of those three. You don't want to give too much emphasis on your stories one day—and then you forget to shut up and be quiet and give your silence. Then maybe you neglect your stats, too. Or one day you're getting really stats heavy and you're neglecting your story telling and your silence. Sometimes your silence is a little heavy and you're neglecting the other sides.

"Ultimately, you're a perfect balance of all three, where you can tell your stories, back them up with your statistics, and then you can be quiet. That's what the best broadcasters are able to do. You get bogged down, especially on the radio side, if you're trying to get too much into statistical minutiae. You could bore your listening audience if they're driving and they hear too many statistics. But it's that nice balance of the three Ss, and that was a really important thing that Brian told me when I got to Milwaukee."

Another tip Levering offered relates to being around the dugout and batting cage at the beginning of batting practice—and just listening. The information you pick up there—a lot of which you cannot look up anywhere—is invaluable. But don't force conversations with players. "There's such a thing as 'being around and being seen but not heard,'" Levering explained. "There's a big difference between 'being around' and 'being heard too much.' If you're hanging around the clubhouse or around the batting cage, you can just be there and hang out. You don't have to talk to anybody. You just take everything in. But if someone wants to come up to you and have a conversation, that's great. Or a conversation happens organically, and you're not forcing a conversation. That's the best way to be, where you're just there, you're being seen, but you're not outwardly pushing an agenda at other people—because that's a great way to lose relationships: if you're being heard too much and not being seen."

"Being heard too much" is a mistake that you can't afford to make in the industry. But of course, you'll make your share of mistakes on air in a broadcast. That's okay; it's part of the learning process. In Levering's case, that's certainly true. He still laughs about his days calling minor-league games when commercial breaks were only sixty seconds long. "When I first started, I was on a radio station which you couldn't hear unless you were, honestly, in the parking lot of the radio station," he said. "It didn't have a very, very big bandwidth. In my first year, having only done a handful of ball games, I could make a lot of mistakes and not a lot of people were going to hear it. And I was very, very thankful for that opportunity. Thinking back, I'm glad that I was by myself and that I didn't have all those breaks, because it taught me so many lessons about who I was as a broadcaster: my tempo, my delivery, what I could do, what I couldn't do, what I could try to pull off, and what I couldn't pull off. I learned more about myself talking to myself, basically, and not knowing if what I was saying was landing on deaf ears. Or if people were reacting in a specific way. It was really important for me to do that. That's how I found out who I was. Even now, when I do have a partner, there are times when it's the fourth inning and I'm working with Bob [Uecker] at a home game, he'll just stand up and go to the back of the booth and eat dinner or just hang out with somebody, and I'm doing the game by myself. And there's nothing wrong with that. There are some days where I'm [comfortable with the idea of], 'I don't need a partner. I'm just going to talk to myself. This is what we're doing, and I'm going to entertain.' If I hadn't had that experience in the minor leagues, I'd have a much harder time with doing games by myself and being confident with it, too. But going back and listening to those tapes is painful." He paused for a laugh. "It's very painful—because I wasn't very good. And I got a lot, lot better as the years went on."

A big part of getting better is gaining that confidence with experience. As for advice for building confidence, Levering's advice is, just keep doing it: "I really didn't think that I was very good until probably my third year. That's 280 baseball games! Two full seasons at 140 games a year before I actually felt confident in what I was doing and that I was on the right path and could do this for a career. And it took a long time to figure that out. You just got to keep doing it."

Developing a personal style, added Levering, is significant in terms of boosting your confidence: "Developing your own style—that's the biggest part of it." And while some broadcasters believe that copying somebody good is the way to start, Levering doesn't subscribe to that theory. "[It won't work] if you're trying to rip off other people's styles because you grew up listening to XYZ broadcaster," he said. "There will always be only one Vin Scully. There's nobody who's ever going to be the same as him. So, why even try and rip off his style? You're going to hurt your own brand. Doing these games and figuring out who *you* are as a broadcaster gives you the confidence to move forward. It's not until you figure yourself out that you can really do that."

Finally, Levering acknowledged that he receives tons of e-mails from students asking him for advice. The two most commonly asked questions: How did you get into the business? How did you get your start?

Levering said his reply is succinct: "Just keep showing up." He elaborated, "It's right place, right time, right people. [It's] putting yourself in the right situations to succeed. For me, it all started with being an intern at Fox. When my internship ended, my baseball career ended, and my school ended, you're in that place where you go, 'Well, what's next?' I just kept showing up after my internship ended, and nobody told me to stop showing up. It turned into a full-time job. The producer started liking me and started hiring me to do different shows. And it was because I just kept showing up. Pure and simple. Not because I was the best. Not because I was good. But I had a good work ethic, I did a good job, and I just kept showing up. That's the biggest thing. Keep showing up."

Sports Radio and Podcasting

Ted Sobel, Radio Sportscaster

Job title: Network studio host/reporter, Sports USA Radio

Education/training: Degrees in radio and television (Los Angeles City College) and sportscasting (Santa Monica College)

Key pieces of advice: Video and audio podcasts now give everyone the opportunity to work on their craft in whatever subject. Take some type of speech class to feel more comfortable speaking to others. To hone my skills in play-by-play, I did six years of sitting in the stands and practicing night after night after night. Even if you cannot get paid for it, do it because that is the best way to get the experience.

Ted Sobel is no stranger to the world of sports radio. The longest current tenured Los Angeles–based radio sports reporter, Sobel began covering sports in 1973 and is the recipient of three Golden Mike awards for his work as a sports reporter/anchor at KFWB 980. He has covered many world-class sporting events, including the World Series, the Super Bowl, NBA Finals, Stanley Cup Finals, BCS Championship Games, and all the major tournaments in golf, tennis, and horse racing.

Sobel has even spent ten years as a pro and college hockey play-by-play announcer, including five seasons with the International Hockey League's Los Angeles/Long Beach Ice Dogs. As the play-by-play voice for the University of Wisconsin, he called two games in 1980 against Team USA, the national team famous for its Miracle on Ice stunner in that year's Winter Olympics.

Since 2004, Sobel has been with Sports USA Radio, where his roles have included sideline reporting and studio hosting for NFL and college football games as well as contributing one-on-one interviews with some of the NFL's biggest

TED SOBEL. *COURTESY OF TED SOBEL*

names. In 2001, he published a memoir titled *Touching Greatness: Tales from the Front Row with Heroes and Legends.*

So you *really* want to work in sports radio? Well, according to Sobel, the industry has changed significantly over the years, and he didn't mince words when asked what one could do to break in and land the ultimate dream job—get paid to talk sports. "I actually don't recommend it so much now [for just radio], but I've got ideas about it and want those interested to know the truth—the good and the not-so-good," said Sobel, who enjoyed a twenty-two-year run with KFWB from 1994 to 2016.

LIKE WITH ACTING GIGS, YOU'LL HAVE TO MAKE SACRIFICES

First, it's important to understand the reality that radio jobs aren't stable. "I don't recommend it now mostly because it's a spiraling downhill industry which is really, really difficult to make a decent living from," Sobel elaborated, "because most of the ownerships now are just big conglomerates that are the cheapest corporations that you'll ever want to work for. They're all trying to get away from being unionized, which means, before, let's just say—I'll throw a number out—if you were making $25 an hour, they'd rather pay you half. And, obviously, it's a little tough to live on $12.50 an hour these days.

"In radio, they don't care. If you're nonunion, they're gonna try to lowball you as much as they can. That's just the reality. They've always been that way, but I worked for a unionized station in LA for many years and so we didn't get screwed over by the big companies. We were CBS-owned and Westinghouse-owned when they were a big company, but we were union so we had contracts and couldn't get screwed over. But now, they'll say, 'Can you work for $4 an hour? [giggling] Great, you're doing drive time.' So, it's really tough, and now, there are examples of the opposite of that, but that's not the norm, unfortunately.

"So, my suggestion is if you want to get into radio, you've *got to be passionate.* You gotta really, really want it, and you're going to sacrifice, too. It's like if you want to get into acting; you know how unstable it is, right? You'll get an acting job, [but then] you don't know when the next one's coming because you're day-by-day, literally, with jobs in acting—unless you're one of the top few hundred fortunate people in the world. The rest of them are waiting tables and trying to make a living, because it's tough. There's a lot of that in radio now, except for the high end. Even Howard Stern, who was the number-one paid guy in radio, got out of [terrestrial] radio. He got out as fast as he could because he knew what was going on. Now, he's on Sirius [XM Satellite Radio]. It's very disappointing because it's an incredible career if it's for somebody who really loves what they're doing. But it's so difficult to feel like you're doing well if you're not fairly compensated."

YOU'LL NEED TO GET YOUR START IN A SMALL TOWN

If your dream job involves working in radio, getting a start in the industry almost always means relocating—especially if you're from a big city. It's simply too difficult to break into the business in a major market. "You've almost got to go to a small market," Sobel continued, "and if you want to be a big fish in a small market, then go for it. There's lots of jobs like that." But before you choose to relocate, you must also consider whether the lifestyle suits you. For some, it's a difficult adjustment. It would be for Sobel: "I'm from LA, so it's difficult for a guy who grew up here to want to go to a small market because, to me, that's going backward."

Still, as Sobel added, working in a small market also has nice upsides, allowing you to hone your skills and establish your credibility more quickly. With less competition in most smaller markets, your name can become more readily associated with sports in that particular community. Then, if a position opens up in a bigger market after two or three years, and you decide to move on, you'll have had those three years of continuous work at a radio station, which will work in your favor as you compete against candidates fresh out of college without as much experience.

And let's say your long-term goal is to transition into other jobs in sports media—for example, a play-by-play broadcaster—in a major market. Well, your chances will be better if you start out in a small market, working as many shows and games as possible. "If you're really good and you got the exposure—you got to know people, too—you could transition into TV or into other forms of the media," added Sobel.

"But if you want to do play-by-play, that's like being a brain surgeon as opposed to being a general practitioner, meaning that's a specialty in broadcasting. [With play-by-play] you're not just talking sports; you're calling a game and you better know how to do it. So if that's your passion and that's your goal, and you have some talent, obviously, that's a great direction to go, anywhere from sports radio. A lot of times, you can't start out doing play-by-play. If you do, you're probably gonna have to start at a very low level, like minor-league something, whatever sport it is. Or small-college or small-town kind of stuff, even doing high school stuff locally. And that's great experience! In LA and other big cities, we don't do much high school on the radio. You go to a small town, and they'll probably have the 'rivalry football game of the week' on in high school because that's what interests them. So that's what I would suggest, whatever it takes.

"I did six years of sitting in the stands with a tape recorder and practicing night after night after night going to LA Kings games—and doing the same at Lakers, Dodgers, Rams, and Angels games. I was there *all* the time. If you can't get paid for it, do it because that's the best way to get the experience! And enjoy the ride."

STARTING YOUR OWN PODCAST

"One important message following the above statements," said Sobel, "[is that] video and audio podcasts now give *everyone* the opportunity to work on your craft in whatever subject and is a huge advantage over those of us who grew up in an era when that option simply didn't exist. And many are not only honing their on-air skills this way, but also getting the online exposure that could lead to bigger and better 'real' jobs out there! So if that is your passion, *go for it!*"

That's right: students looking to practice speaking into a mic can also consider podcasting, which literally anybody can start these days with only a smartphone. Even Sobel himself is doing a podcast, called *Touching Greatness*. There are some important points, according to Sobel, for those wanting to launch their own podcasts: Do lots of practice first and be interesting and prepared. Showing some personality is also a huge plus!

"It might be a good idea to just do it with your friends first, if you don't have a radio background. And I always highly recommend taking some type of speech class to feel most comfortable speaking to others, whatever your future has in store," said Sobel. "[On a podcast] you need to keep it interesting, to the point where there's a flow to it instead of you being all over the place. You gotta ask good questions and have good topics and, of course, *be prepared*, and just general stuff that the average person wouldn't know until they did it. I mean, if [you've] been a plumber [your] whole lives but [you] love sports and just want to do a podcast, then [you] better learn how to talk into a microphone to the point where people would want to listen to you as opposed to you're just babbling. You really must be interesting, and I hope you have a personality that comes across in your delivery. Don't be afraid to show it. On the air, it's very important. It bugs me that you get some of these cookie-cutter kind of broadcasters that are so afraid to show their personality. They're all voice and no substance. So they sound wonderful but they don't say anything, and they don't keep it interesting to most. So, I stress: if you got a personality, don't be afraid to show it. Don't hold back at all. Enjoy it. It's sports! This isn't brain surgery. Too many people take sports so damn seriously. It's a damn game! Enjoy it!"

Additionally, Sobel suggested that you think about the podcasts you listen to yourself and understand why you do tune in. That could help you to understand what to do in your own podcasts. "Are you going to listen to something more than once if you hear someone who's not only just sort of generic in whatever they say, but also has no personality and is just talking—let's just say, hockey—for the sake of it?" Sobel asked. "And it's not just because they're saying what you want them to say about the sport, but because [they are] interesting and it sounds like they know what they're talking about. And they're very much prepared. To me, there's so much involved in just being yourself. If you're qualified from a standpoint that you actually follow a specific sport—or sports in general—you could do a generic [podcast] like me. I cover everything, even horse racing, tennis, and golf, because I've covered it all and feel comfortable with it all. If I don't feel comfortable with the sport, I certainly wouldn't do a podcast on it. If you do, you're going to be exposed, and certainly the listeners are going to know it in a very short time, like, 'Wow, this guy doesn't know what he's talking about!' You're not going to have many listeners that way!"

When you first start out, Sobel emphasized, be realistic with your expectations: "Because it's hard to build it up. It's very difficult to make money off it—I don't want to say you can't make money off it, but it's simply usually a bumpy road. I mean, you need to get tons of listeners, and you just can't put your name out there and say, 'Hey, I'm great! Listen to me!' It usually takes a while unless you're incredibly good at marketing yourself, which most people aren't.

"[To summarize], my suggestion is this: If I don't have any broadcasting experience, I would sit there and record something with a friend, like you're sitting at a bar and talking sports. I would do that until you feel really comfortable about it, and then let the world listen to it. But I don't want the world to listen to my first twenty-five audition tapes. They're usually awful! So, I'm not sending out my practice tapes and I would hope somebody wouldn't want to do that with a podcast, but sometimes you listen and it's like watching paint dry. So no thanks!"

Another consideration for your own podcast, said Sobel, is to include a cohost or a guest: "I would practice until you at least say, 'Hey, that sounds pretty good.' Then, you can get out there and, of course, if you have guests or if it's just you and another person or just you talking, you better be damn interesting if you think you're going to hold an audience. I think I'm very interesting—but I wouldn't want to listen to me talk to myself! That's why I like guests. I would never want to listen to one guy who thinks he knows the world. That's the most boring sports talk radio in the world. It's always good to be able to banter with another person."

REMEMBER TO ASK THE QUESTIONS THAT NEED TO BE ASKED

Students wanting to work in sports media "need to be able to generate their own persona out there," advised Sobel. "They need to let people know who they are, why they are, what they're all about, and it's very important because [the athlete being interviewed would say], 'Oh, it's Joe Smith. Yeah, I know him; he's a good reporter and he's fair. He's not just ripping people just to rip them because he's bored and just a negative person.' I've been called 'negative' at times because they didn't know me or my motives in interviews—and I made sure they got to know me. I'd say, 'Because I ask a question that needs to be asked doesn't mean I'm negative. It means I'm not one of the kiss-asses in the room who's afraid to ask it.' I'm not asking it because I'm trying to be controversial. I'm asking it because it's simply *the* question that needed to be asked."

Sobel gave an example from the 2011 NBA Finals, a series won by the Dallas Mavericks over LeBron James and the Miami Heat. A newcomer to the Heat that season, James had predicted a dynasty for Miami and alluded to multiple championships with his proclamation, "Not two, not three, not four, not five, not six, not seven" the day after signing with the club.

"Think back to the last game [of the Finals]," said Sobel, who was in Miami for Game 6 when the Heat lost to Dallas. "LeBron's reputation in that series specifically, and certainly throughout the playoffs, was that he just passed the ball and didn't want to shoot. We were saying at the time that he was being too passive aggressive, that he was 'afraid' to be the guy. He was, 'Here, Dwyane Wade, you take the ball; I don't wanna have to take the clutch shot.' That's because he's a pass-first kind of a guy. That's a great attribute in many ways, but it's also not great when you have this talent and you're in crunch time to win a championship." Fast forward to the postgame press conference after Miami lost the final game. "I don't know if you remember that somebody asked LeBron James, 'Did you guys choke?' Now, is that a fair question to ask at the time?"

Based on the circumstances, many sports fans would say yes. Sobel himself believed so. "I mean, 'choke' is a negative word," he continued. "It's overused and often used unfairly. I've used it maybe three or four times in my life, and I've interviewed thousands of athletes. But I stood there in that room and I watched question after question—LeBron was up on the podium with Dwyane Wade— and nobody asked the only question that needed to be asked.

"So, I raised my hand and they gave me the mic. I said, 'This is for both of you, but LeBron first. LeBron, this is not the kind of word I like to use. I'm not trying to be disrespectful at all. But with your expectations and what you guys have been saying all year long—and you had home-court advantage tonight but couldn't extend the series—I want to know if you feel that you guys choked.' LeBron looked at me like he couldn't believe that I even asked that question. Then he quickly turned his head and looked over to D-Wade, like, 'Okay, it's yours'—just like he did on the court! 'Here's the ball, baby! I don't want it!'"

In that situation, Sobel felt the "choke" question was one needed to be asked. But, he cautioned, asking a fair question based on the situation isn't the same as just being mean-spirited and ripping athletes. You can be honest without being negative. For instance, if a shortstop makes a career-high four errors in a game, you don't have to say he was awful; all you have to say is that he made four errors, the most he's ever made in a game. Be factual without emotion. On the other hand, let's say you're doing a podcast and all you do is criticize athletes for making misplays or not coming through in the clutch. If you're known for doing this, athletes are not likely going to come on your show, ever.

But say you're lucky enough to land athletes or coaches as guests on your podcast. Is it ever okay to be critical of them? After all, you can't act like everything is going well when it's not, or you will lose credibility. Can you ever tell your guests, "Boy, that was an awful play," or "That was a horrible play call"—even in jest—or must you always choose your words carefully?

"I have to say it all depends on the person," Sobel opined. "Like, if you know a subject, if you know them personally and you have them on the air, whether they're a college or pro athlete, you have them all on a podcast with you. You know you could joke with them and tell them that they had an awful year last year, and they can handle it. If you don't know them, then you can still do it, but you're going to take a chance. You've got to walk that tightrope of, okay, is this person going to tell all of his teammates, 'Hey, don't go on Ted's show. He'll just rip you . . .' There's no straight answer to it. You need to be confident of what you do, and if you're really good and if you've earned the respect of people out there, if they already know that your shtick isn't just ripping athletes, just to be controversial—that's a major hurdle, don't you think?" The bottom line, advised Sobel, is to be respectful.

YOU STILL GOTTA ASK THE QUESTIONS THAT NEED TO BE ASKED, PART II

Finally, Sobel cautioned that not every moment of working in sports is appealing: "Yeah, I get to go to a lot of games for free. But do you like being in a smelly locker room after a team lost in the last second and nobody wants to talk to you and you're basically the enemy?"

Sobel brought up two examples from 2012 of devastating losses in golf—and how he handled those interviews. The cheat sheet version is that after an athlete has suffered a devastating defeat, you still have to ask the questions, but at the same time, you should always be tactful. "I had back-to-back interviews where both of them choked on the 18th green. One of them was a major. The golfer was I. K. Kim, one of the nicest people on the planet. And I had to be the first one to ask her a question. She missed a very short putt [one foot away]—a [foot] away to win a major, but she missed it on the 18th green and lost in a playoff," Sobel said, referring to the 2012 Kraft Nabisco Championship in Rancho Mirage, California.

"I was there as the 18th green announcer, but I was also there doing my radio stuff, so I was also covering it as a reporter. When it was all over, I was standing on the end of the green, whereas all the reporters were way back in another place as I got a special pass because I was supposed to be there. I asked the person who was running the tournament if it was possible to talk to I. K. Kim before she went into the [media] room because I needed it for immediate use [for radio] to feed my report back to the station.

"They made an exception for me, and Kim walked over and said, 'Nice to meet you.' I did not know her personally. I had to say, 'I know this is difficult. But I just have to ask you: What's going through your mind when this happens? I mean, you know that you've never won a major. This is such a big deal. What's going through your mind as this unfolds?' I wasn't going to use the word 'choke' because I didn't want to get her more upset than she already was. Before she could open her mouth, she started crying. I was standing there but suddenly didn't want to be here. I wish I didn't have to, but as a reporter, we *must* ask the necessary question. She just missed the shortest putt to ever (potentially) win a major in golf history, and I'm the first person to ask her about it. What was I supposed to do, not bring it up? I couldn't just say, 'Hey, how's your day?' I've got to mention it.

"But she was able to gather her thoughts; she took a few deep breaths and was able to give me a couple of comments. And I said, 'Thank you. I don't wanna bother you any longer than need be. You need to go into the room and deal with the other [media members]. All the best to you moving forward.' Thank goodness she won a major four years after that. [But] that's another time I ask [people interested in working in sports media]: 'You still want my job? You wanna be the person to ask this young lady who's just lost a major with the shortest putt in the history of golf?'"

Sobel then shared a story involving golfer Kyle Stanley, who'd suffered a similar collapse at a PGA Tour event in San Diego several weeks prior to Kim's disappointing finish: "He had a five-shot lead with two holes to play, which is almost impossible to lose. But Kyle unfortunately blew it. He was breaking down afterward, crying. And, again, I was the first person to ask him a question in his postmatch news conference. That was back-to-back tournaments I covered, this one being five weeks [earlier]. Kyle was losing his breath and breaking down because he was so upset. The good news is that the following week he came back and had his first PGA Tour win [at a different event in Phoenix]. So after Kim blew it [just weeks after Stanley did], here I was again, thinking, 'Wow, I can't believe this. Two times in a row.'"

But even when the athlete is crying, you still have to ask the questions that need to be asked. Just make sure you're tactful.

For more stories from his career along with tips for aspiring broadcasters, check out Ted Sobel, *Touching Greatness: Tales from the Front Row with Heroes and Legends* (Monterey, CA: Coaches Choice, 2021).

4

Minor League Baseball Play-by-Play

Chris King, Sports Broadcaster

Job title: Radio play-by-play broadcaster, Tri-City Dust Devils (High-A West, Minor League Baseball) and Idaho Vandals (men's basketball and football)

Education/training: Degree in communications (Washington State University, Edward R. Murrow College of Communication); announcing sports in high school

Key pieces of advice: Cultivate a broad array of skills such as audio and video editing, graphic design, social media. Look for ways to make yourself as valuable as possible. Keep the big picture in mind, always looking for ways to promote business. Communicate a sense of energy and fun. Be a self-starter. Have a positive attitude and be persistent.

Play-by-play broadcaster Chris King, who calls the action for men's basketball and football at the University of Idaho and announces MiLB games for the High-A West Tri-City Dust Devils, shared some advice for aspiring broadcasters and others on how to "get into the game." The 2017 Idaho Sportscaster of the Year, who has been doing play-by-play since high school, also recounted the thrill of calling no-hitters for the Dust Devils and talked about long bus rides in MiLB.

For King, being a play-by-play announcer is something he knew he wanted to do from a young age. "I'm from Marysville, Washington, a little bit north of Seattle, just right next to Everett," he said. "And as long as I can remember, I wanted to be involved in sports. I also knew very early on it wasn't going to be as a player. So you have to find your path to be around it and to be a part of it. I was very fortunate in my high school that I had a great video production program. I was able to call my first game when I was fifteen. Even then, I felt like, 'Oh my gosh, I've been preparing all my life for this, and here's my opportunity.' From

CHRIS KING. *COURTESY OF CHRIS KING*

there, it seemed like one thing led to another, in a real great way, in that more doors opened. From there, it seemed like I'd take one opportunity and it would lead to something bigger.

"And I went off to college at Washington State, where they have a really good communications program, the Edward R. Murrow College of Communication, where students receive a lot of opportunities through there. But for me personally, what I love the most is play-by-play. It's calling a game and it's just, you go into a game, and—this goes for covering a game in any number of ways and not that there aren't a lot of ways to be involved in sports media where you can tell great stories, but—what just really resonates with me is when you call a game and when you show up at the ballpark that day, or you show up at the arena or the stadium or wherever it is, you just don't know what's going to happen. And you feel special in the sense you feel really privileged to have the role of however many people are on the other end listening. You get to be the eyes and the ears, and you get to be the one relaying what's going on to them. That's something that just strikes a chord with me that I absolutely love. And really, you don't know, you could have what you'd consider a stinker of a game or the team you cover is down, 8–0, early, but then that you kind of have to have different muscles. You've got to flex your muscles then to just tell some stories and to keep the listener engaged. Or you show up at the ballpark—and I've been fortunate and I've called two no-hitters for the team I've covered. You just don't know if you're going to show up and you get that kind of excitement and the anticipation and building up into that final out. So that's kind of how I got into it. I've worked for the Dust Devils for a number of years. Before that, I worked for a summer collegiate baseball team, the Wenatchee AppleSox, in the West Coast League. Basketball-wise, I worked at Boise State for two years, announcing women's basketball. That led to the opportunity at the University of Idaho to announce men's basketball."

For the two no-hitters, King described what went on in his mind as those games were unfolding: "Probably about the fifth or the sixth inning is when you really become just conscious of the fact like, 'Wow, okay . . .' You're looking down at the score book or up at the scoreboard and you're seeing the goose egg under the hit column. The two I've called had been combined no-hitters. I wouldn't say that either time I had a phrase in the back of my mind [for the final out of the no-hitter]. It depends on that last outcome, but I know in baseball, there's been a lot of talk about if you're jinxing the perfect game or a no-hitter. And I do not subscribe to that theory. For one, Vin Scully didn't subscribe to that theory. And if it's good enough for Vin, it's good enough for me as a broadcaster. Two, just on principle, I need to do my job effectively. Not everyone's going to be listening to all three hours of a baseball game. And the job is I want to capture people's attention. I want to tell the story of what's happening at the ballpark that night, and on a night where there's a no-hitter, that's a huge story. If you're burying it, then you're not doing the listener a service if someone's tuning in or tuning out or checking on the score."

King referenced Scully in the context of how the legendary broadcaster approached calling a no-hitter. For young people aspiring to become a play-by-play announcer, learning from great broadcasters such as Scully is important, in King's opinion. At the same time, you have to develop your own style. "You've got to learn from those people that you were influenced by," he said, "and there's no way you couldn't be influenced by listening to the announcers with the team that you're immersed in as a fan growing up. But [you have] to be conscious and aware of not doing a poor impersonation, but instead taking the best of what they do and adding it into just your own personal style. I think that happens sometimes where you can maybe tell by listening to someone, especially if they're really inexperienced, what region they're from or who their favorite team is because they've taken on some of the characteristics of their favorite announcers. So I think you gotta be aware of taking the things that you like and making it your own, as opposed to maybe just trying to and turning out to be just a poor impersonation."

For students who might not know what it's like working as a minor-league broadcaster—in particular baseball, which has games virtually every day—King shared his experiences about traveling with the Dust Devils. Life on the road as a broadcaster in the minors can be both grueling and exhilarating with lots of fitful sleep on the bus, he said. "It's like a marathon and a sprint at the same time. It ends up being seventy-six games in eighty-one days [which was the schedule in the former Short-Season Single-A Northwest League at the time of this interview, but beginning in 2022 the Dust Devils, as part of the new High-A West League, were expected to play a 132-game schedule], traveling with the team and you're there for every game. You learn how to sleep on a bus as best as you can.

"My advice for anyone who wants to travel with the team on a bus is to bring a pillow no matter what. Also, always bring a pair of pants or a blanket, because normally if you're staff, you're sitting closer to the front of the bus. The coaches and trainer are probably in front of me and then I'm somewhere in the third or fourth row behind them typically. And the AC is usually on at the front of the bus, so it can get cold at the front. Sleep on a bus is more like a sleep purgatory. You try to, if you can, zone out; that's about the best you can hope for.

"But getting back from a trip, as long as you get back before the sun comes up and you get back and maybe your head hits the pillow in your own bed before the sun comes up, that's a victory. It's hard to describe just how fun it is, but it's almost like traveling with the circus because there have been times I've looked behind me and there have been guys who were shoulder to shoulder sharing seats—although it's gotten better now. The trend has gone toward teams traveling with two buses as opposed to just one bus. But if you're trying to pack all those people with the coaches, the trainer, the strength coach, and all the players on one bus; it's tight in there and players are pretty much all doubling up. And I've turned around before and at times looked at guys doubling up behind me and I've been fortunate to always get my own seat. But guys who've just freshly got a million-dollar signing bonus or multiple millions and they're shoulder to shoulder or doubling up on a bus trip that's going to take from 10:30 at night to 4:30 in the morning, really, where else do you get an experience quite like that? It really does feel like you're traveling with the circus.

"When the season comes to an end, it takes time to get reacclimated to normal life, and you can't compete with the level of energy and excitement that comes with being there, game in and game out. It's a fun level, too [being in what was then the Northwest League, a low-A chain], because you're seeing guys who are just starting their professional careers and there have been guys I've been able to see who have gone on to great things where there are times you're either one of the first people they see when they show up at the ballpark, or the taxi or the Uber or the Lyft drops them off, and boom, they're there at Gesa Stadium. And this is the beginning of their professional baseball journey. I even laugh when I see Mike Tauchman on TV today. He got up with the Rockies and I ended up picking him up at the airport when he landed after he got drafted. So the first person who greeted him to begin his professional baseball journey was me at the airport, picking him up in my 2006 Chevy Cobalt. They were low on people and he needed a ride at that point. By now, people use pretty much Uber and Lyft, but at that point this was probably 2013. It was, 'Hey, who's got a minute and who's got a car? They can go pick up this guy who just landed.' So, anytime I see him on MLB Network, I laugh to myself thinking, 'His professional baseball journey started in the passenger seat of my 2006 Chevy Cobalt.' It's little things like that, that you don't really get anywhere else in life experiences."

Life as a MiLB broadcaster also involves handling media relations and often sales. In King's case, he not only handles interview requests but also prepares media notes and all other responsibilities related to media relations. In terms of the skills required for the role for students interested in what he does, he offered the following advice: "There's a number of things. I would say it really doesn't hurt the wider array of skills you have, the more marketable and, most importantly, the more valuable you are. I would say [as far as] the skills that you can learn at school and have handy, [it's a major plus if you're] good at graphic design and good at social media. With social media, though, it's hard [when you're doing play-by-play]. I know some guys who have to do social media while they're calling the game—and I admire them because I don't. So I'd really say graphic design, any sort of video editing, audio editing that you can do. The more creative that you can be, the better.

"I would say, too, that you have to understand the whole ecosystem, and this is maybe a question that I'm answering more on the baseball side—or just maybe not the college sports side, but how the professional minor-league side is. You just have to make yourself as valuable as possible. You've got to understand, it's not just if you've got a great interview—and you do want to have a great interview—but you got to just have an idea of the bigger picture working for a team that's trying to turn as big of a profit as possible. And that's not a bad thing. You want to be able to see the big picture; it's good for everyone who works for a team when there's more tickets being sold and more hot dogs being sold and more hats being sold. So I would give people the idea that when you do something, how does this improve what the team is doing? I think it especially applies to broadcasting, too, because I think one of the great commercials for a team is if you're listening to a broadcast and hopefully that broadcaster is making it sound like, 'Hey, this ballpark, there's something special going on here. This sounds like fun. I want to be out there, even regardless of what the score is.' And it's always more fun when your team is doing better than not doing better. With anything in life, winning's more fun than losing, but especially on the minor-league side, it's not all that. Even on the major-league side, you can only control what you can control. So I would say, too, that you got to understand the bigger picture. I think that, as well, just—if I can, on a broadcast, get in to help promote something that's coming up and I can slip that in, even though I don't have that in front of me. You just have to keep an eye on the fact that it's not just the broadcasts, but you're part of this whole big thing of this team and being successful in this brand. And fortunately, the team I work for has been so great and the people I work for have been just awesome. It's not always the case where the people you work for are just so fantastic to work for. But there's a bigger picture at play and why you want to have as many skills as possible to make yourself as valuable as possible.

"I'd also say, too, that your job is not going to be someone comes and tells you to do X, Y, and Z. Have the freedom and creativity to be forward thinking. If you see something that you can do better, then do it better and say, 'I see we're doing it this way. Why don't we do it this way? I could do this.' Or just say, 'We've never done this before, but I've got a plan to do this.' Just because something hasn't been done before doesn't mean it can't be done in the future, but if you have a good plan and show how you'd do it, I think overall, no matter what you do, you just want to make yourself more valuable and be a good team player on top of all those other skills that I think, whatever you do, don't hurt.

"Then, there's the sales side to it, too, where maybe if you're not directly a ticket sales rep or a sponsorship rep that, like I was mentioning before, you keep that in mind, whether it's the Dodgers or the Dust Devils or the Seahawks, that you all want the team to be successful. It goes back to the idea that it's a good thing to sell more hats, sell more tickets, sell more hot dogs, all that stuff."

Since King does football and basketball along with baseball, it seemed only fitting to ask how he approaches those sports differently in terms of preparation. "Football probably takes the most time when it comes to prep," he explained. "The work begins on Sunday to call a game the next Saturday. Knowing how to ID and have info prepped that you might need to reference at any point with twenty-two players on the field takes a good amount of time. It is the most important—for me, at least—to watch film so I know how to tell guys apart, on top of getting to watch the actual action to get an idea of what the teams try to do.

"With basketball, it also especially helps to be able to watch film. Even though there are only ten guys to worry about on the court at the same time, knowing the physical differences and traits to tell them all apart is super helpful going into a game. Again, that's on top of getting a feel for what they like to do when watching previous games.

"Baseball also takes a lot of prep, but it is almost more like a daily pop quiz. With a game nearly each day during the season, there is a lot less buildup compared to football or basketball, but it's almost more like you're telling a small part of a much bigger story each game."

As he mentioned earlier, the job of a broadcaster is to let listeners know what's going on, as people aren't necessarily tuning in for all three hours of a broadcast. In his case, he prefers giving out the scores frequently in each sport. "I'm a believer that there's no such thing as telling the score enough," he said. "I've never heard a listener complain that a broadcaster told the score too much. I've heard countless times listeners complain that a broadcaster isn't telling the score enough. Not every listener is tuned in for the entire game. When people turn on a game, that's the first thing they want to know. Constantly telling the score and recapping what's happened so far is crucial for a broadcaster. That goes for any sport."

When asked for final words of wisdom for students aspiring to work in sports, King offered the following: "I would just go with the old saying, 'If it's to be, it's up to me.' If you do want to work in sports, it's so competitive that someone's not necessarily going to knock on your door. You have to go knock on someone else's door, give them a call, or e-mail them. It doesn't hurt to be aggressive. There's a difference between aggressive and annoying, but you make the case for yourself, what value you bring, and—we discussed skills before, and I really do think that as much as those skills are great, probably the most important variable that you can have is just a good attitude and a willingness to learn. I think you can go a long way in life if you're reliable and you're someone that people want to be around. If you have the ability to be someone that coworkers still want to have a beer with after a long day working in sports, then that's a really good sign.

"So you don't have to have all the answers right away, but if you have the right attitude, you can find a way to be around the people who can help give you all those answers. It's a different time for sports right now [because of the COVID-19 pandemic]. I don't know if any of us can say with 100 percent confidence we're going to know exactly what things are gonna look like when we're on the other side of this pandemic, but I do think all those traits, the formula to being someone who is successful in sports before, will ring true going into the future."

5

Media Relations and Play-by-Play

Steve Granado, Sports Broadcaster

Job title: Sports play-by-play broadcaster; media relations director

Education/training: Degree in broadcast journalism, with a radio/television/film minor (Cal State Fullerton)

Key pieces of advice: Graphic design and some sort of video editing will go a long way if you're an aspiring play-by-play broadcaster. And if you're looking to get into this, you need to jump into it with realistic expectations. And you have to love it, plain and simple. If you don't put your whole heart into it, you're not going to be able to make a career out of it. If you really, really want this, you have to go out and get it. It's not going to be handed to you.

Steve Granado is still working his way up in the world of sports broadcasting, but his journey up to this point has been impressive given the fact he had something of a late start. After all, he'd originally wanted to major in engineering, and it wasn't until his sophomore year at Cal State Fullerton that he realized sports broadcasting was his true passion. At that point, Granado followed his passion and declared a broadcast journalism major alongside a radio/television/film minor, focusing on sports reporting.

Upon graduating in 2015, Granado shifted into Minor League Baseball, beginning with the Rancho Cucamonga Quakes that summer as a member of the media relations department. In 2016, he began his MiLB broadcasting career with the Boise Hawks, touring the Pacific Northwest. The following year, the West Virginia Power brought him in to provide color and play-by-play commentary. Since then, Granado has voiced varsity prep and NCAA sports around the country, including nationally recognized collegiate and high school talent from UCLA softball and JSerra Catholic baseball, to Wilson Tobs baseball and USA Hockey. Seven years into his career, he has broadcast baseball, softball, hockey, basketball, soccer, football, water polo, and volleyball for nearly eight hundred games behind the mic.

If you had told him in his final year of high school that he'd have called that many games—and be working in the realm of sports broadcasting, period—he wouldn't have believed you. It's true that Granado began loving sports at a young age, and as a teen he was always a confident speaker within his own social circle. "But I wasn't really vocal through high school until I made a graduation speech," he said. "I'd written a speech and won a competition. There were two speeches, the valedictorian and salutatorian speeches, and then it was kind of like a wild card. That was the wild card, the play-in game, so to speak, where I wrote a speech and submitted it to the school. They liked it, and I made that speech at my high school and it went really well, to the point where still today when I go back to my hometown and I run into somebody, they'll still bring it up. But that was the first time where I was, like, 'Oh, I can speak in front of people.' I was nervous to a degree but wasn't overtly nervous. And that's where the idea started, the seed in my mind, like, 'Hey, I can present. I'm well-spoken. And I have some ideas.'"

Still, being a good presenter isn't exactly the same as announcing sports, and Granado didn't start thinking seriously about pursuing a career in broadcasting until later that summer. "I first got the idea of jumping into broadcasting right after I graduated high school," he recalled. "That summer, I was watching the Angels game with my dad and we're just talking about the game. I'd said something and I don't remember what I said but immediately after I said it, Victor Rojas, the Angels play-by-play [broadcaster], said it. The idea at that point had been floated by my sister that I might study some sort of communications.

"And that was the first time my dad was like, 'Hey, maybe you should put more thought into this.' I was an engineering major going into school and I wanted to [be] in [the] environmental [field] working with renewable energy, so I stuck it out for a little bit. I took three semesters of engineering classes, chemistry, and calculus, but the math and science just became too much for me by the end of my first semester in my sophomore year. It still sounded good in theory, money-wise and security-wise, but I decided to take a leap and switched to broadcast journalism.

"I guess the story starts there, at Cal State Fullerton, and I started doing that. I started taking some classes in journalism, completely switching my brain around from math and science, which had been my whole life leading up to that point. I mean, from elementary school through high school, I thought I wanted to be in biology."

Being in broadcast journalism allowed him to have on-air opportunities and become comfortable in doing announcing. "I started calling Cal State Fullerton ice hockey during the end of my junior year in 2014," he said. "I was doing a little PA announcing for them before that, just filling in. I was doing PA announcing for the school's baseball team. So I had these chances just to be on-air, just figuring out my voice, finding out my style, and getting more comfortable with speaking into a microphone. I was taking my broadcast classes where I was doing the school's TV show news program during my senior year. I was doing a little blogging for an Angels blog. So I started to weave my path into some sort of journalism, some sort of sports coverage—and even during my senior capstone class, which is doing the school news broadcast. Every time I did it, it was sports. Whatever sports coverage I could do, I was doing."

Since his passion was baseball, Granado also went to the Winter Meetings in his final year of college to network and explore job opportunities: "I ended up getting an internship through going down there in 2014. It was a media relations position with the Rancho Cucamonga Quakes. It wasn't on-air when I took the job, but it was an internship. I needed an internship to graduate, so I needed that out of the way and it was close enough to home where it was only twenty to thirty miles away. It was an unpaid internship, like many are. We won a championship and we hosted the All-Star Game. We had Cody Bellinger, Alex Verdugo, José De León, Kyle Farmer, and all these now–major leaguers on that team. It was just this absolutely incredible experience. It just opened my eyes."

It also helped that he was given numerous on-air opportunities by Mike Lindskog, the Quakes' director of public relations and broadcaster. "Mike gave me a chance to do postgame radio where I was doing MLB scores," he said. "And so, I actually got on the air that July—for the first time on terrestrial radio, on Fox Sports 1350, and it took off from there. Mike gave me some chances on the road and some Wednesday night games where he's like, 'I'll take care of the Twitter and the media relations stuff. Why don't you go call the game down in the other booth?' So I'd be doing a game on a random Wednesday night, and that's how I built my first baseball demo tape. I got a Bellinger homer on my first demo. I had a Verdugo ball in the gap that he caught. I had a double play ball in there. It was a terrible demo, but it ended up landing a gig in Idaho [for the Boise Hawks]."

While it feels cool to be able to say that you're calling professional baseball for a living, life in the minor leagues can be a struggle. That certainly was the case for Granado in Boise. The lesson learned: You simply have to have a tremendous amount of passion to work in the industry. "That was the first time I'd moved away from home," Granado elaborated. "It was the first time I'd gone to a state I'd never been to before. And it was a very tough, gut-wrenching situation. It tested me a lot, and it burst the bubble a little bit, and gave me more insight into what the real world was like. It was a gut punch. It was gritty. It was exhausting. I was working for next to nothing, money-wise. But I stuck through it and got through the seventy-six games in minor-league short season. But it was tough. That was one of the more trying times in my life, was to get through that summer, and that's the first time I was on the air regularly every night doing [play-by-play]. It was internet-only, but it was still on the air calling pre- and post[game]. I was doing the play-by-play by myself for every single game. I was running the media relations department. I was running the press box. I was the liaison with the [Colorado] Rockies [who, at the time, were the Boise Hawks' parent club] and so it's a lot to ask out of a twenty-three-year-old."

But Granado got through it, and that Boise job led to an opportunity in West Virginia the following year in 2017: "And without getting too personal, I went through some personal stuff while I was out there, too. And that tested me, too. So, my career path to get to this point where I'm 'comfortable'—I'm working, obviously, but I still want to get to bigger and better things—has been, to put it bluntly, rough. It's been a bumpy road. For a lot of guys and gals in this profession that are making their way into play-by-play or sideline reporting or anchoring, whatever it is in sports, it's a very tough path and the odds are severely stacked against you. You gotta move. You gotta work for zero money. You gotta scrape together what you can. Luckily for me, I have a good support system where my parents have helped me and continue to help me when I need it.

"As your situation gets worse and worse, the hill gets steeper. Sometimes it almost seems impossible. It's easier to make it as a player than it is as a broadcaster. There's twenty-six spots on a baseball field in a major-league club. For play-by-play, there's three on a major-league club if you're lucky: TV, radio, and Spanish.

And now some teams are simulcasting radio and TV. So it's tough. If you're trying to be a play-by-play broadcaster, it's not for the faint of heart. It's exhausting. It's heartbreaking, over and over again. I liken it to being an actor. You're auditioning, and everything is so subjective. You just hope the person (A) watches or listens to your stuff, and (B) likes you. You can have all the qualifications in the world, but if they don't like you—just that random person—then it's over.

"The odds are so stacked against you. Although I'm doing it, being allowed to do it and finding a team that will listen and let you do it is hard. You gotta just take what you can get and just keep truckin' forward and hoping that one day, it pays off and you can make a decent living at it. But I wouldn't trade it for anything else. I love it."

HAVE A BROAD SPECTRUM OF SKILLS AND COMPETENCIES

As Granado handles media relations duties in his role as a minor-league broadcaster—which is the norm in minor-league sports—he's tasked with preparing media notes for both home and away games, along with updating the team website with stories and press releases. In terms of software skills for an aspiring minor-league play-by-play broadcaster/media relations assistant or director, he recommended, for starters, being able to edit videos using Adobe products: "[That includes] Premiere, Photoshop, Illustrator, and After Effects, if you're getting crazy. I literally have Adobe InDesign open up right now working on game notes for a game today."

Fortunately for Granado, he'd always had an interest in learning how to create and edit videos. "I started making videos when I was a kid, like eight or nine, making home movies on the cassette [recorder], which was what we used back then," he said. "I started taking some classes in high school about graphic design that didn't necessarily fit into the curriculum, but I was interested in doing it. I had an interest in animation at one point. I thought I was going to work in special effects when I was in high school, too—my brain's all over the place, obviously— but I started doing that and got interested in it. And it, weirdly enough, translated into this, because when you're working in minor-league baseball or for a college, you gotta do more than one thing. So being able to diversify that portfolio, to being able to go, 'Hey, I've used this software before. I enjoy doing this,' and just get used to doing it in your free time—especially in a world where content creation is king. You gotta be able to at least say that you can do it—maybe not pumping out MLB-worthy or Cut4-worthy stuff, but you're also pumping out stuff that's worthy enough where you're going to get a double tap and a like and a retweet.

"But graphic design is a massive aspect of it, and some sort of video editing is gonna go a long way if you're an aspiring play-by-play [broadcaster]. I didn't think about that when I was getting into it for the first time. That was the furthest thing from my mind. I was thinking, 'Yeah, I can do it,' but I didn't think it was gonna be the job. But a lot of times what you doing most of your time isn't calling the game. It's working with these Adobe products. They're the industry standard, at least right now, to work from. You can do Movie Maker or iMovie if you have absolutely nothing else, but these are the industry standards, and having that Swiss Army knife of 'everything media relations' and [knowing how to work] with Excel, being able to be flexible in that, being able to be that Swiss Army knife, goes a long way. It keeps you working. It makes you look better than the next person applying for that job if you [can say], 'Look at these videos I've edited,' or, 'I can edit these audio samples and fix these audio files in [Adobe] Audition,' or, 'I've run media relations through InDesign and Excel.' It's never gonna hurt you."

BE CURIOUS. ASK QUESTIONS. FOLLOW UP.

In the baseball off-season, Granado returns home to Los Angeles, where he continues to work in sports. On weekends in the fall and winter, for instance, he does play-by-play for the LA Kings High School Hockey League (LAKHSHL), a league designed to continue the growth of hockey in Southern California. The league began play in 2015–2016, featuring high school players from the Los Angeles, Ventura, Santa Barbara, and Kern counties. It's not the NHL, but the LAKHSHL gives Granado an opportunity to regularly call what's known as the "coolest game on earth."

And Granado received that opportunity because he was curious, asked questions, and followed up: "I first started in 2016, when I called two games. Now, I'm one of the main guys there, but I got that gig out of doing Cal State Fullerton ice hockey. We called a game—Fullerton against USC—in Anaheim at Anaheim Ice, the old training facility for the Ducks. There was a guy there calling another game before us. I talked to him, and he said, 'I do this for a company called Black Dog Hockey. We do streaming for this, this, and this. Here's a business card. Reach out to this person.' They were looking for people and they had me on for a couple of games to fill in. That turned into calling games every weekend for this league."

What can people looking for an opportunity in sports learn from Granado's example? "Just be curious," he said. "I was like, 'Hey, you're calling something. Do you ever need a fill-in? I'm looking for work.' It just fell in my lap. I reached out to the company, and their response was, 'Hey, you're local? You like it and you can do it? Okay, because we need people.' So, it's just being curious, asking questions, and following up."

FINAL WORD

Granado shared a few final pieces of advice for aspiring broadcasters: "If you're looking to get into this, you need to jump into it with some realistic expectations. You're not gonna be in the majors in two years. There's a reason why your Vin Scullys of the world sit around for sixty-seven years, right? There's a reason why these people hang on to jobs for fifteen to twenty years at a time; it's because they're hard to get. If I'd gotten that reality gut check in the beginning, a little earlier, it would make things a little easier, but I had to learn it as I went, that this isn't just gonna wind up in my lap. Obviously, I knew it's going to take hard work and I knew I *could* struggle, but I didn't think I'd struggle as much as I've had [to].

"Six years in, I thought I would've had a full-time minor-league job, easily, and that I would've been there for two or three years at this point. So it's definitely not easy. You gotta really love it, and that's what I tell everybody, because it's gonna test you in ways that you never thought you'd be tested. It's a labor of love and it's tough, and you have to make decisions that aren't necessarily always the best for, maybe, your mental health or your family. You gotta be selfish sometimes. But if it truly is your dream, and you think you have talent—and you think you can have the drive and you think that you can be somebody in this world and share these moments and make these memories for people last a lifetime—then what the hell? Go for it. It's not gonna hurt trying, and that's what I'm still trying to do. I know it's still a long path ahead, and it's exhausting. But I love it and I want to keep doing it, and I believe in myself.

"But you gotta love it, plain and simple. If you don't absolutely 100 percent put your whole heart into it, you're not gonna be able to make a career out of it. Sure, you can make it a hobby, calling your local high school games on Friday night, and there's no shame in that. But if you really, really want this, you gotta go out and get it. It's not going to be handed to you."

6

Sideline Reporting

Kris Budden, Sideline Reporter

Job title: Sideline reporter, ESPN

Education/training: Degree in broadcast journalism (University of Missouri)

Key pieces of advice: When phrasing a question to a coach, making sure that it's always neutral will get you a lot further in the interview. Always make sure there's not a negative or positive tone to it—because they could be up 40-something points but he might not be pleased. We might think so based on their play, but he might be upset about something. So, if you asked him how pleased he was in the first half and he replied that he's ticked, then that makes it look like a stupid question.

Kris Budden is a college sports sideline reporter for ESPN's football, basketball, and baseball coverage. Prior to joining ESPN, Budden was a sideline and feature reporter for Fox Sports, covering NFL and college football from 2013 to 2015.

During that time, she also worked for Fox Sports San Diego as a host and reporter for the regional sports network's coverage of Major League Baseball's San Diego Padres.

As a teenager, Budden already knew she wanted to be in broadcasting. To prepare for this career, she'd shadow her godfather, an anchor at WFAA-TV in Dallas, and for additional practice, she'd sit at home with the closed captioning on and try to read the sentences like a teleprompter. After high school, she decided to pursue her broadcasting dream and attended the prestigious University of Missouri, where she would graduate from Mizzou's School of Journalism with a broadcast journalism degree.

Although she didn't originally plan on working in sports broadcasting, she ultimately realized that path was the one that would allow her to do what she enjoys. "I just love telling people's stories," Budden said on sportscaster Alex Feuz's *The Whole Story* podcast, explaining that she originally wanted to be a news reporter. "And at the end of the day, I'm someone who takes my work home with me, and I thought I wouldn't be very happy standing outside of a fire and talking about murders every day, and at the root of it I wanted to tell people's stories to audiences.

"In sports, you'd get a chance to do that a lot more than you do with news. Whatever path it took me on, I wanted to be in a place where I could tell those stories. I started in local news. I was a photographer, an editor, a producer, and on-air . . . and that's what attracted me to being a sideline reporter. It was getting a chance to share the stories on the field. I love being able to interview people on the best days of their lives." An example she brings up is the day she interviewed Mike Bercovici, a backup quarterback who threw a game-winning touchdown pass for Arizona State against USC. "Most people won't even remember that name. He beat USC on a last-second Hail Mary. I got to interview him while he was crying. That's the best day of his life, and I got to be a part of that. That's what still drives me every day: Getting to be a part of people's best days."

Budden's first job in sports out of college was as a weekend sports anchor at WCAV-TV in Charlottesville, Virginia. Within eighteen months, she moved to WBIR-TV in Knoxville, Tennessee, to work as both a sports anchor and reporter covering the Tennessee Volunteers athletics programs. Over the course of six years, Budden covered the men's and women's NCAA, SEC, and Big 12 basketball tournaments, the 2012 London Olympics, and legendary women's basketball coach Pat Summitt's retirement in 2013.

While Budden has already checked off many of her career goals in sports broadcasting, she's also thrived as a working mom. When asked to offer some insights on creating an effective work–life balance, she shared what works best in her case:

"I didn't know until I got into it, and you can give as much advice as you want, but until you're in it, you don't really realize how best to manage it.

"For me, I live by the quote, 'Be where your feet are.' So if I'm at home, and those are the hours I'm meant to be with my family, then my phone gets put away. I have an Apple Watch, so someone could contact me if I have to take player calls or coach calls. But for the most part, those hours are designed to be with family. I'm 98 percent in with my family. And the times where I'm at work, that work gets 98 percent of me—I say 98 percent because there's always 2 percent [just in case] there's an emergency at home. You just learn to work smarter, not work more. Before I had family, I could spend fourteen hours a day studying notes for a football game. Did I necessarily need to do that? No, but I felt like I had to. Now that I'm [where I am] in my career, I know how to study, how to prepare the best. Sometimes that's waking up before my kids, during their nap time, after they go to bed, so that I can figure out a way to give each a different piece of me—because you can't give yourself 100 percent to both worlds."

Preparing for a game requires hours of studying information, whether it's from team websites, newspapers, game notes, media guides, game films, or other sources. For those who might not appreciate the work that goes into the preparation for a game, Budden explained what her day-to-day routine for a Saturday college football contest looks like: "[With football], it's the longest prep just because of the [number of] players. You also have to know all of the games that led up to that game for a sense of perspective of that season."

For college football, the new week begins on Sunday. "We get our game assignment," she explained. "First thing I really do is contact the sports information directors. Each week, I try to talk to three or four players from each team—a couple on offense, a couple on defense. That's for my own storylines so that I have stuff [to say during a sideline report] that the guys in the booth don't necessarily have conversations with. Then, from there, it's watching the game film from the week before. What people don't realize is if you're working on a Saturday, you didn't see all the other games on that Saturday.

"Mondays are conference calls with our production crew, player calls, notes. I start my [spotting] boards on Mondays.

"Then Tuesday and Wednesday are player calls, taking notes, and putting together my boards. Thursday is usually a travel day. Friday is meetings all day with coaches. We'll have a production meeting either Friday night or Saturday morning.

"And honestly, the day of the game is the easiest stuff because if you've done all your prep, there isn't much else to do. For my job, two hours before a game, I'm on the sidelines. I'm watching warm-ups [trying to figure out], 'Is everybody there?' You don't always have coaches that will tell you if someone's not going to play. So you go through it two-deep to make sure everyone of note is out there during the warm-up. Who's injured? [There's] watching those players, talking with the equipment guys, [and] familiarizing yourself with the medical team—random things like if there was an injury, what hospital would the ambulance go to? Those are all things to find out ahead of time, because once you're in a game, that information is really hard to find out."

(When discussing her preparation for a college football game, Budden mentions the use of a spotting board, a visual reference tool that instantly provides key information on vital statistics and information at a quick glance. A spotting board is usually an oversized, one-page chart of all the players on a team, along with player jersey number and stats, head-to-head results against the opponent, previous results, leaders, standings, and other useful nuggets of information. Information from spotting boards comes from team websites, newspapers, discussions with players and coaches, game notes, stat packs, and team media guides.)

For those who might wonder how a sideline reporter's job differs from that of a play-by-play announcer or an analyst, Budden explains that the sideline reporter acts as the "eyes and ears" for the colleagues in the booth and production truck: "You're there for a purpose, and it's not to relay a bunch of feature stories that you read in newspapers and magazines and websites—because that's everything that a play-by-play [broadcaster] or analyst could do. The purpose of the sideline reporter is to be the eyes and ears on the field that the booth and the production truck can't hear. And sometimes that makes the air; sometimes it doesn't. Sometimes, it's me just telling a director, 'Hey, get a shot of this,' or, 'So-and-so is walking off the field.' That's not necessarily [going to be part of my sideline] report, but if you're [part of a college game crew] that doesn't have a lot of cameras, that sideline reporter is helpful to the director and the producer, so that they don't miss things with the camera."

As far as what makes a great sideline reporter, Budden brings up a comment made by fellow sideline reporter Allison Williams, an ESPN colleague. "She said, 'It's really easy to be an okay sideline reporter. It's really, really hard to be a great sideline reporter.' And I agree with her 100 percent. You can do an interview and do a couple feature stories, and you can get away with being just okay and not being exposed. To be a really, really good one is finding the moments, finding the conversations, witnessing things that change the elements and the story of the game. If I didn't report on something, if I missed an injury, no one really knows that I missed it. So that's where you can really figure out how you can and cannot get exposed. But say I noticed something: There was a minute injury that no one really noticed and the coaches don't give you any information on it, but that quarterback doesn't come out in the second half. That's where what I saw and what I heard on the sidelines really pays dividends, especially nowadays when the coaching staffs aren't giving a lot of information. So to me, it's just always keeping your eyes and ears open as to what you're seeing, and a lot of times that means not paying attention to the action on the field but everything else that's going around it."

Budden cautioned, too, that it's important to make sure that everything is factually correct during a sideline report. "Sometimes it's hard because you're also lip reading. Unless you know 100 percent that that's what that person says, don't say it. It's okay." When doing a sideline report, it's also important to be succinct: "In my mind, what people also have a hard time with is the guys in the booth get to talk endlessly. We have to talk in twenty-second snippets. We have to be done by the time of the snap of the next play. So it's going through the report, keeping an eye on the field so that you're not talking over the next play. In my mind, I start with [point] A and I want to get to point F—from A through F. I might notice that they're getting up to the line, [so] you have to figure out quickly in your head how to get to F and what can you drop out. What can you drop out that's not necessary to the story? What's essential to telling the story? Especially with injury reports, it's just, 'Here's the nuggets. Here's what I know.' It's okay to not know stuff. You don't necessarily have to say that, but just give what you know. If it's more of a complicated feature story, then know the elements that you might need to drop out if you don't always have the time to get through all of it."

As far as interviewing skills, Budden likened handling sideline interviews to taking somebody on the road. "I definitely have a map in my head of how to interview," she said. "You have a place where you want to get to, and a place where you want to start. That road may have a lot of curves or it may be a straight line, but it's on the shoulders of the interviewer to make sure that you get the most out of that road. You can go 100 miles an hour and get from A to B really easily, but did you miss a lot of turns along the way that would've made the interview great?"

Confidence plays a key role, she continued, and that builds as one gains more experience: "When you first start out, you have these questions that you want to ask, and then you stop listening for the answers. As your confidence grows, I always know that if I don't get a great answer, there's a couple questions in the back of my mind. But as you get better at it, you learn to listen. People like Tom Rinaldi are the best at this. They can just listen, and they know how to respond. The best interviewers take those answers, you're still getting them to point B, where you want to get to, but within that time maybe you brought up some emotion, maybe you brought up some details, that people didn't know."

Budden remembered interviewing Vanderbilt baseball coach Tim Corbin after the team won the SEC baseball tournament in 2019: "Tim Corbin started crying during a question that wasn't even meant to go there. But they had a player, Donny Everett, [who] passed away [three years earlier], and whatever jogged up in Tim Corbin's mind, he thought of him and got emotional. So in that moment, you have to know to pause. [You] have an innate reaction as [a] human when you see someone crying is you want to jump in and hug them. And the hardest part of those interviews is just letting it breathe and letting that emotion play out. I even had my producer in my ear, who was just like, 'Let this breathe.' Because I had the knowledge of the background of Donny Everett, I was able to follow up with that and say, 'What does this title mean for your program?' Had I not paid attention to the answer or let the moment breathe, and my next question was, 'What do you think of Kumar Rocker's outing?' then you've lost all emotion out of it. So [it makes a huge difference] the more prepared you are and the more knowledgeable you are—and the prep you've done helps you have that confidence to say, 'It's okay to not have ten questions lined up in my head.' Sometimes, the really easy 'Why?' or 'How?' questions as a follow-up can get really great responses."

With regard to using an "easy" question, Budden pointed to something Rinaldi once used with Alabama head football coach Nick Saban after the Crimson Tide lost in the National Championship. "He had to go to the locker room and he was jogging his mind, like, 'What's the best, the smartest question? You know Saban's going to be ticked,'" she said. "He said the best question was the easiest question, and sometimes we don't think of the easiest question. But the question was, 'What went wrong?' I remember [being blown away hearing that] because I would never think of that. That's such a simple question. But it's almost so simple that we don't think about it. That gets the answer that you're looking for there. When you're younger in your career, you feel like you have to have all these stats. 'So, you guys are plus-five on the boards with only five turnovers. . . . ' Take that out of it because it's that time where you're taking the words out of the interviewee's mouth. Sometimes, just, 'What went wrong?' is the best question."

Then, explained Budden, you allow the interview subject to share his or her thoughts, and hopefully the response will give you many follow-up questions to ask. "But that comes with confidence. You're always like, 'What if a question doesn't come to mind? Then I'm stuck here in this dead space and I don't have anything.' It takes some more confidence and some screw-ups along the way."

But a sideline reporter will also encounter coaches who may not say much or who may not answer the questions. However, if the sideline reporter goes in knowing the tendencies of the interview subject, Budden explained, there are no surprises: "Part of it is knowing who you're interviewing. Mike Leach will talk to you forever about pirates. I know it's not my questions. He just doesn't give [the expected answers] to anyone. I go back to the 'How?' and the 'Why?' Those are questions that always will get you something that's more than one-word answers. I sometimes rely on 'What's important?' Like, 'What'll be important in the second half?' That requires them to give a detailed answer. 'How did this happen?' or, 'How were they able to jump out to a 10-point lead?'

"Then, there [are others] like John Calipari, who's going to take the interview wherever he wants to go, no matter what the question is. So if you ask about rebounding and he doesn't want to talk about rebounding, he's not going to talk about it. He's going to talk about scoring or turnovers or mentality, or whatever. So, sometimes with [Calipari], my question just is, 'What were your thoughts in the first half?' or, 'How do you think your team played in the first half?'"

Finally, Budden suggested being neutral when phrasing a question to a coach. "Always make sure there's not a negative or positive tone to it—because they could be up 40-something points but he could be pissed," she said. "So, you can't say, 'How *pleased* were you with your team?' because he might not be pleased. We

AN EXAMPLE OF A SPOTTING BOARD USED BY CHRIS KING FOR A BASKETBALL BROADCAST. *COURTESY OF CHRIS KING* might think so based on their play, but he might be upset about something. So if you say, 'How pleased were you in the first half?' and he goes, 'Well, I'm ticked,' then that makes it look like a stupid question. Making sure that it's always neutral will also get you a lot further in the interview."

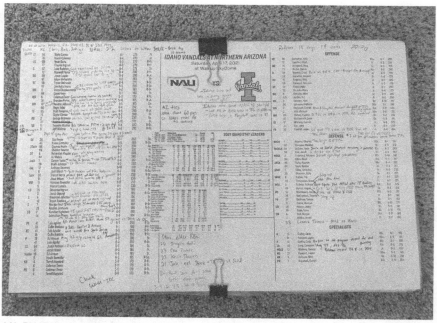

AN EXAMPLE OF A SPOTTING BOARD USED BY CHRIS KING FOR A FOOTBALL BROADCAST. *COURTESY OF CHRIS KING*

II

JOURNALISM AND PHOTOGRAPHY

Sports Photography

Richard Kee, Baseball Team Photographer

Job title: Former official team photographer, Los Angeles Dodgers

Education/training: Associate of arts degree (Brooks Institute of Photography)

Key pieces of advice: Whether it's 1976 or today, the principles are still the same: Do your homework. Find out what you want to do. Be honest with yourself and be prepared to put all your energy into that, but do it wisely.

Richard Kee, currently a lifestyle photographer based in Southern California, was the official team photographer of the LA Dodgers in the 1970s and 1980s. After working a decade in that role, he left baseball and opened his own business in food and commercial work. A graduate of the prestigious Brooks Institute of Photography, Kee is concentrating today on lifestyle portraits, capturing photos of individuals who have interesting life stories behind them.

Having built a solid reputation in the photography industry, Kee also continues to be called on by major companies—including Nike, UPS, NBC, American

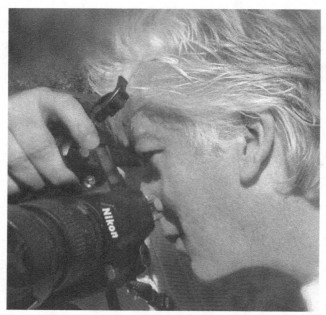

RICHARD KEE. *COURTESY OF RICHARD KEE*

Airlines, General Motors, Coca-Cola, *Sports Illustrated*, the Rose Bowl, and baseball's Dodgers, San Francisco Giants, and New York Mets—to handle their advertising campaigns.

In our interview, Kee discussed how he got his start working for one of the most storied franchises in sports and offered advice to students and others on how to get into the game.

"I wanted to get a job with the Dodgers in 1976 as a photographer," Kee said. "I did not have any past experience shooting sports. I did have college experience as far as photography at Santa Barbara, at a place called Brooks Institute. I graduated from there and I wanted to do sports because that was my love. So if I could combine the two, especially with it being baseball, I had that passion to be able to figure out—or try to figure out—how the best way to go about it was. And that's what I did; I approached and contacted Fred Claire and asked him if I could do it.

"Keep in mind this was in 1976, so not many ball clubs were doing extensive marketing back then. The Dodgers were. They were big on building up a season-ticket base, so they were ideal for me because they did do quite a bit of marketing. I approached them, and at that point, I met with Fred. He wanted to know exactly what I wanted to do. I said, 'I simply want a chance to photograph [the ball club].

If you give me a chance to photograph the ball club for four or five games, I would be able to put together a multimedia presentation of the fan experience of Dodger baseball.' He afforded me those games, and I photographed it.

"Then, I met back up with him within the week and showed him the presentation. Even before he saw the presentation, on the way to the boardroom, he stopped and said to [team owner] Peter O'Malley, 'Peter, I have something that I want you to see.' Right off the bat, he gave me that confidence and he knew that—and felt that—I was going to come through. Fortunately, everything went well. Peter enjoyed it. Fred wanted it. [At] that moment, Fred said, 'Rich, this is terrific.' I said, 'Fred, my goal is not just this, but that was an introduction to be able to go and get a job with the Dodgers.' And that's what happened. I wound up being their team photographer. I was with them for the better part of a decade during the 1970s and 1980s. It was basically sheer passion to do the job. I wanted it, and I wasn't going to let anybody get in my way.

"But Fred admired the way that I went about securing that position, and he hired me. And essentially, I hustled it. There was not a job opening, but rather, I contacted the Dodgers. And being politely aggressive, I worked out that trial period with them and [it] eventually led me to spending close to a decade with the Dodgers."

Although Kee's approach came nearly half a century ago, the former Dodgers photographer believes it's still applicable even today. "Whether it was 1976 or today, the principles are still the same, at least in the way that I approach it," he said. "And that is to do your homework. Find out what you want to do. And you have to be honest with yourself and be prepared to put all your energy into that, but you do it wisely. Let's say, for instance, for me as a self-employed photographer, whether it's an account that may involve food or sports, whatever it may be, if I want it, I have to do the homework ahead of time and find out as much as I can before I have that opportunity to make that face-to-face proposal. And it means knowing what your competition is. Who's their current supplier? Are they happy with them? And in most cases, your point person, whether that's an art director or a marketing director, they're always looking to improve. With that being said, you have to find out how or what they need to improve on.

"Then you start by looking at the competition and seeing or learning as much as you can about them. How long have they been handling that particular account? Are they getting lazy? Are they getting too comfortable? Do they still have that fire in their belly? You want to know what you're up against.

"Then you go about—once you've learned as much as you can about the present situation, especially if you can learn from that particular art director or within the company—[giving them] what they're looking for that they're not getting. More often than not, you're not going to be offering something that's unique to your customer. What you're hoping to offer is an improvement over what they have. If that's the case, it has to be significant enough for them to consider a change. So you'll need to do your homework: Know your competition; know your customer and what your customer isn't currently getting from their provider. And that's what you would want to focus on. So it requires as much homework as possible so that you go in and you can make the best of your efforts toward where their interest is. And don't feel like you have to fine-tune it to the point where it paralyzes you. Keep your enthusiasm, show that you want that account, and that you'll over deliver. And that's essentially what you do. That's worked for me. You keep it as simple as possible and you focus on what their greatest interests are. After all, they're the ones who make that decision. So that's a simple formula that I've stuck with that's worked well.

"And that's where you funnel down your energy into making your best case. It's a lot of research and then you make your case and be honest. You tell them what you bring to the table is your passion. And that passion may be the difference between what they're getting and what you're offering.

"And what I did with that slide show when I approached the Dodgers was I did it on speculation. That was no investment, no risk, by the Dodgers. I'd never photographed baseball before. I took on that risk so that the ball club goes, 'We don't have a problem with Rich's request. It's not costing us a penny. We don't have to buy anything until we see the product. And if we like it, we'll buy it.' So if you can come up with something that's conceptual that takes the risk away and makes it an easy yes for your client to give you a chance, then I think that's your way to get your foot in the door."

Kee also suggested having a backup plan. In his case, if he hadn't been successful getting a job with the Dodgers, he would've taken those images from the five games at Dodger Stadium and driven across town to Anaheim to make a similar pitch to the Angels.

With respect to having done your homework on the competition—the sports organization's current supplier or photographer—Kee said you don't necessarily have to go the route of approaching the club: "At that point, you have a choice. Either you go directly to the club and ask them to do something, as I did [with the Dodgers], or the other way is you would most likely have to go to the existing account holder—the photographer that's handling it then—and ask if you could be an assistant to some degree. Now that's a risk, because they'll immediately look at you as a threat, that you obviously want their job. So that may be less successful than having your own game plan to offer the ball club.

"Then, once you get your foot in the door, you network. You'll have to be very careful about the other person that you're trying to steal the job away from. But you can navigate that once you're on the scene, because you're somewhat insulated and protected because if the employer likes you, the other photographer is going to be tempered on not trying to destroy you, and will be forced to accept your presence, to whatever degree. I just think you need to find a tactful way to make an offer that they can't refuse."

Like any young person starting out in the industry, Kee had valuable mentors when he first joined the Dodgers, none bigger than Fred Claire. Even after Kee left the Dodgers in the 1980s, Claire remained his mentor—and that relationship, Kee said, continues even to this day. For students looking to work in sports, having a mentor is crucial as they navigate their careers. For those wanting to be sports photographers, Kee offered advice about how to seek out a mentor in the business: "I think it's important to have a mentor both on the inside and the out, in the sense that since the day Fred hired me—and especially after my time with the ball club—I've gone to him on numerous occasions for advice and counsel. He's always been very generous with sharing advice. He's had a huge influence on not just myself but many others.

"For a young person that's going out in a particular field—whether it's photography, or it involves studio work, or if it's sports—find somebody in that business. Try to develop a relationship and a friendship with them. Especially if you're young, if that mentor or that particular photographer is a good person, he'll give you the time if he feels that you're dedicated. And you'll get the advice of an experienced person who's gone through that process. And that information, that advice you get, is invaluable. It's better than going to a structured school because you learn what's important and relevant in the field. So I would say you find a mentor ahead of time, and if you're fortunate to land that particular job, find a mentor within that you feel comfortable [with] that you can share your thoughts [and] your enthusiasm, because that way it then becomes a partnership of growth where you can advance within that account. Then it's not just that particular photographer trying to make headway. You'll have the support of somebody within, and usually they would be a decision maker. So if you're young, you want to find somebody that knows the business who'll help you and give you that advantage going in."

For young people and students looking to get into sports, although times have changed since Kee entered and left the industry, some of the principles that worked for him still apply today. And these principles aren't solely for photographers; they apply in other areas in sports. Kee elaborated, "Come up with a hook that would grab that particular ball club's attention. If it was in my case, I put together a multimedia slide presentation. When I contacted the Dodgers, in my case, I did it on a proposal that it was conditional. If they didn't like it, they didn't have to purchase it. All I was asking for was a trade of giving me an opportunity to actually shoot, show what I can do. And then afterward, if they liked it, we [could] talk about purchasing it. That allowed me in the door and gave me an opportunity because they had nothing to lose. So first, come up with some type of proposal that's updated to today's times that you can offer that particular sports franchise.

"If you can come up with that and you're given an opportunity to show them your talent, that you can handle it, you're dependable, and that you deliver, I believe that's your best way to be able to get in. Once you get in, then you can spread your roots and grow within the organization and responsibilities, but all you need is that one trial, that chance. So whatever it is, whether you're a photographer or a reporter or an intern that wants to do something within the organization, make it an easy yes for them. Then, once you're there, you're in their presence and then you could work it. But don't shoot for the stars right out of the gate. Get yourself inside the door. Then, at that point, you can work forward.

"One other thing that I would suggest to people, especially youngsters that are trying out: Do the unexpected. In today's times, everybody e-mails each other. The best suggestion that I could tell you is the best investment is go out and buy a roll of postage stamps. Because what you want to do is when you have an opportunity to meet with that particular person from that organization, before the sun sets, you've already taken the time to do a handwritten thank-you note that's short and to the point, and you mail it off to that particular person. For that person to receive a handwritten, hand-addressed note is as good as a second interview and you blow your competition out of the water simply because you did what they didn't do. That will make you stand out. It's a very simple and inexpensive advantage if you do it."

That philosophy of doing the unexpected to stand out from the crowd applies even in the work that you do, added Kee: "In my case, during that period of time in the 1970s, most photographers were photographing 90 percent action shots. My style of shooting is quite different where 50 percent of my shooting of a sport was, I would say, illustrative as opposed to pure action. I would be able to tell, and anybody else can do this. I enjoyed photographing the elements of the game. That would be whether it was close-up macro shots of a baseball in a glove or a bat in the bat rack. To me, that spoke of the sport of baseball, just as much as it may have been Steve Garvey standing with his batting stance at home plate ready to swing through. That was the difference. And I found that what Fred Claire and his staff was getting was pure action. I was able to, in that trial period, show them more of a lifestyle . . . a different approach to recording the game, the fans, the entire experience. That's what made the difference between me and my competition. So look for some different ways to approach it."

Certainly, the way Kee originally approached the Dodgers and his photography style exhibit his creativity. But he also gave a more recent example. At the time of our interview, he was operating his own business focusing on lifestyle photography. "I concentrate on individuals that have interesting life stories behind them, whether they're in sports, business, or the entertainment field," he explained. "I enjoy that interaction and working with the individuals and doing unconventional portraits, or nontraditional. So that's what I enjoy the most at this point.

"One example of the portraits which was unique was the San Diego Chicken, Ted Giannoulas. We made plans to photograph him in that I didn't want to photograph him in any traditional way, so I wanted to do the exception. As it turned out, we approached Ted and said, 'We'd like to take you and take you back home and photograph you where you were born and raised.' Ted's immediate reaction was, 'Why do we have to go to Ontario, Canada?' which is his birthplace. I said, 'No, Ted. I want to take you back to the hood. I want to photograph you in an egg farm, a chicken farm. I want to put you in the middle of a thousand chickens.' After he stopped laughing, he readily agreed, and I photographed him in a San Diego egg farm, in amongst thousands of chickens around himself and me. And it's a shot that we both enjoy and are proud of."

That concept of the lifestyle portrait at the egg farm is an example of Kee's creativity—something completely unexpected by the client—which impressed even an experienced entertainer like Giannoulas, the man who's portrayed the Chicken for six decades and seen it all, making more than seven thousand appearances in eight different countries. But the idea of having the portrait taken at the egg farm still cracked Giannoulas up. For Kee, the principle is simple: "Add something compelling to each image or don't bother. Each individual brings a different situation in a storyline that you could depict in your image."

Doing lifestyle photos might be fun, but—switching back to sports—is the job of a sports photographer stressful? After all, working at games over the course of a six-month-long season is a huge commitment, and given baseball's languid pace of play, many contests run longer than four hours, meaning plenty of long days at the ballpark. Even trying to take the perfect in-game shots can be stressful. Considering all these factors, one could argue that being a sports photographer doesn't seem as straightforward as just showing up at the ballpark and enjoying the game.

Kee, however, doesn't see it that way. He addressed those challenges this way: "I would answer it very simply. I would welcome the chance to spend as much time in that particular arena or stadium. If you want that position as a team photographer, you're there and you want as much time to be able to do what you love."

As far as the stress level of the job, Kee considered his role as the Dodgers' official team photographer to be fun. "It was surreal [working for the franchise] because I was a baseball fan from five years onward," he said. "So that was my dream job. And I wanted it. I hustled. I worked for it. I obtained it and I kept it and I enjoyed the hell out of it. To develop friendships from the folks within that organization was priceless. Technology has changed the way that you go about handling a role as a photographer. We did not have digital during that time and it was manual lenses. So it was different. It was a whole different process, a different set of demands, but I sure appreciated my time there.

"There was a lot of hard work and a lot of stress, but it was always a joy. The reason was that's where I wanted to be. I wanted to be in the mix. I wanted the pressure. That was part of the return for being in that position, for being a team photographer. When it comes to throughout the year, we would take head-and-shoulder portraits. We would do two sessions of those, twice a year—first at the beginning of the year, and then mid- to late fall. We were constantly doing head-and-shoulder shots. In this role, you were dealing with ballplayers with all sorts of personalities. But it was mostly fun, and I enjoyed a terrific relationship with the players. When it came time to do team photos, we would do those twice a year. They would be done just before an evening game, so typically 4:00 in the afternoon, before batting practice. We would have it set up. Players would walk out to left field, get on the risers, and I was set and ready to photograph them. So the actual process of taking the team photo in itself with the players was less than five minutes. It was the setup beforehand [that took more time]. If there was pressure put on, pressure was only there as a result of exciting times, exciting baseball, whether it was the playoffs or World Series, and that was what your dream was each year. But I never looked at any of it as 'pressure.' I loved it. Sure, there was pressure. But it wasn't pressure like, 'I hate it.' It was quite the opposite. I embraced it."

Key offered some final words of wisdom for students wanting to work in sports: "I would just simply tell them to put together a game plan, and be able to figure out a very fair and attractive offering to whatever client they want to engage with initially. They have to realize that they may have all the credentials, all the degrees in the world, but it comes down to what the potential client or employer needs the most. And if you can figure out how to deliver it and do it and still have

RICHARD KEE COLLECTION
PRESERVING THE GAME

AN IMAGE TAKEN BY RICHARD KEE IN 1984 WITH THE JAPANESE OLYMPIC BASE-
BALL TEAM HAVING A MEETING ON THE FIELD AT DODGER STADIUM. *COURTESY
OF RICHARD KEE*

this job that you would thoroughly enjoy, then that's up to you to conceive that.
Once you have that, just go after it and be as politely aggressive as you can. You
don't want to be obnoxious. But you want to remind that potential client, 'I want
to work for you. I want this job.' And they'll never be upset with you.

"So that just calls for tactful persistence. They will take note that this person
wants this. And that's eventually going to make its mark. [Be] politely aggressive, be creative, and be very unselfish when you initially go out to get a job. I'm
not saying you undercut yourself. The answer is not to go and say, 'Well, this
man is charging you $200 a game to photograph, and I'll do it for $175.' In the
end, that employer does not care about the $200 or the $175. Your offer of [a]
discount probably hurts you more than it helps you. What you want to do is you
want to tell them, 'Look, I'll do it for the same amount. But I'm going to deliver
this to you. And what I deliver is more than what you're getting now.' So I think
you have to be very careful about making a wise offer that's fair for all parties
involved. But initially, you want to present an offer that they can't refuse, to give
you a chance, because . . . the best way to demonstrate what talents you have is if
you can actually get to do something, whether it's to photograph or it's anything
else, whatever that trade pertains to in that field that you're working in. But have
the confidence and enjoy it, because that's what it's all about. And as long as
you're polite about it, you cannot go wrong."

Baseball Writer

J. P. Hoornstra, Sportswriter and Author

Job title: Baseball writer, Southern California News Group

Education/training: Bachelor's degree in psychology (UCLA); writing for school newspapers

Key piece of advice: Understand you'll be going into an industry that has a lot of constraints, a lot of volatility.

J. P. Hoornstra covers Major League Baseball as a sportswriter for the Southern California News Group, an umbrella group of local daily newspapers published in the Greater Los Angeles area that includes the *Los Angeles Daily News* and *Orange County Register*, and is the author of the 2015 book *The 50 Greatest Dodger Games of All Time.*

A regular panelist on Spectrum SportsNet LA's *Access SportsNet: Dodgers* nightly highlights show and an occasional guest on ESPN's *SportsCenter* and *Outside the Lines*, Hoornstra has also done some travel writing for the *New York Daily News.*

HOW I BECAME INTERESTED IN SPORTSWRITING AS A CAREER

Hoornstra can definitely thank his parents for the fact that he's a sportswriter to-day. If they'd taken away the sports section when he was a child and left him with something else at the breakfast table, who knows what he might be doing now? "When I was a kid, I liked writing and I enjoyed sports," Hoornstra recalled. "I grew up in Cupertino [a city in California's Silicon Valley that borders San Jose], and my parents had a newspaper subscription to the *San Jose Mercury News*. Every morning, the paper would be sitting there and I'd have something to read before school while I was eating my cereal. The one section that my parents didn't care for was the sports section. News was gone. Local was gone. Entertainment, forget it. Sports? Yes. I had free rein and free access to it every day.

"I would read the *Mercury* every day as a kid, and so by the time I went to high school, I had a great interest in writing [sports] for my high school student newspaper—and I did that for the high school monthly paper. I took high school journalism classes as a senior, and then I took journalism again in junior college. I wrote for the student newspaper at a junior college there in Cupertino—De Anza College—and I was sports editor of the weekly newspaper there.

"I majored in psychology, mainly because I wanted to transfer to one of the University of California schools, and the University of California schools don't

J. P. HOORNSTRA WITH MLB PITCHER BRETT ANDERSON. *COURTESY OF J. P. HOORNSTRA*

offer journalism as an undergraduate major. So I picked a major that I enjoyed, that I was good at, that I didn't really have to work too hard to get good grades at while still being able to do whatever I wanted to in my spare time. So I majored in psychology and ended up transferring to UCLA after a couple of years at De Anza—and again I [wrote for] the student newspaper at UCLA. I was an assistant sports editor for the student newspaper there in my junior year, I was the sports editor my senior year, and all the while I just finished my psychology [degree] and my interest [in writing sports] had never waned.

"So just from the time of reading a newspaper as a kid, at seven, eight years old, to the time I was actually writing articles for a newspaper in high school and college, I always enjoyed it. And that's how I started."

OVERCOMING CHALLENGES IN THE EARLY GOING

When Hoornstra was beginning his sportswriting career, "the biggest challenge was making ends meet." He elaborated, "Even in my first year writing for a newspaper as a staff writer in 2003, I was living in the city of Benicia, which is about thirty minutes north of Berkeley in the Bay Area. And even though it's not a super-rich town, the cost of living is crazy high. Just to make ends meet, I needed to substitute teach in my spare time. That was just to have a studio apartment on my own! That's how bad it was."

Hoornstra said that he was fortunate he received those side jobs. "I [basically] taught anything," he recalled with a laugh. "I never took a day of Spanish in high school or college, but I substitute taught a Spanish class once. I taught fourth graders. I taught junior high. I taught high school. Any subject you can imagine, I probably filled in.

"So that [making ends meet] was the biggest challenge, and I did that for three years. Then I moved to Southern California to work for the company I'm with now, and even then, still, for a year I substitute taught and I had roommates. I always had to do other things to supplement my income, whether that was teaching or freelance writing. I just set aside the time to do it because you have to eat [and] you have to live.

"But professionally, the act of writing and reporting in doing the daily grind was never that much of a grind for me. It didn't feel like work most of the time. So, work-related challenges, as far as the actual practice of journalism, there weren't that many challenges to overcome. At least I didn't find it that difficult. The difficult part, for me, was paying rent. Never had a check bounce, but I often needed roommates."

FREELANCE WRITING

While substitute teaching was something Hoornstra did simply to supplement his income, his freelance writing gigs were probably assignments he took more seriously. At the time, the availability of such freelance gigs was much different than it is today, as more opportunities exist now.

"[In terms of] freelance writing, now you have Upwork—they have a website and an app—where a new freelance writing gig is posted literally every five minutes," said Hoornstra. "Before Upwork, it was about who you know. For example, Japanese publications often rely on reporters here in America to write about the Japanese players, whether that's Kenta Maeda or Shohei Ohtani or whoever. So there's this loose, unofficial network of writers over here and editors over there who will be in contact to see if you can write five hundred words about how you think Ohtani's going to do this season. Stuff like that. And that's just word of mouth: 'Hey, somebody passed along your name. Can you write this? It'll pay this much. Yes or no.' That's a fairly reliable avenue, just because of the demand for news over there in Japan about the players who are over here.

"But then, even before that, before I was covering baseball professionally, it was really about who you knew."

Hoornstra said he was fortunate that he also has a sister who referred freelance writing gigs to him: "She'd been a travel writer for a number of years, so she'd have assignments that took me to places like Europe, Alaska, Australia, and Machu Picchu. In my case, it really helped that she had those connections because she's been a constant source of support, on a very practical level, as far as getting me work and opening avenues for freelance gigs that I wouldn't have had otherwise. Especially because she's never ventured into sports, but she's somebody who's opened doors for me to write about other things, which—if I ever want to supplement my income or travel anyplace cool—I can do because of her. Not because of anything I've done as a sportswriter."

ADVICE FOR STUDENTS WANTING TO BECOME SPORTSWRITERS

Hoornstra considers himself fortunate that he enjoys his career as a sportswriter—but, he cautions, it's not as glamorous as people might think. And if you're serious about getting into the industry, understand what you'll be getting into: There will be struggles, and you will have to make sacrifices.

He elaborated in some detail: "My advice would be that if you just want to ask the questions that you want to ask, write the stories that you want to write, and not really have to answer to anybody else's definition of what makes the 'ideal' content, being a sportswriter is the only way to go. And the only way to go doesn't pay all that well.

"Now, if you want to write what somebody else wants you to write, want to ask the questions somebody else wants you to ask, you can probably get more money there. You can work for a team. You can work for an agency. You can work for any other different number of contractors.

"But if you want to write for a truly independent news outlet, it's going to be a tough road just because you have to be in the 1 percent of the 1 percent to make a living doing this. I'm sure there are tons of people who'd want to do what I do: have a full-time job with benefits as a sportswriter. [But] it's just so hard [compared to other careers in terms of the money you could be making]. It's tough. It's a struggle. There are going to be sacrifices you have to make for the rest of your life—whether that's living modestly, having part-time work, or having roommates—just to be able to make ends meet. Or just being able to make repairs to your home or enjoy craft beers. These are all things you have to struggle to earn."

The name Austin Murphy comes to mind, said Hoornstra, when fellow sports journalists worry about just how unstable the profession can be and the reality of making ends meet. Murphy, a well-respected journalist who wrote for *Sports Illustrated*, penned an article in 2018 about how he picked up a job as an Amazon delivery driver to supplement his work because *SI* had laid him off. According to the article, he was freelancing, but he wanted to refinance his home, so he needed some sort of more steady employment than just freelancing work. He applied for a job with Amazon and wrote about what that experience was like. "If I'd graduated from college the same time Austin Murphy graduated from college and had followed the steps that he did in his career," Hoornstra acknowledged, "I would've thought I had made it. Yet here he was in 2018 delivering packages so that he [could] just live the way that he wants to live. These are the things that really great sports journalists have to deal with now."

For Hoornstra, who receives many e-mails from students asking about the industry, it's about being candid when answering these questions about what a young person can expect in the world of sportswriting. "I get high schoolers and college kids asking me that periodically," he said. "I have to confront this question a lot. My answer generally stays the same, because at the end of the day, I understand what that itch feels like to try to pursue this as a career because you just can't imagine yourself doing anything else. And I'm not gonna tell that kid not to do it, because even if you give it your best shot in some other industry, and you succeed beyond your wildest dreams—however the industry defines 'success'—there's still going to be some part of you that always wondered, 'Gosh. Couldn't I have made it in journalism? Could I have been one of those people who gets to do this full-time for a living?' And I don't want to tell that kid not to try. So I always will [encourage them to try].

"But I'll try to prepare them for the reality of the job . . . in my case, I graduated from college in 2003, I took a vacation to Hawaii with some of my high school friends to celebrate our graduation, I came back and interviewed for a job, two weeks later got it, and I've been with the same company basically for seventeen years. I don't know who can say that in 2020, but probably not a lot of people. As for the number of sportswriters who can say something like that? I can probably count them on one hand or two. And I don't think that's a realistic expectation for today's college graduates, and I tell them that. I tell them, 'Have a backup plan. Value your time because nobody else is going to value your time for you. You have to decide what a balance looks like in your life.'"

And for people who are accustomed to a certain lifestyle, Hoornstra added, it might be difficult for some to adjust if their first sportswriting job, say, takes them far away from home: "You'll probably have to sacrifice some comfortability in the quality of your life. If you grew up in a major city or a suburb, and the only place that hires you out of college is a very small-market newspaper where you're on a staff with ten people or fewer—and you're the one sportswriter, you miss the home cooking, there's an Arby's, there's a McDonald's, there's a Chipotle, and those are the only three restaurants in town—is that quality of life worth it for you? That's a question you need to be asking yourself.

"I want to tell these kids that what I do is possible. But I also have to tell them that what I do, and the trajectory that I've followed, and the career I've been able to have, is unlikely. And you need to be prepared for that. You need to be prepared for sacrificing in ways that you don't want to. A lot of that will be time. A lot of that will be money. So you have to ask yourself, 'Are the things that I'm sacrificing in order to follow this path worth it? Is that second job the thing that I should be considering as my first job, and should I be doing the sportswriting thing on the side?' Those are really important questions you, as a young journalist, need to be asking yourself a lot, because that's the position many young journalists that I know find themselves in.

"But the broader thing is that doing this job requires sacrifices no matter how good you are. Only you are going to know whether it's worth it or not."

THE NEWSPAPER INDUSTRY AND THE CORONAVIRUS

For anybody assuming it's the COVID-19 pandemic that has hit the newspaper industry hard—just like it has decimated many industries globally—the reality is that the decline of the newspaper actually began well before this novel virus. "Necessity had forced the newspaper industry to look toward changing their economic incentives before a lot of other industries did, in such a way that would help them weather the coronavirus," Hoornstra explained. "The reality for the newspaper industry is that once the coronavirus hit, a lot of advertising dollars dried up. If you were running a newspaper in 2015 and you weren't already thinking about how to tether your revenue stream less to advertising and more to digital subscriptions and web traffic, you were already behind the game."

Conservatively speaking, according to Hoornstra, for at least five years prior to COVID-19, newspapers had already begun to rely a lot less on advertising and more heavily on web traffic and digital subscriptions in order to survive. In simple terms, many newspapers let readers have access to a small amount of their news online before a pop-up window appeared notifying readers they could have full access after purchasing a subscription. "Even newsletter subscriptions, for example the Dodgers newsletters I put out all the time," Hoornstra said. "These were things that newspapers [had already been depending on], consecutively speaking, for at least five years [before COVID]—and, more realistically, the last ten to twenty years. That's when newspapers should've been making that pivot. Again, once the advertising revenue stream further eroded because of the coronavirus, that became even more essential than ever."

The business operations of the newspaper he writes for are obviously not Hoornstra's department, although as a reporter employed by the paper he is a primary stakeholder and has responsibilities toward the company and an interest in its success. "There are certain things I can do when I put out my Dodgers newsletters to help grow revenue," he explained. "But that's really small relative to the grand scheme of the mechanics of my job. For me, personally, it's more like, 'Keep doing what you're doing.' I want the transparency from my bosses in terms of what our financial state is and what I can do to improve it, but realistically, I just really want to be able to focus on being a good reporter. That's true now. It was true five years ago. It was true ten years ago, which was probably the first time I had to think about getting furloughed or getting a pay cut, when the internet really started to erode our business model."

That's not to say the pandemic didn't affect newspaper writers, as the restrictions brought about by COVID-19 made the sports reporters' jobs a little trickier when sports resumed in the summer of 2020. "The biggest impediment to my day-to-day being normal is just the lack of access to the athletes at the games that sportswriters are usually afforded," Hoornstra said. "Major League Baseball [in 2020] barred reporters from clubhouses, from the dugout prior to the game, from being on the field prior to the game, from any of those places after the game. We were basically confined to walking into the ballpark, going to our seats, staying there for however long the game lasted, filing our story, and leaving. On the one hand, you respect all of that, understanding that it's in the best interest of public health. On the other hand, it makes it a lot harder to do your job well.

"Even aside from that, there was the issue of travel. My newspaper sent one reporter to the World Series in Arlington. This was the first year that I did not cover any Dodgers playoff games since 2012, when they didn't make the playoffs for the last time. Intellectually, it's easy for me to separate my personal point of view from my professional. Emotionally, it's very conflicting, because I want to be there to do the best work that I can possibly do. But I also have my own health interests in mind as well as that of my family. The last place I'd want to be [during a pandemic] is an airport. Maybe the second-to-last place is the back of a rideshare car, like an Uber or a Lyft. Maybe the third-to-last place is a very large hotel with a lot of people in it, depending on the agent and depending on who's running the hotel. There are some caveats there, but you get the point. There's a degree of safety that I feel at home watching the game on my television that I don't feel when I'm out in public in major cities. There's a heck of a lot of tension there, and I didn't feel any resolution to that tension for as long as the season lasted."

DEALING WITH ATHLETES WHO REFUSE TO COOPERATE

Writing about sports is certainly "awesome," as Hoornstra acknowledged. Unfortunately, there are times when athletes simply don't want to be interviewed for a story. In his years covering baseball, Hoornstra has come across his fair share of players who aren't exactly cooperative. How does he handle such situations?

"There are two ways to approach that problem when it comes up," Hoornstra said, "and it will come up. One is to look them square in the eyes and say, 'Look, if you don't wanna do this, I won't waste your time.' That's honestly the best way to do it, really. And then you get the story some other way."

Hoornstra provided a recent example of such a scenario when he was doing a story on a Dodgers player: "I can think of an athlete who I ran into that problem with within the [last couple of years]. . . . I got three questions out of him for a story that was about him. He'd been playing for the Dodgers for about a month [following a trade]. He was playing average to above-average defense, and he hadn't done that for years. And now that we had a sample size that allowed us to say that, I wanted to ask him if he noticed it. It would've been nice, but I didn't need him to tell me that, ultimately. I talked to his coaches, I talked to his manager, I talked to somebody he played with [on his previous team], and I got the story. The numbers and the anecdotes from the coaches told the story. But [the player himself] was quoted in that story about him maybe once.

"So you get the story from the people who'll give it to you. And if the athlete is being difficult, you look him square in the eyes and you say, 'Look, if you don't wanna do this, I won't waste your time.' And sometimes they'll just tell you to go away. Other times, they'll respect you for it and they'll open up."

But this tactic won't work if you absolutely need to have quotes provided by that specific athlete. "[In that situation] you really need to just keep asking the questions, because you can't run the risk of him blowing you off—in which case, you just persist." But what if the athlete in question is rude? Hoornstra said that's something a sportswriter will have to learn to deal with. After all, if you're getting paid to write these stories and you absolutely need to chase down those particular athletes to get their quotes, you just have to persist. It's part of the job. "If you can deal with the paycheck, you can deal with an athlete being a dick," added Hoornstra.

THE PROCESS OF WRITING AND PUBLISHING ARTICLES

As Hoornstra said, the act of writing and reporting doesn't feel like work most of the time. But what exactly is the process of writing an article and getting it published? "Getting a story published is the easy part," he explained. "When I'm assigned to cover a baseball game, my editors generally know what articles to expect from me. I'll communicate with them throughout the day to keep them updated on specifics. I write it; they publish it."

The actual process varies greatly depending on the assignment. Hoornstra writes a baseball-focused column that runs every Thursday—and is due on Wednesday. "By the end of the day on Monday," he said, "I at least have my topic, if not a few words scribbled down. If I need to interview people, I've made that request or I've done that interview. Tuesday is scribbling more, following up on requests, maybe doing interviews. Wednesday is writing, polishing, self-editing—hoping my editors aren't ready to kill me because I'm filing it later than they want it."

When games weren't being played during COVID and little was happening in the sense of baseball news (because transactions were on hold due to the labor dispute), Hoornstra said he was able to buy more time to work on his weekly column. That's also true during the off-season, for instance, when Kim Ng and Perry Minasian were named general managers of the Marlins and Angels, respectively. "I was happy to wait for them to give their first press conferences so I could get a sense for what kind of attributes they'd bring to the job and then write a column in response to that," Hoornstra explained. "Off-season and in-season, there are a lot of differences. With the unique situation [during the COVID-19 season], I really needed to be thinking about these topics beforehand, and I had plenty of time to do that."

With breaking news stories, it's different. But Hoornstra has a method for that: "If I'm covering a breaking news event, my process is frantic, but it's confined. Write, text, call. Write, text, call. Write, text, call. Over and over again until I've filed. That's what breaking news is like: It's simple but frantic."

When he said, "Write, text, call," Hoornstra meant texting and calling both his sources and his editors. He provided an example that came following the 2020 baseball season: "A source tipped me off to some of the changes that were coming to the Dodgers' minor-league affiliates. That was a pretty big deal, as far as off-season stories go, because the changes coming to Minor League Baseball were really extensive." In this case, LA was cutting ties with its rookie-level affiliate in Ogden, Utah. Although the team had been a Dodgers affiliate only since 2003, a previous franchise in Ogden was affiliated with LA from 1966 to 1973, with Hall of Famer Tommy Lasorda managing that club. "There was a lot of history there with Ogden," continued Hoornstra. "There were some other affiliation changes which my sources tipped me off to that were also important. So first thing I did was I wrote. I texted my editor and said, 'Here's the lead to this story that I have. Tell me if you think this is a good angle to take.' He wrote back and said, 'Yup. That's good. Let's run with it.' So I wrote, I wrote, I wrote. I texted the source back. I e-mailed somebody else. I texted somebody else just to say, 'Hey, here's what I'm writing. Tell me if you can add a comment to this or if I'm off.' Somebody who should've been able to add to the story, if they were at liberty to, and that was it. And I put the story out."

An issue that can arise when breaking a story is not having all the facts right, although this happens infrequently. "This sometimes happens with breaking news," Hoornstra explained. "With this story, somebody read it and went, 'Well, that's not true!' So, they e-mailed me and said, 'I read your story. Just letting you know, this is wrong!' And I said, 'Oh, really? What more can you tell me?' So now we're going back to this circular process. We're e-mailing back and forth. Now that I have this information, I'm texting back my original source, and I'm saying, 'Hey, this other person told me this. What can you say about that?' As I'm hearing these things, I'm going back to my editor and saying, 'We're gonna have to update this,' going back into my story, taking notes on what people are telling me, revising the copy of my article, and going back to my editor and saying, 'Okay, here's what I have now.' In the meantime, I'm asking other people to call me back, and they're getting back to me throughout the day.

"I started on that probably at about noon. I don't think I felt like I was done until maybe 5:30. That was a story that I thought was good to go at about 1:30 in the afternoon. Four hours later, I've got a lot more information that I didn't have at the beginning of the day. Fortunately, this wasn't 9:00 at night. The copy desk wasn't worried about what needed to go in print, what kind of headline they needed to put in the next day's newspaper, because I'd started early enough. But sometimes that will happen, where now I'm not just communicating with one editor who's updating the website; I'm communicating with the guy who's updating the website and the guy who's writing the headline and the guy who needs to know when the story is going to come in so he can plan out the rest of his evening because he's worried about the pages in print. But particularly when there are no games to play, I'll try to break news that nobody else has, and if I'm lucky, it will be accurate the first time. So that's how that works."

When covering an actual baseball game, Hoornstra said, "the process is such that I have to improvise based on what's going on. [But typically,] I try to arrive at least four hours before the first pitch. I pick up on a story before the game that needs to hit the internet as soon as possible. Then I rush to my computer as soon as possible. Sometimes I'll start typing it on my phone first. If I don't, which is most days, I'd use the hours before the game to just talk to as many people as I can, mostly off the record. You never know what you'll hear once you get people talking. Then, come game time, if I haven't filed my pregame story, I'll be typing from the first pitch. If I have filed my pregame story, I'll probably just eat my dinner during the first inning. Then, from there, I'm just taking notes on what I'm watching during the game. A lot of checking Twitter to see what other people are picking up on and talking about. By the final pitch, I have to have a story that's ready to file."

WRITING BOOKS—YOU'VE GOTTA HAVE PASSION

In addition to his daily sportswriting duties and regular appearances on Spectrum SportsNet LA, Hoornstra also found the time to write a book titled *The Top 50 Dodger Games of All Time*, published in 2015. At the time of our interview, though, he did not have an other similar projects in the works. It's simply a time-consuming process, and he was not sure he'd be able to commit the time needed for another book.

"When I started that book," he explained, "I had enough spare time where I knew that if I worked diligently enough during the baseball off-season and spring training that I could knock that out in less than a year—and it ended up taking me two years. And my wife was cool with me setting aside the time to write that book. She understood that that was an important foot in the door to that world where, now, if another publisher wanted me to write a book and asked if I've ever committed myself to such a project, I can say yes.

"Now, often—at least from my understanding—if you're working with a major publishing company that gives you an advance, they're also going to give you a deadline and that's going to be a hard deadline. And you have to look at that and be honest with yourself and with your publisher and give a yes or no as to whether you can meet that deadline. And if you're working full-time as a sportswriter for a daily newspaper, as I am, the answer may very well be no.

"If you have a little bit more flexibility, like you're a full-time freelancer, let's say, with some recurring freelance gigs but those gigs allow you to say, 'No, I can't do it this month; I'm writing a book,' or you have a job where you're not having daily and weekly deadlines like I do, then your answer might very well be yes.

"But you have to be really honest with yourself about the commitment and what your life looks like and whether you can put other things aside to take on a project that's going to require daily work—at least an hour every day and probably more than that.

"Those are huge projects and you don't see the fruits of your labor for a long time. But if you have a good idea for a book, you have a publisher who's willing to publish it, and you're willing to just work at that for that long, knowing you're only going to see small royalty checks down the road, [then you should go for it,]" he added with a laugh.

Passion, said Hoornstra, is a necessity, too, when writing a book: "Because if you don't have the passion but you have the talent, at least if you're writing articles daily or weekly, you're getting feedback every day or every week—and that can fuel your passion because you're constantly getting that feedback. If you don't have the passion for the book or for anything long-term, you're not going to see feedback on your work for months, if not years. Like Jane Leavy—I heard an interview with her; she was working on the Babe Ruth book for two or three years. And she's one of the best sports biographers living, at least in this country, and if she didn't have the passion for that project, I don't know how you'd spend two to three years working on it.

"But if you're writing an article or a blog on a daily or weekly basis, you're getting feedback from readers who will tell you, 'You're doing great and I love your work and keep it up'—and that fuels your passion—or they'll say, 'You suck at this. Don't be wasting your time; I'm never gonna read you.' Or, arguably worse than that, you're not getting any feedback at all because nobody's reading what you're writing. Then you know, at least, 'I shouldn't be wasting my time on this because I'm not any good at it.'"

III

SPORTS MARKETING, PUBLICITY, AND SALES

9

Sports Marketing

Marsha Collier, Sports Business for Dummies

Job title: Former general manager of *Dodger Blue*, the LA Dodgers newspaper; tech podcaster; freelance author

Education/training: Degree in English literature (University of Miami); media skills training (CommCore Consulting); asking questions and learning on the job while at the *Miami Herald*

Key pieces of advice: Love what you do. Keep learning. No matter who you meet, always be kind and understanding. And take advice from and listen to people; you'll be able to make better decisions with your career.

Marsha Collier, an award-winning tech author who has sold more than 1 million books, is an entrepreneur, radio personality, podcast host, and educator specializing in technology, internet marketing, and e-commerce.

Probably best known for being the author of the For Dummies reference book series about eBay and social media, Collier has also done work in the sports marketing business—in auto racing and baseball. Her stint in baseball came during the 1980s, when Collier, then working for the *Los Angeles Daily News*, was part of the marketing team that helped the LA Dodgers launch the campaign "Dodger Blue."

Collier, who is no longer involved in sports marketing, has since carved out a major career working in social media. She took some time out of her busy schedule in August 2019—two weeks after being in New York for the unveiling of the Samsung Galaxy Note 10—to chat about her life in sports and outside of sports.

Interestingly, Collier didn't seek out a job in sports out of college. After graduating from the University of Miami, she worked briefly in fashion advertising for the *Miami Herald* before relocating to Southern California. "I was working for the *Los Angeles Daily News*, and the company that owned the *Daily News* was the *Chicago Tribune*, who owned the Chicago Cubs," said Collier when recounting how she got involved with sports marketing. "They decided to build a relationship between the newspaper and the Dodgers. Of course, I was just an innocent

MARSHA COLLIER WITH HALL OF FAME MANAGER TOMMY LASORDA. *COURTESY OF MARSHA COLLIER*

bystander at this time. I didn't know what was going on, but one day I was the special projects manager for the newspaper where I [handled] marketing. [Long story short], the Dodgers gave [the paper] an opportunity to have their own [official Dodgers] newspaper, and we printed it and distributed it for them."

As Collier explained, she was simply told to head down to Dodger Stadium and was not given any specifics. But the assignment taught her a valuable lesson: "I really didn't know what was going on, and I went down there. And being a baseball fan myself—I grew up in New York [and] listened to the Dodgers on the radio and on TV as a kid—the Dodgers were sacrosanct to me, and here I was talking to people from the Dodgers! I knew all about baseball because I love the game, but it was stepping into this other magical world, which is something young people should remember: You never know what's going to lead to anything. I mean, no matter who you meet, no matter what kind of person they are, always be kind and understanding. And take advice from people and listen to people. And by that, you'll be able to make better decisions with your career."

One important realization Collier had was that you couldn't go into a sports job being just a fan. Continuing to learn and improve was part of the game, not simply showing up and hanging out. "My key was to learn," she said. "If I had to be at the game at a certain time, I'd be there two hours earlier, just to be there to learn. And [it wasn't all that common] being a woman [in sports] in those days. We're talking the 1980s, because I have a picture of my daughter. She was maybe one year old, in the dugout being held up by the players. So it was in the '80s, and there weren't a lot of women in sports at the time. And the guys were very smart and very well-learned in sports. I tended to doubt myself only because I was around these people who did know so much.

"So I worked hard and learned as much as I could about the game. The guys would tease me in the press box. One famous writer would lean over me to another famous writer and say, 'Charlie! Dodgers in the American League this year or the National League?' And I'd see them [casting a] side-look at me. I knew the Dodgers were in the National League, but I thought, 'Maybe I missed something. Maybe there's a new rule! Oh my! I'm gonna sit here and be a fool!' They had great fun at my expense a lot of the time. But I just kept my mouth shut and I learned. And keeping your mouth shut is one of the best ways to learn. Keeping your ears open twice as long as you move your lips—or maybe three times as long—will definitely help you learn.

"Like I said, you never know what direction things will go for you. My daughter is in marketing at a university—she is marketing and promotions manager of Cal State Northridge, but she may be moving into sports—because, like I said, she was with me at Dodger Stadium when she was just a baby. She saw my career in marketing, and she went to university and majored in marketing. I mean, if you love something—and marketing really is fun—[you go after it]. And sports marketing . . . who doesn't love sports?

"So learning from these people [and] asking questions made me love it even more. I mean, can you just imagine your head exploding? You're getting to work for the Dodgers! You don't know everything, but you're willing to learn as much as you can learn—and you're on the field with the Dodgers! It was amazing because sports is something that just holds together human beings if they let it, if they open themselves to it."

After Collier moved on from baseball, she was a member of the California-based American Auto Racing Writers and Broadcasters Association (AARWBA). Her involvement with the AARWBA, the oldest and largest organization devoted to auto racing coverage, came about because of her background in marketing along with the contacts she'd made in baseball. "People knew me [because of] the work [I'd done] with the Dodgers," she said. "So, I was approached originally by the Southern California Off Road Enthusiasts—the acronym is SCORE—and it was auto racing in the desert. But before that, I'd already had my own marketing company and my own publication on car racing. I mean, I loved sports. I loved NASCAR racing. I loved car racing. I thought this was amazing. And way back in the day, we had a track here, Riverside Raceway, so what I'd do is I had a publication. It was only six times a year, and I would base it around the Winternationals—the NHRA; NASCAR, which was two races a year out here; and Formula One, which had races twice a year also. So, it was six races a year.

"And I'd go, in an entrepreneurial way, to auto shops, to auto repair places—anything that was car-oriented—for advertising. And we printed a tabloid newspaper, [which] was distributed free at these same places where I had the advertising. So it was a free publication, like it was the early internet. It was free, and [it had everything] you wanted to read [with] photographs, and there was a color spread in the center where people could have their favorite car. And they wrote in. I had major advertisers, which was super. And I enjoyed that, but it kept me away from home a lot—and that's another thing about sports. Depending on what your job is, you're away from home. So you have to consider that once you have a family.

"Well, after I left the newspaper—that was when the *Daily News* had been sold and they were no longer doing *Dodger Blue*—I still had my own marketing company. After a brief hiatus, I was approached by SCORE. It was the people who do the Baja 1000 and stuff like that, which is pretty big-time racing, and I never knew how tough a racing it was. But I'd go out to the desert and work with photographers and writers. Now, I didn't do the writing on any of these. I put it together for *Dodger Blue*—that was the newspaper for the Dodgers. On the masthead, it had me as general manager. So basically, I put all the pieces in place and let the experts do what they do best—which is also an important thing in marketing: Let people do what they do best.

"So sports marketing is also great for those of us who love sports who can't do it. I mean, how many people do you know love basketball? And then, how many people do you know who can actually play basketball? But by being in marketing, you get to participate. You get to be part of the action. And it hinges on your energy as well.

"And marketing is such an amazing career for anybody, and I didn't start out to be in marketing. It was interesting: [At] my first job, I was told they didn't want a woman in the writing area of the *Miami Herald*. (I actually have evidence; I do have letters, whether they wanted a woman in the department.) At that time, I said, 'Can they do this?' The state assemblywoman was somebody I knew, and she wrote a note to the executive editor. And I got to go into the newspaper for a week, taking all kinds of tests—psychological tests, knowledge tests—all those tests that they can give prospective employees. For some reason, even though I majored in English literature—because I love writing, and that was my next career change, and I'm working on my fiftieth book now—I scored 100 percent on the marketing test. Not even the top quartile, but 100 percent! And this was something I never, never studied—never really had any interest in, never thought about—but because I'd made such a big stink about getting a job, I figured I'd better take whatever job they offered me.

"That started me on the road of something [I hadn't studied] even though I'd been to college. And since a newspaper worked twenty-four hours, I could go to different departments. I'd do that and ask what they're doing. Could I watch? How does this work? What's going on? And the whole thing about life—baseball, sports, and marketing—is learning, because if you don't keep thinking and you don't keep changing, you'll never succeed."

That last piece of advice, of course, applies to anybody wanting to get not just into sports but other fields, too. And just as an athlete would study film or work on, say, hitting technique in baseball, anybody with aspirations for working in sports can and should also do their homework, so to speak. "[That's true] even in today's computer era," Collier continued. "Like, if you're in marketing, are you familiar with social media? Well, there are all these different platforms: Facebook, Snapchat, TikTok, and all kinds of things. And the different demographics move from one to the next—and unless marketers keep their eyes open in today's world of digital marketing, it's the same thing. Every day has to be a learning curve. Every day, you have to read and study. Otherwise, in the busy world that we live in now, you'll fall behind and be easily replaced by somebody who stayed up to date or is on top of what's happening."

Of course, with Collier's writing background, she was able to offer suggestions on how to become successful in writing. The first piece of advice goes back to that willingness to listen: "You don't have to be the greatest writer, but if you listen early on in your career—to your editors and your teachers—you're going to be a much better writer. I mean, people today say, 'Oh, I'm writing a book! I'm going to publish it on Amazon!'

"I say, 'Well, who's your editor?'

"'Well, I don't need an editor!'

"'You what?' Well, everybody needs an editor! Every book—every long form, every short form piece of writing—you need somebody to [take a] second look at it. If you have nobody to [take a] second look at it, you put it away and look at it yourself a little later. That's what I always do. Even if you're on deadline, you walk away from it, and then you come back to it before you post. It's just common sense. But writing books is a team effort—and editors have told me that they have a hard time with writers because they'll come back to me and say, 'Wait a minute. Didn't you say this before? Shouldn't that come before this point?'"

Another common example one of Collier's editors used to send her was her unnecessary use of the pronoun "it." That piece of advice has, to this day, stuck with her: "What is 'it'? You said, 'It blah blah blah . . .' What is 'it'? Tell the reader what 'it' is. [Doing this] doesn't hurt your content, and the reader has everything spelled out clearly."

As Collier acknowledged, she has learned a great deal about writing from her editors over the years. Remembering to apply that knowledge, as far as she's concerned, makes a huge difference. But so does the willingness to adapt and change with the times. "That's part of continual learning," she said. "Don't you feel like you get better as a writer with everything you write? Well, right now, the book I'm working on is the tenth edition of *eBay for Dummies*. And over the years, I update the book, and the jokes change and the pop culture references change. I remember one [example] in the book [saying] you were going to sit down and binge watch *The Sopranos*. In the latest book, I changed it to *Game of Thrones*, because you have to change! So even updating an older edition makes a huge difference. And it's all from the editors. It's all what you learn. Learning is never ending."

For Collier, lifelong learning is a must if you want to succeed in your field, whether it's sports or marketing or social media—or any other area you're pursuing. At Dodger Stadium, she learned by listening. When she was working for the newspaper, she learned by asking questions. Collier even takes classes to further her learning, something she suggested that students and young people do. In her case, she took a class on podcasting before launching her own weekly tech podcast, *Computer & Technology Radio*, which receives thirty thousand downloads a month. "With podcasting, I went to somebody who knew what they were doing—not somebody [who] was going to sell me something," she said. "I'd rather go to someone and pay them to teach me—rather than someone who wants to teach me for free and sell me stuff. I went and I studied voice—voiceover lessons. And I studied media when I was in New York, [in terms of] how to talk to the media. So I paid. I took a media skills workshop in 2004 from a company called CommCore Consulting Group—one of the largest crisis communicators, PR people. I went to classes to learn. And when you pay and take the classes, it pays off."

What also pays off is having passion for whatever you're doing, which is crucial in sports because working in the industry—with its long hours at the ballpark, stadium, or arena—is a grind. You have to have passion to want to keep showing up. Collier's advice for having that motivation to continue showing up every single day or every single week—especially when trying to juggle everything else that might be happening in life—was succinct, quoting the famous trademark of the world's largest supplier of athletic shoes and apparel: "I'm very enthusiastic about everything I do. I just love it all. Sometimes I just don't want to do it, but you know what? Doing it keeps you centered. Like the old Nike saying, 'Just do it,' it's true. Just do it."

She brought up her own examples with her weekly Twitter Customer Service #CustServ chat, which she started in 2008, and her podcast. "I started a chat on Twitter for people interested in customer service and customer service professionals, and they join in for an hour," she said. "We ask questions and people answer, and it's an educational experience for everybody. I do that every Tuesday night. Every Saturday at noon, I do the podcast, which I've been doing for over ten years. Obviously, I do miss some when I'm traveling, because I travel quite a bit. But it centers you. Having something you always have to report to—say, you're a teacher and you know you have to be somewhere at a certain time every week or whenever—that's a center. That helps you. I think [it also helps to] organize your life. Once you start saying, 'I don't feel like doing that, this is just not what I want to do,' it's going to fall apart and crumble, like an old cookie. Because focus is what you have to have—and continue doing it."

And continuing to do it can lead to other opportunities or perks. At least it has in Collier's case: "I was just in New York for the unveiling for Samsung's Note 10. Huawei invites me to their phone launches, which is exciting because they're all over the world, and they pay me to go. I get to do a lot of that, and I think that's one of the benefits of the podcast. I may not be making a ton of money off of it, but [I do receive] a lot of good side things."

But everything, concluded Collier, goes back to just loving what you do: "I love what I do, and it all came from marketing—because marketing spins everything. So my advice for students—it could be for people going into sports but also into other areas, too—is love what you do. Keep learning. You'll get the opportunity when you're good. And keep learning. And just do it."

Publicity

Steve Brener, PR Director

Job title: Former director of publicity, Los Angeles Dodgers

Education/training: Degree in journalism (Cal State Northridge); writing for school newspapers

Key pieces of advice: In the world of public relations, it's important to have a good education. Be proficient in writing and grammar. Be a good editor. Stay abreast of what's happening in the world.

Steve Brener is another individual working in the sports industry who initially never thought about a career related to sports.

Although he grew up loving sports, he had an interest in becoming an accountant when he started high school. A chance meeting with the sports editor of a local daily newspaper, however, led him to the path of sportswriting, which ultimately took him into the realm of public relations (PR) in sports. From 1970 to 1987, Brener worked in the publicity department of his childhood team, the LA Dodgers. Despite his youth—he joined the organization while still attending college—he rose to the top quickly. At the age of twenty-four, Brener was named the club's publicity director in 1975, and during his dozen years in that role he became known throughout the baseball world as one of the best PR executives in the business.

Shortly after Brener left the Dodgers in 1987, he and Toby Zwikel, another former Dodgers PR executive, founded Brener Zwikel & Associates, Inc. (BZA), a sports PR and marketing firm. Providing counsel and support for regional and national sporting events, BZA has become one of the nation's leading PR firms and has handled some of the most prestigious events in sports, including the Super Bowl, Rose Bowl, BCS Championship, and soccer's World Cup. BZA has also been hired for men's and women's professional golf tour events as well as world championship boxing matches—including, at one point, nine of the top eleven biggest pay-per-view boxing telecasts in history. The firm's client list includes the National Football League, Major League Baseball, the National Hockey League, Showtime Sports, Red Bull, Auto Club Speedway, MGM Resorts International, and many more.

Looking back at his career journey, Brener acknowledged that he never thought he would be in the world of sports publicity and marketing. "I always had a love for sports," he said, "so I thought my niche might be as a sportswriter."

Actually, he initially thought his niche would be in accounting. While attending Ulysses S. Grant High School in Los Angeles, Brener figured he was going to be an accountant someday. But his plans changed in tenth grade after a chance meeting with Pete Kokon, the sports editor at the *Valley Times*, a now-defunct San Fernando Valley daily newspaper. On that particular day, Brener was helping out the school's track coach at Los Angeles Valley College when he overheard Kokon, who was there looking for a volunteer to cover that day's track meet, asking around to see if anyone would be willing to do it. Brener raised his hand and said, "I'll do it. I'm your man." Although Kokon didn't know who he was, he trusted the young Brener to do the job.

And that, according to Brener, is how he first became involved in sportswriting.

"All of a sudden, this changed my course of direction," he said. "I became the sports editor with the high school newspaper. I began covering a few sports for the *Valley Times*. Pete took me under his wing and taught me a lot about journalism and covering sports. So, after I got involved in covering sports and sports editing in high school, I switched gears and decided my passion was sports and sportswriting." Then, after high school, he attended Valley College, where he became sports information director in his first semester.

The chance meeting with Kokon and then having him as a mentor was a lucky break for Brener, but he said that's what the sports industry is all about. "This business," Brener continued, "is all about contacts and relationships." That's also how he ended up working for the the team then known as the California Angels in 1969, while he was still in college. Through his sports connections, he knew former Dodgers players Norm Sherry and Roger Craig, who had become scouts for the Angels and Dodgers, respectively. During a Valley College baseball game, he asked the two former players what his chances were of getting into baseball. Told his odds were a million to one, Brener was undaunted. He ultimately convinced Sherry to introduce him to George Lederer, the Angels' director of promotions and public relations, and Brener was offered a part-time job with the club's publicity department. Although he was still attending college and lived in the San Fernando Valley—it took an hour to drive to Anaheim Stadium (now known as Angel Stadium of Anaheim) in Orange County every day—Brener jumped at the opportunity to work for the American League ball club. "I'd drive to Anaheim every day right after my classes. I made $25 a day for the Angels and got the opportunity to write scorecard features and do the lineup [sheets]," Brener said.

In 1970, he decided to jump ship to the crosstown Dodgers and was hired by Fred Claire, who'd just become the club's publicity director in 1969. After joining the Dodgers, Brener transferred to Cal State Northridge; he graduated in 1973 with a journalism degree. In 1975, when Claire was promoted to the position of vice president of public relations and promotions, he personally recommended Brener for the role of publicity director for the Dodgers. "Fred gave me the opportunity of a lifetime, to come a little closer to home and work for the Dodgers," Brener said. "Back in my younger days, I was a big fan of the Dodgers, so it was a lifelong dream to work for the club that I loved and followed. And I found my niche in sports public relations, and eventually became the youngest PR director in baseball history there in 1975 at the age of twenty-four."

As far as what it was like to work in the publicity department of a sports franchise, Brener shared some of his experience from his Dodger days: "Working in baseball's probably the most difficult sport because the season's 162 games, plus you spend about six weeks in spring training before the season even gets going. Then, if you're fortunate enough in the postseason, the season can go even another month until the beginning of November."

For Brener, as the PR director, he was putting in a workaholic's hours. He arrived at his office by 10:00 in the morning daily and left about an hour after each home game, which on many nights could be past 12:30 the next morning. But he didn't mind. "I enjoyed waking up each and every day, going to Dodger Stadium, because every day brought another chapter in the Dodger story," he explained. When the Dodgers were at home, he had a seven-days-a-week job. When they traveled, he was often with the club, making half the trips. On road trips, about ten reporters traveled with the team regularly, along with two radio broadcast teams, and as the PR director, Brener was responsible for handling their requests. Even when he didn't travel, he worked at the office from 9:00 in the morning to 6:00 at night, before returning home to keep score of the game by radio or television.

During game days at Dodger Stadium, Brener stayed busy during the day working on statistics and handling requests from fans and players. He dealt with people on all levels, not only fans and players—everybody from owner Peter O'Malley to interns and from the visiting teams to members of the media. The phone in the Dodgers publicity office rang nonstop every day, and the mail never stopped coming in. He might, for example, receive letters from Little League teams wanting a dozen baseballs signed by Dodgers players, and he'd make sure those requests were handled.

The media notes in the press box were also his responsibility, and Brener and his assistant Toby Zwikel compiled up to ten pages of notes for the press prior to every home game, with information such as the Dodgers' record in day games versus night games, on artificial turf, in one-run games, against left-handers, and much, much more. Throughout the game (and even after the game), Brener fielded questions from reporters, such as, "When did so-and-so go on the disabled list?" and, "When was the last time a Dodger player did this and that?"

It was also Brener's job to clear the clubhouse of nonplayers a half hour before each home game. He even had the responsibility of checking on last-minute details such as player transactions and injuries. "I'm a troubleshooter," he said of his pregame routine.

And his work year didn't end with the final out of the season. The day after the season ended, he was already preparing for the following season, work that included doing a final wrap-up on statistics, working on the highlight film, and starting on the next season's media guide.

With so many PR responsibilities in such a long season, what does it take to be able to handle this type of job? "It's a long grueling season, and you really have to be dedicated and love the game of baseball to be in it," Brener said. "The other thing that's important in the world of public relations is having a good education. Being proficient in writing and grammar as well as being a good editor—those are important things also. And you have to stay abreast of what's happening in the world as well.

"If I had to do it all over again—I was a journalism major and business administration minor—I'd probably take some political science [classes] or something along those lines. The business minor certainly helped me in the various areas of the business world. I learned accounting and took a real estate class and some other courses, so it's all important. I think it's important from the standpoint of, like, being a good utility man in Major League Baseball who's around for twenty years, who's able to play more than one position. You're more likely going to have a longer career and be able to do more things. So if the journalism or sports public relations didn't work out, I'd probably be an accountant for some other field in the business area."

Brener also clarified that when he mentions being up to date with what's happening in the world, he isn't referring to only the specific sport you're involved in—and not just only sports, either. In Los Angeles, for instance, the Dodgers aren't competing just with the other local sports teams because of all the various forms of entertainment available in the city, and as a PR director, that's something he has to consider. "When we were working at Dodger Stadium in the early days, we felt like we were working 24/7 at that time," he said. "But now, it really is 24/7 with the advent of the internet. It's a 24/7 news cycle now with everything that's going on with all the social media, radio, TV, and online. There's a lot going on and you just have to stay abreast of everything and keep up with everything not only in the world of baseball but in the world of sports and entertainment. We're all competing with all the major-league and professional franchises in this city [Los Angeles] and college football and college basketball. And you got the beach, and you can go to the movies. You've got theme parks, concerts, and everything. The competition's heavy. So you gotta do the best to promote your product—your team, in this case—and get the word out on what's happening with the Dodgers and at Dodger Stadium."

And because it's a 24/7 news cycle today, Brener said, knowing social media is crucial: "In this day and age, this is a social and a digital world. In the world of PR, you have to be well-rounded for the changes that are happening each and every day in this society. That means having a good social media background, with Instagram, Twitter, and Facebook. [Obviously] doing what you do in college to get your degree and doing the internships are very important, but you'll have a longer career if you can grasp the social and digital world, writing, and sales—being a great salesperson. Again, it's like being that utility man in baseball: Playing more positions means you're more likely going to have a longer career and do more things. [But on top of that] the most important is contacts and relationships, getting to know people, and helping one another."

For college students still in school, Brener offered the following words of wisdom: "Work hard. [Have] dedication. Enjoy people. Enjoy your life. Don't forget to take Spanish. I think Spanish is important. [With the Dodgers in the early 1980s, we] had Fernandomania [with superstar pitcher Fernando Valenzuela on the ball club]. Unfortunately, what little Spanish I had, it didn't work for me. Luckily, Jaime Jarrin, who's our broadcaster, handled the translation of Fernando and all those press conferences that we put together. So having the Spanish language as a second language is important in this day and age. [Looking at baseball specifically,] we have players from Japan and Korea. [On the Dodgers] we had a player from Cuba, and having that other language can certainly assist a PR director. Major League Baseball recognized that [in the mid-2010s and implemented a policy stating] each club had to have a PR representative as a translator on the road. So we have an additional rep that goes with our team, home and away, that is a translator for our players that need translation with the media. [MLB has] recognized the importance of it and so each club has a rep now."

Media Sales

Barry Turbow, Media Sales Professional

Job title: National sales manager, Lakers and Dodgers television networks

Education/training: Bachelor's degree in business administration (California State University, Northridge)

Key pieces of advice: Simply being a fan alone probably won't help you get a job in sports media sales. Personal and professional integrity are paramount. Interning and networking are critical to professional success. Be able to read body language and nonverbals. Really spend time getting to know the client. It's important to establish rapport before going in for the ask.

Barry Turbow works in sales in the sports media industry, enjoying the role of national sales manager for the LA Lakers and Dodgers television networks. His career path, as he said in our interview, is unconventional in that he began in a nonsports industry before transitioning into sports. That wasn't his original plan,

BARRY TURBOW. *COURTESY OF BARRY TURBOW*

though; he'd always thought he was going to go straight into sports out of college.

"I grew up a die-hard sports fan," he said. "Born and raised in Los Angeles. I was a big homer fan—Dodgers, Lakers, Rams, Raiders—because back in the day, you couldn't watch anybody except your home team. All the national cable deals didn't exist. In college, I interned for Kareem Abdul-Jabbar and his production company. With baseball being my passion, they were going to help me get a job in baseball when I graduated, whatever it took."

But things didn't work out that way. When he graduated in June 1994 with a bachelor's degree in business administration at California State University, Northridge (CSUN), baseball was experiencing a labor dispute—with players eventually going on strike two months later, leading to the cancellation of the World Series. Realizing it wasn't the best time to get into baseball, Turbow had to pivot: "To make a long story short, I wasn't sure what I wanted to do. I studied business marketing—that was my major—with a finance minor. I ended up answering a couple ads in the back of the advertising magazine *Adweek*, because I thought the whole advertising agency thing was cool, and ended up getting into media sales."

Turbow worked in media sales for Petry Television (which focused on broadcast television across the country in different markets) from 1994 to 1999, eventually being promoted to senior account executive. His duties included providing advertising sales and support services to client television stations nationwide. But seeking other opportunities, he left media sales briefly from 1999 to 2002. "That was a time when high-tech start-ups were coming left and right, throwing money at people," he said, "and it was a heck of an opportunity. I rode the wave up and I rode the wave down, and I was able to segue based on my relationships that I had in media before I left back to it, and I started working at Fox Sports in 2002. That really started my career in sports media sales."

A key lesson from Turbow's story is that the relationships he'd built with people within the industry helped him land the Fox Sports job. "Thankfully," he said, "I was able to network with some of the executive management at Fox Sports and I was able to get hired in 2002. And I've been working locally here in Los Angeles, whether it was for Fox Sports, nationally, then I went locally for Fox Sports West and Prime Ticket. And we had literally every single team in Los Angeles back then on our air, which was great. Born and raised in Los Angeles, I couldn't think of a better place for me to be.

"When the Lakers branched out and started their own regional sports network with, at the time it was Time Warner, and then the Dodgers left us at Fox Sports and started their own network, again under the Time Warner umbrella, I was able to leave Fox Sports for [my current] opportunity. And I've been with this organization since about 2016. I love the product I represent. I love the sports teams in Los Angeles, and I wouldn't want to sell anybody other than the teams that I truly have a passion for.

"Long story short, with my marketing degree, I first got into media sales with Petry Television, stayed in media sales [after taking that brief break], and that's where I still am to this day, but with the sports focus. So you could say it took me eight years into my career, from 1994 to 2002, to truly get into sports, which is ultimately where I wanted to be. And I think sports is a great place to end your career, not really start it. I say that because it's sexy. Everybody wants to get a job in sports. Everybody wants to work and be affiliated with their favorite teams, whatever it is. So when the demand for the entry-level jobs is high, the pay isn't so great and it's grunt work. If you've talked to people that work in an entry-level position with their team, it's usually cold-calling—250 calls a day—to get people to buy a pack of tickets or season tickets. If they get good, then they'll move up and they'll start selling premium seats. It's a tough gig, and you're not going to make the money that you want."

Having successfully found his niche in sports media sales, Turbow tries to help out young people he comes across daily: "When I talk to our interns and our entry-level people, I'm like, 'What do you want to do? What's your long-term approach? How do you want to approach [your career]?' If they're working with me, I ask, 'Do you like what I do? Do you not like what I do?' That's part of the process, too, because there are so many jobs that are now affiliated with sports that, when I graduated, I didn't even know existed. The job I'm in right now technically didn't even exist back then, because local rights fees were just emerging in the mid-1990s, so it's a completely different world.

"So I'm fortunate that I got a decent amount of media experience before I segued into sports, [and] I think [one of the keys to success] is taking a long-term approach. [Also,] being able to network—for the right reasons—with people in important positions, is critical."

What's also critical is how you come across. Young people seeking a career in sports should conduct themselves in a professional manner, Turbow said, to not come across as being a fan: "I handle the sales for the Lakers and Dodgers television networks, and one of the biggest flaws that I see from people that come in and interview: They tell me they're a fan. When somebody comes in and tells me they're a Laker fan or a Dodger fan, that doesn't impress me. Frankly, in Los Angeles, nine out of ten people you talk to are probably a Laker fan or a Dodger fan.

"Of course, it depends on what level we're hiring. If we're looking at entry level, it's a little bit different. If we find somebody that's interned in media or interned with some type of sports background, that helps. But it's not just saying that you're a fan. That doesn't mean a thing to me, because that, to me, says I don't know if you can handle working here because if you're not gonna be going to every single game or to the high-profile stuff, I don't need somebody salty. So that doesn't impress. And I think sometimes people think that if they come in and they say, 'I'm a big fan of' whatever team they'd be affiliated with, [it would impress the interviewer—when in reality] that doesn't mean much. I think the credibility of your résumé and your background will speak volumes more in whatever type of job you're looking for—in the long run."

This means that while it's great to be able to talk water-cooler talk about what happened in the game last night, getting hired is more about relevant experience for the job. "It's great to have that passion for the local team," he said. "That's almost a prerequisite. If you want to work in sports or you want to work for us, you're going to be a sports fan. So it's a given. I don't think it's the main reason to hire someone.

"So what kind of relevant experience or internships do you have that make you qualified for the position we're hiring? That's much more important, at least to me, in the way we hire. In my case, starting in the advertising world and then moving into a sales position before segueing into sports, I've brought relevant experience to the job that I ultimately got at Fox Sports. That means a lot more and will lead to much more success because the perception is, 'It's great. That's all we do is get around and talk sports around the water cooler.' And that's the job, and my job is to go out and entertain clients at games, and that's part of it. That's the *best* part of it. But it's not the only part. A lot of it tends to be what happens when you're out to a game till midnight but you still got to be at the office at 7:30 in the morning and follow up on deliverables for clients. People see the sexy side. They don't see the pressure that comes just from a sales side or from just being in the day-to-day office. It's still a job, and it needs to be treated that way, with relevant experience."

Since networking is important and finding a mentor in the industry can be tricky, Turbow ensures his interns know he's there to assist them if they reach out.

"I dare you guys to stay in touch with me," he normally tells them. "Now, I don't want you to drop me an e-mail and say, 'Hey, awesome game last night!' Instead, I think the best way to make an impact on somebody that you'd want to mentor you, would be: (A) When we talk, listen. (B) A great follow-up to that would be [for] you [to] find an article applicable to a topic we discussed."

Because so much information can be found online, there's simply no excuse not to follow up on a topic that was previously discussed. "For example," Turbow said, "one of the main things I just talked about to our interns was [the idea that] everybody perceives sports to be male-dominated. It's actually more family-friendly programming, with the Lakers and Dodgers [having] a huge female audience. So [in this particular example], I'd love to have one of those interns that was in that room send me an article talking about female fans of teams or something involved with sports. I'm sure I could, in two seconds, do a Google search and find something that's applicable. So I think you have to show that you think strategically, that you have a good head on your shoulders, that you listen to what we discussed, and 'Here's something applicable to it.'"

Being able to research such information online and bring it up in conversation makes any young person just entering the industry look much more impressive, as far as Turbow is concerned: "That's a great way to get credibility from someone, because, again, if someone comes in and all they want to do is talk about how Clayton Kershaw gave up two home runs—and he sucks and should be traded—that doesn't impress me. Talk to me about some of the topics we went over, let's go over them, and show me that you listened and that you retained the information and want to know more about it. That's 1,000 percent more engaging than just talking water-cooler talk."

What also doesn't impress organizations, added Turbow, is a lack of awareness of social media etiquette. "That's all part of the entire new world of vetting a qualified candidate. Whatever you post online, pretend either your boss or your parents are going to see it, so post and act accordingly. It's very much an HR practice to check somebody's profile, whether it's their Facebook or Instagram or Snapchat. People are going to look at that, and it's going to affect your personal opportunities. And it's going to live for perpetuity on the web. So act very carefully and professionally in it. Again, things that you may have done as a freshman in college may come back and haunt you.

"So, as part of getting ready to enter the real world as a college graduate, you need to vet your social media presence, look at what people would see from their perspective if they just Googled you, and what comes up, and what they'll see on your social media that may impact your ability to get that job or show them that this person isn't somebody that I'd want to put in front of a client or have them work for us internally. So it's very important to clean that up and make sure that you stay on the straight and narrow in anything and everything you post."

While many young people enjoy using social media, not everybody is comfortable with the idea of doing sales. An introvert, for instance, might be nervous just at the idea of talking to prospective clients. As Turbow said, though, one doesn't need to be super outgoing to be effective in sales: "I come from a sales background and what I do primarily is sales—and it's a very quantifiable job, meaning the scoreboard doesn't lie. Either you put numbers up or you don't. And especially with interns or younger people with less experience, they come in as almost afraid of sales. I think that's because they think they can't stand up in front of a boardroom and talk to a room full of fifty people." The organization hiring you will typically provide you with in-depth training to help you succeed; Turbow's does this. "We have a curriculum for our interns, and one of the questions that I make sure I'm asked every time we sit down in front of them is, 'If I'm not a people person—I'm not an extrovert—do you think I could do sales?' I tell them, 'Absolutely!' The people that buy from us have many different personality types, so when we put a sales team together and we put clients together with sales people, it's primarily based on relationships [where] I think these personalities will be compatible."

This means that, within Turbow's organization, sales interns and staff are put in positions where they're most likely to succeed. "From a sales perspective," he said, "you have to match personalities [between] a salesperson [and] that potential client. So to have a successful sales team, you need a very diverse set of personalities. And part of the decision on what account goes where is based upon that client and their personality. We have several clients that are very shy and don't want somebody who's that stereotypical salesperson that might be louder or more boisterous. They're going to want somebody that they can relate to, that they believe, that they trust. And I don't even really see my job as sales. I'm more of a sports marketing consultant. My job is knowing my product and being able to communicate that to whoever's potentially going to buy my assets. And, really, what it comes down to [is] establishing that credibility, that integrity with the client, and that doesn't necessarily mean you're jumping up and down on a table with a boisterous personality. It means you're actually delivering something they're looking for, and you're being honest and factual about what they happen to be talking about.

"I don't think sales needs to be someone that would be a stereotypical salesperson at all. The part of my job I enjoy is that consultative approach and coming up with a solution for someone that meets their needs, ultimately. And I don't think it has to be done in the stereotypical sales manner. If you're on the sales side, the main key is being authentic—and not trying to sell somebody something that you shouldn't. I think it's more of a consultative job. I really, truly try to say I'm more of a sports marketing consultant than in sales, because I'm trying to get involved with clients, learn their marketing initiatives, and how the assets that I represent can help them meet their marketing objectives.

"With that being said, people shouldn't be scared of getting into sales, because there are many different personalities that need to be in sales and work with people—but if you're authentic and you're genuine and you have integrity, that's going to make an exponential difference in your success."

Those qualities—being authentic and genuine, along with having integrity— are essential for any sports business professional, according to Turbow: "Being able to do more than you say you're going to do is important. Whether it's internal or external—whether you're dealing with clients directly or whether you're in finance and you're dealing with the billing department—always do more than you say you're going to do. The cliché would be 'under promise and over deliver.' But there's truth to that. There's follow-up—that truly is almost lost nowadays in a lot of ways, because there's so much less communication because everything is sent via either e-mail or text now. The one-on-one communication gets lost. Sometimes, that gets lost in translation. What you meant to say may not be what they heard when you type something out, versus a conversation like you and I are having now. So I think clear communication is critical. And knowing when to ask and make sure that if you're not talking, that your point that you were trying to get across was delivered—and it wasn't misinterpreted for something else.

"But it all comes down to personal follow-up and back to professional integrity and even personal integrity with it, because when you get to know people and if you're relationship-based—and even if you're not—it's very important that you hold yourself in a manner that demands respect."

Turbow noted that communication is sometimes misinterpreted simply because of a trend away from one-on-one conversations in today's work culture. How might one navigate around that? "Unfortunately, that's why this is called 'work,' not 'fun.' I go to work every day; I don't go to 'fun,' even though sometimes it's more fun than not," he said with a laugh. "But it's inevitable that crises will come up. The best way to handle it—again, it might be a recurring theme that I'm talking about—is professional integrity. You gotta communicate bad news as much [as]—if not more than—good news, so some things will be in your control [while] some things will be out of your control.

"[To give an example], we had the Dodgers sold through the [2019] National League Championship Series. Well, they went out in five games in the National League Divisional Series. So that's something that was, as an example, out of my control. In aggregate, we had about $1.8 million in Dodgers, just National League Championship Series games alone. So that's a dilemma. We now have several people to appease. I now have the clients that spent with me that time is of the essence, that I needed to get a hold of them immediately, and let them know, because a lot of them are not in Los Angeles, that these games that they purchased are not going to air and what do [they] want us to do with the money? Sometimes, in that situation, you may say, 'I'm gonna do everything possible to hold on to that $1.8 million,' but the right decision with a few of the clients was to give them the money back, and say, 'You know what? You bought the Dodgers. I can't sell you the Cardinals versus the Nationals, obviously, at the same rate as the Dodgers, and you're only specifically focusing on local sports and local markets.'

"Obviously, I'll come up with a solution for the Lakers, but if it's sports-based, whatever it is, it might be timing. There's sales-based based on timing. Right now, all we have is postseason baseball and preseason basketball.

"So I didn't have a solution. So I gave $80,000, for example, back to Subway because they have a special promotion going on over the next two weeks that was critical for them. I wasn't even going to say, 'I can put something together,' because if I did, it probably would've discredited me. And I'm, of course, focused on business going forward. It's not about just getting business once. It's about getting them to renew and spend more with you as your relationship builds—and they see that you're gonna take good care of them.

"So I think the best way to [handle] any type of situation is you have to deliver bad news in person, ideally; if not, over the phone, where you can communicate—not just in a short e-mail because I think that'll get lost in translation. So I think taking it on head-on is better received. And usually when I'm trying to come up with a solution, if I don't have something that fits into their marketing needs, then I'm gonna say, 'You know what, here, take it back and you guys will find a better home for it, because I know what you bought and I can't deliver that to you, unfortunately.' That's very difficult to do at times, but it helps with the end result. That, again, establishes that credibility that is so integral. I don't care if you're in sales or if you're in finance—or whatever you're doing with whatever organization you're looking at—I think that's critical."

The entire world, of course, was introduced to an unexpected crisis with the COVID-19 pandemic in 2020. "It was surreal," Turbow said when discussing how the pandemic has affected his industry. "My perspective is that everything is relationship based. When not only the sports world but the entire world seemed to pause in mid-March—I've never canceled more business in my life. At that point, it seemed to be more of, 'Okay, let's hold it together. Let's just make sure everybody's okay.' It humanized the entire business. So where you've had people that you've dealt with for so long, now the business almost became secondary to me; it was more like, 'How are you doing?' and, 'How's your family?'

"We're all going from face-to-face meetings or traveling across the country for a meeting or in your backyard, to almost no communication at all, and all over the phone or a Zoom meeting or WebEx. Of course, in sports, I didn't have the assets that we traditionally do in sports—whether it was heading into the NBA playoffs, being able to host clients at a game, or baseball season, being able to host people at Dodger Stadium. Instead of being able to have a casual conversation over a three- or four-hour game, you have to get very concise and a much more consultative approach, and listen, and being able to provide a need. Because when you're on the other line of a WebEx or a Zoom call, it's much different than being in person. So being able to listen and provide a solution for what people are looking for, once they started to normalize. But at first it was just, okay, no problem. If a car dealership, as an example, isn't open and can't get any foot traffic, there's no point in advertising. So it was time to be a good partner.

"[With] some of our very best clients, during COVID, a lot more people were home watching television. Whether it was ratings were up or there were more eyeballs aggregated to consume our content, even though we didn't have any live sports, we still had some airtime to fill. So we were able to take care of all of the clients the best we could. And even though they didn't have any schedules running that they were paying for, we still wanted to be a good partner and keep them at least, bring them some type of awareness or presence in the LA marketplace. And hopefully, when things normalize here, whenever that may be, it's going to mean we're all going to be better off for it. It really comes down to relationship and how you treat people. Ultimately, it's what's going to make things go better. There's still many businesses struggling. So as opposed to trying to go in and sell them the media schedule, 'How can I help the business grow or sustain or survive?' has been the narrative, as opposed to what it was previous to COVID."

Even when you do the best you can, though, there will be times when you're criticized. Turbow had the following pointers when it comes to handling criticism: "You have to get thick skin first, with criticism, because people are going to criticize you no matter what, internal versus external. It's just a way of life. But if it's constructive criticism from a superior, that's very different than criticism from a peer because you're outperforming them. So I think it's being able to delineate between the two, and if it's constructive, it's being able to take it and always strive to evolve and become better. So I don't think criticism is necessarily a bad thing. When you do an annual review, even if I killed in my job and I did an amazing job, there are still going to be people that will find something bad to say about it. Okay, well, I'd have things to learn and improve on. Now, if it's somebody next to me that's just jealous because I've done my job that they should have done better, then you got to not let that affect you—and brush it off."

Finally, Turbow reemphasized the idea of thinking about the long term when it comes to career choices: "One of the key things I would say when I'm giving advice to students is, 'Keep your eye on the long-term growth opportunities.' You may get yourself into a job that you don't like when you're starting out a career. That's just as good as if you found something you love. That way, it can help you narrow it down to say, 'I never want to do that again,' and help you find something you love. But the key is keeping your eye on the long-term.

"If you want to run sales for your favorite team or if you want to get into media sales, [you might be thinking,] 'Okay, I want to go sell the Lakers and Dodgers in Los Angeles.' That sounds pretty sexy, right? Well, guess what? If you come in here and start as an assistant, it's going to take you a long time and they're going to underpay you eventually, because you're internal. I think you need to go out and build a long-term [plan]—I'd say your own business plan—on what it's going to take to get [you] where [you] want to go. So if [you] start someplace else, [you might] say, 'Okay, I'm gonna give this two years. While I'm there for two years, I'm gonna network my ass off. I'm gonna get to know everybody I can. When I can go to a game, I'm not gonna sit there and watch as a fan. I'm gonna be up asking questions of people at that game and networking. And who do I know that knows people here or there? How can I leverage the people that I know to make an introduction? And when they make that introduction, I have to be impactful and impress whomever I'm talking to.'

"You never know what that's going to lead to. And that might be two or three years down the line [before it] leads to something, but you're never going to get a job in sports by answering something online from Indeed, or something [like that], because there's too much demand for it. So part of the process, I think, would be narrow it down to something you truly, sincerely enjoy doing—whether it's sports-related or not, at that time. And see if there's something applicable in sports that you can do, and then, 'How am I going to weave my way to get to where I want to be—whether it's in one, two, three, four, or five years?' For me, from 1994 to 2002, that took eight years for me to get into sports officially when I started media. So always keep your eye on the long term, not just short-term gratification, for your career building."

Ticket Sales

Russell Robards, Ticket Sales and Fan Experience

Job title: Former ticket sales and experience manager, LA Wildcats (XFL)

Education/training: Master's degree in sport management (California State University, Long Beach); internships

Key piece of advice: You gotta sacrifice if you do want to work in sports.

Sports has always been a huge part of Russell Robards's family. Like his siblings, he grew up playing sports. His brother and sister both played college sports. He played junior college football. Both of his parents are PE teachers. "With sports being such a big part of my family, I wanted to be open-minded when it came to having a career," Robards admitted. "So I thought if I could get a good job working in sports, I might enjoy that."

He had the opportunity to work for a pair of professional football teams from 2018 to 2020, parlaying a 2018 internship with the Rose Bowl to positions with the NFL's LA Chargers (2018–2019) and the XFL's LA Wildcats (2019–2020): "I interned for the Rose Bowl concierge services for events, which led to the Chargers fan experience and game operations, and then I did ticket sales and experience for the XFL [Wildcats]." Although the XFL season ended prematurely halfway into the 2020 campaign because of the COVID-19 pandemic, Robards had already been leaning toward leaving the sports industry. The pandemic simply expedited the process, he explained. Now working in a nonsports field, he's planning to eventually return to school to pursue higher education so that he can follow his parents' footsteps and become a PE teacher.

For sports fans who'd like to work for their favorite team, it's important to understand that working in sports typically means not being able to watch every game. This is the case for anybody working on the sales and fan experience side. "When I was working for the XFL on game days, we'd be able to catch little snippets, mainly at the end," said Robards. "But for the most part we're busy talking to fans trying to do upsales. [On the fan] experience side, we're trying to get the fans together who are doing something at halftime or at the end of the game. So we're trying to coordinate that. That was the biggest thing."

For athletes who grew up playing sports, it might also take time to adjust to the realization that working in sports has a totally different feel from what they are used to: "I loved playing, the teamwork, the camaraderie, performing athletically and physically. Once you start working in sports, sales is a grind. You're in the office, selling on the phones or on the laptop trying to meet with people. The product I was selling was for sports. At the same time, it wasn't sports. That's what I realized." It's tempting, then, to try and pursue a similar position outside of sports because the paycheck is often bigger. "[You come to realize], 'Hey, I can get into sales [in another industry] making [a better income],' especially [considering the fact that] people I knew who were doing sales [outside of sports] were making way more money than I was. That's the hardest part, I think, about sports. So many people are willing to take pay cuts and work like that because they want to work for the Rams or their favorite team—and be able to say that. For me, I lost some of that 'sparkle in my eye' for working in sports, in a sense. I'd go to work and realize, 'I'm not out on the field. I'm not participating in anything. I'm in the office making calls.' So I wanted to get out and see more about [what the] business [world offers], make more money, and have more freedom in that sense—because it *is* a grind. I just wanted to try something else."

But let's say you want to work for the Rams—or your favorite team—but aren't sure what area you could work in. Don't forget to consider game operations/ticket sales and fan experience, especially if you enjoy interacting with sports fans.

Anybody who's attended a sporting event knows that teams pay a lot of attention to creating a unique fan experience at every game, putting on events to entertain the crowd during intermission or between innings or at halftime, depending on the sport. Working in fan experience means getting fans ready for those events every game day, and those events are scripted. For game days in professional football, the typical workday runs approximately eight hours. "For the XFL, let's say the game starts at 1:00; we'd get there around 10:00. Most of it was just to make sure everybody's there on time and early. So the first bit is maybe helping get some stuff set up at tables and booths. We'd all meet and game plan on what we're doing, get our game-plan sheets of schedules—with times, where we're going, and what we're doing," Robards explained, referring to the pregame and in-game itineraries distributed to staff that list the times and notes for the various events during that game, such as halftime fan experiences and in-game promotions.

"We'd go over that," he continued. "Pregame, we'd go and help people check in for their event that day, whether it's special packages and halftime shows. When gates open, we had to make sure that we were prepared and at our booths and areas. If we were part of the halftime crew for the experience that day, we'd go and get our fans together and bring them down, and monitor things and make sure everyone's in place, and do their little halftime experience. And then come back up. At our booths, we'd try to talk to different fans, see if they have season tickets, and try to get them in for season tickets, see if we can upsell them on where they're at, making sure they're enjoying their seats. At the end of the game, we'd have an end-of-the-game experience, so we'd have to get fans together for that and do that after the game. Then it's pick everything up and head back. Say the game starts at 1:00, you'd have to be there at 10:00, and then be out of there around 5:30 or 6:00. So, you're looking at a 10-to-6 schedule on game days— without watching much of the game, either."

Of course, depending on your department, working in sports might also mean commuting to the team's facility or office on days when the club isn't playing. Although for many sports organizations, the stadium, arena, or ballpark serves as the club's headquarters, that wasn't the case for the LA Wildcats, which proved inconvenient for Robards in terms of commute. For nongame days when he was working in the team's sales office, it meant extra-long days. "For the XFL, we had a separate office in a different location, which was in Beverly Hills," he said. "That was cool—at first. But I was commuting to get to the office two hours each way, which made my days really long." The good news: he got to work with an amazing team in the office. "We had a great sales team, and our boss was awesome. It was a grind, making a lot of calls and reaching out [trying to make sales]. We weren't making very much, but that was the grind of that."

For those sales calls, it's not necessarily volume of calls but building a rapport with the person at the other end that is important. "I'd try and be around one hundred calls per day," he said when asked how many people he'd talk to on a given day. "If I was having long conversations, it'd be less—which is good if I'm able to convert those long conversations into sales. Sometimes, too, I was working on experiences. I had different packages that I was trying to set up, so I'd be working with a colleague on making a ticket package flyer or something to post. Or we'd have meetings or needed to help with other parts of the office. Since the XFL was basically a start-up—it was our first season trying to get everything going, marketing the team, figuring out who's our target market and who's our audience—it was a grind, but at the same time, it was also fun and I learned a lot."

When working for a brand-new team (especially in a brand-new league)—even in a big, established sports market such as Los Angeles—you have to be willing to go the extra mile to make sales and find new fans. For Robards, working for the Wildcats meant getting out into the community to seek fans willing to give the XFL a chance: "[Management would] ask us for a lot of input and get ideas flowing, try and figure it out. We had to prospect. We found some success with NFL fan groups. I'd go to some of the watch parties and tailgates of NFL games, and try and talk to people, and see if we could try to get them to be a part of the XFL. We tried doing some special packages with Boy Scouts and Girl Scouts. We were trying to touch base with people, whoever would be interested in the XFL."

For Robards, approaching people and talking to them—often outside of office hours—was part of his normal routine. So before the Wildcats ever played their first game, Robards was often working weekends trying to connect with new XFL fans: "I'd actually go out to football camps. I went out to the NFL games when they had it at the Coliseum for the Rams, and I'd just go to the tailgate and walk around and talk to people." (The Rams, who left Southern California after the 1994 season and played in St. Louis between 1995 and 2015, used the Los Angeles Memorial Coliseum as their temporary home from 2016 to 2019 when the team returned to Los Angeles. Beginning in 2020, the team played in the brand-new SoFi Stadium, which also serves as the home for the LA Chargers.)

"Then," he continued, "once I went to some of their tailgates or talked to people from the fan clubs about where they had their watch parties, I'd go to different sports bars and do all that—which wasn't necessarily required [as part of my job], but I was trying to make sales and get people involved. I was doing that on weekends, so it was a few extra hours [outside of the normal office hours]."

With the established NFL Chargers, there was less of that, simply because the NFL is a known commodity: "It was more just in-house calls and having people come to the stadium for a walk-through if they were interested in tickets. It was a little more 9-to-5. Commute was way better for me, about twenty to thirty minutes instead of two hours, which was a big difference. The NFL kind of sells itself. They have plenty of fans. It was just getting those fans' butts in seats. But we had a list to call and people to try and reach out to, whereas it was a lot more prospecting and in-person [interactions] for the XFL."

For anybody wanting to work for the Rose Bowl or in-game operations/ ticket sales and fan experience for their favorite football team, Robards said a sport management degree certainly helps because of two key elements it offers: networking and internship opportunities. Although the courses in his sport management program helped—Robards has a master's degree in sport management from California State University, Long Beach—the positions with the NFL and XFL wouldn't have been possible without the networking and internships. "I'd say it was much more of the guest speakers and them pushing you to network, and the internships they were able to provide," he said when asked his thoughts about what he learned in the classroom. "We had some pretty cool insights from people in the sports world, whether it was professors or guest speakers. We heard a lot of insights and different people's perspectives. [Among guest speakers,] we had someone working for Monster Energy for the extreme sports side, people involved in the Olympics, and others in the sports field. [At the same time,] there were obviously things I learned in class that helped. Our [Sport] Finance class was taught by Andy Roundtree, the former CFO of the Angels [and Anaheim Ducks]. Otto Benedict, who does operations for SoFi Stadium, taught our Operations class. Dr. Stephen Hawn, the managing director of the Long Beach State Sport Management Program, has been tremendous even after I've left sports.

"But so much of it was you yourself going and signing up for internships, working extra, meeting people, trying to get a coffee with someone and learn from them. [These were things] that I found to be much more valuable and helping in getting that job and learning more; it was putting yourself out there, networking, not the subject of the class that day—at least for me. It was a matter of whether you yourself were going to be able to find the time to get the internship, go up and talk to the guest speakers afterward and try to connect, get their e-mail, keep reaching out. With the internships, you're thrown into the fire and get to see an inside look. It's very hands-on and you get that experience, which I tend to enjoy more versus seeing something on a whiteboard or on a PowerPoint.

"The internships themselves are worth the class alone, doing the sport management program, and it does give you almost a speed course into business. So you do get some knowledge in that, whether it's finance or operations or marketing or sales, and you can find out which area most interests you. I was able to find out through those classes that sales was my niche, and something I wanted to approach in sports, and I think that's great for people who take such a program."

For students wanting to network with mentors in the industry, Robards believes in the philosophy of being persistent. Be dogged when it comes to connecting with people. Sometimes it takes that extra one or two calls, and it's well worth the effort. "I'd almost say go until you do become a pest," Robards advised. "I'm fairly certain that everyone you can probably talk to in our program wishes that maybe they would've done one or two more, maybe they would've networked with one or two more people, maybe they would've reached out just a little more. I have yet to hear someone say, 'Yeah, I just kept reaching out, reaching out, reaching out, and they told me to leave them alone or stop.' Everyone who guest spoke and every instructor who taught us was willing to meet, talk, and go over things and help out. It was just whether people wanted that extra time with them to have a more personalized meeting in reaching out for help. So I would almost push people to try and be a pest."

According to Robards, if you're worried about being bothersome to others, you're not doing yourself any favors, career-wise. When you think that way, you're preventing yourself from getting a recommendation or finding out more about the industry, because somebody else even more persistent and more consistent in following up might receive that opportunity. The bottom line? The person who says "I need this" might ultimately have a better shot at achieving their dream. "Every single person that comes in [to guest speak in your class], e-mail them, talk to them, and try and get that connection," added Robards.

Robards provided a couple of personal examples to illustrate this point: his undergrad professor Dr. Hawn and his former boss with the Wildcats: "I saw Dr. Hawn when I was last in Los Angeles. He's been a big help. Even if I'm leaving sports, he's still trying to help out. My old boss with the XFL was helping me with the résumé for getting a job not in sports. He had connections with jobs that I was looking for, too. Just network with people; they can help you get to the next spot. I really recommend people to just try and be open, honest, and willing to make a connection with others."

Working in sports can be fun, but this career isn't for everybody. Having gone through that grind himself, Robards determined that he doesn't think it's for him. "You gotta sacrifice if you do want to work in sports," he cautioned. "You're going to have to sacrifice a lot of your time, and a lot of your effort and energy for that. And just know it's not going to be the lucrative deals like you think, especially in the beginning. Like most things, you're going to have to work hard to get to the top. But with sports especially, it's definitely a grind."

Marketing

Pat Gallagher, Consultant and Senior Executive in Sports

Job title: Former director of marketing, San Francisco Giants; Former president, San Francisco Giants Enterprises

Education/training: Art major (San Diego State and Humboldt State); marketing experience with SeaWorld amusement parks

Key pieces of advice: Maintain a positive attitude. Be a problem solver, not a problem creator. Remember the reason we do all this stuff, being in the fun business, is to create a "wow" if we can—and to exceed expectations.

Pat Gallagher, a key contributor to the creation of the privately funded Pacific Bell (now Oracle) Park in San Francisco, is best known as one of the longest-serving and most influential executives in Giants history during his thirty-two-year career with the franchise.

You might think that working in marketing—which was Gallagher's job—for a franchise that featured superstars Willie McCovey, Will Clark, and Barry Bonds over the decades would be an easy gig, but in reality, it was challenging because of the lack of a great ballpark during the Candlestick Park days and also, particularly during the 1970s and 1980s, the lack of competitive Giants ballclubs.

As the team's first director of marketing, Gallagher created memorable marketing campaigns selling cold and windy Candlestick Park with humor in the 1980s, and his contributions as senior vice president of business operations in the 1990s and beyond helped reinvigorate the franchise. He also eventually served as the president of Giants Enterprises, concentrating on bringing nonbaseball events to the Giants ballpark.

Today, Gallagher, who left the Giants in 2009, is a frequent speaker and guest instructor at colleges and universities across the country. He's currently a management consultant, mentor, and speaker in the sports and entertainment industry.

Like several other contributors to this book, Gallagher never really thought he would get involved with sports as a career. "I played sports as a kid," he said, "but I was not a hardcore baseball fan at all. My first job in high school—I grew up in San Diego—I worked for SeaWorld in San Diego. It was a great summer job. I parked cars. I directed traffic. I swept cigarette butts. I even, at one point, had the chance to help train extra animals. But it was a great hourly job while you

PAT GALLAGHER. *COURTESY OF PAT GALLAGHER*

were finishing up high school and, really, my first experience with the entertainment business. Then I wound up going to San Diego State and just kept this job; I worked full-time during the summer and then part-time in the winter.

"[As for] my direction at that point, well, I was interested in art and became an art major in college. I liked to draw and sketch and paint, and I drew cartoons for my high school newspaper. I got through almost three years of college and realized that anytime anybody criticized anything I did in art, or if anybody put me on a deadline, I totally fell apart. So, I realized maybe I should start thinking about something else as a vocation. At the same time, I had the opportunity at SeaWorld to go from the operations side of the business to the sales side of the business, and that was truly a key development for me.

"So the theme park business is really where I grew up. I was [still] in San Diego [and at that point] working full-time, and then they sent me to SeaWorld of Ohio, which isn't there anymore, but it was twenty-five miles southeast of Cleveland. It was a theme park that was a marine animal park that was operated during the summer months. And I spent some time at SeaWorld of Florida and eventually had the opportunity to come back to California as the sales and promotion manager for a park that was in Redwood City called Marine World/Africa USA. So I was the theme park marketing guy.

"And this was [in] 1976. [At the time] the Giants—Horace Stoneham had brought the [franchise from New York] to San Francisco in 1958—struggled. They had to deal with Candlestick Park and so the team almost moved to Toronto. A local guy, Bob Lurie, stepped in and bought the Giants [to keep them in San Francisco], and he was looking for a marketing person. A mutual acquaintance said, 'Hey, you ought to interview for that job.' So [in November 1976,] I went in and interviewed to become the Giants' director of marketing. They'd never had anybody like that before and we hit it off, and he offered me the job.

"I wound up in a variety of different roles and stayed with the Giants for thirty-two years. I was their director of marketing, then director of marketing business affairs, and then vice-president of business operations. Like a lot of people in the business, I had a chance to grow. [At the time,] the front offices were small. It was really a much different business than it is now, but it was a fantastic business where I had the opportunity to make my mark, if you will, and what I'm known for is Candlestick Park."

Candlestick, as Gallagher explains, was the coldest and windiest ballpark in the country. It had a reputation, in fact, for being the worst ballpark in the country, and his job was to figure out a way to try to sell it. The team itself, meanwhile, was always losing, and fans just weren't coming out to Candlestick. To sell tickets,

Gallagher had to be innovative in coming up with successful marketing campaigns: "The first couple of years [on the job], I tried to say, 'Come on out and bring your family! It's a great day at the ballpark!' I always was envious of Fred Claire and Steve Brener at Dodger Stadium because [Dodger Stadium] to me was the ultimate ballpark and we didn't [have anything close to that]. We were trying to get people to come to something that really was pretty uncomfortable."

Gallagher used the weather to his advantage when creating marketing campaigns. "Fortunately, I had an owner who appreciated a lot of the things that I [did]," he said. "[For example,] I came up with this little badge called the 'Croix de Candlestick.' It was a little orange button that we gave to people who did what the ultimate act of being a Giants fan was: that is, if they stayed until the end of an extra-inning night game. So we began to exaggerate how bad the weather was, and we did it tongue-in-cheek. Our theme was, 'The Giants hang in there, which as a fan we're saying to you: Please hang in there.' What was great about it is the fans got it—even though it was sort of a joke—and it became a thing.

"And it allowed us to do some things from a marketing standpoint that, if you had a good ballpark and a good team, you never would do. So that followed with an antimascot called the 'Crazy Crab,' which was designed for people to boo at, which sounds ridiculous but it wasn't even supposed to be a mascot. We did a commercial with this crab, a guy in this crab outfit. That was the era where, fortunately, the Dodgers didn't do this. But a lot of other teams—the San Diego Padres and others—came up with these fuzzy mascots. We did a survey that [asked], 'If the Giants had a mascot, would you boo it?' And 67 percent of the people that we surveyed—it was rigged—said, 'Yes, we would boo it!' So we did this commercial. We had this mascot. We put him out on the field. All we were trying to do was say, 'Giants fans are different, they expect something different, they're tougher, they have special grit and determination, [and] they wouldn't put up with something as dumb as a mascot.'

"Well, since we had the costume, we actually wound up putting the mascot out on the field. This was 1984, and for every game for one of the half innings, this goofy mascot would emerge from the dugout or from the tunnel, and do this dance out on the field, and the fans would boo it off the field. That was the shtick. [But the fans] eventually started throwing things at it [and] we were worried for the mascot's safety. The 1984 Giants weren't very good. It was just a series, during that time, of teams that just weren't very good. And as the marketing guy, I began to realize that if I could drum up some interest early and do some things that were interesting, maybe people would buy tickets and come out to the ballpark before [it was finally revealed] how bad our team was. It was like, if we were going to be bad, let's keep it a secret until maybe the end of August. To be honest, during these years, some of these were desperation moves."

But Gallagher continued to come up with ideas to promote the team: "I was able to talk our owner into letting me schedule mostly day games one year, in 1985. Our theme was 'Real grass, real sunshine, real baseball.' We are going to be like the Chicago Cubs of the West—where Candlestick was not a very good place at night, but during the day, it could've been a good experience."

The following year, management decided to promote young stars Will Clark and Robby Thompson to the majors, which gave Gallagher an idea for a theme in 1986. "To try and come up with a theme," he said, "I tried to listen to [general manager] Al Rosen to pick up something that we could say. Al said, 'You gotta like these kids. We're gonna have a bunch of kids.' So our theme became, 'You gotta like these kids.' By some miracle, we actually had a pretty good team in 1986, [which] all of a sudden turned our fan base around and it really became fun. The 1987 team actually won the division, so it went on from there."

The signing of superstar Barry Bonds following the 1992 season helped turn San Francisco into a winning team and led to more excitement about the ball club. Eventually, the Giants moved to Pacific Bell (now Oracle) Park and enjoyed more success. But during the early years of Gallagher's time as director of marketing, it was no easy task to sell the Giants to the fans. Would his outside-the-box marketing campaigns and his offbeat ideas work today? "When I look back on it," he said, "I just didn't know any better, because some of it was fun and it got some visibility, but I really didn't know what else to do." So what would he tell youngsters who find themselves in a position similar to the one he was in then? "I'm big on sales experience. It doesn't matter what you sell. The way you'd create and sell an idea might be totally different from the way I would do it, but I think the ability to do that, every business needs it. The ability to boil down an idea to its basic elements and figure out a way to just sell it and communicate it, that's a skill that is needed. I do think also the ability to put together a team of people—and the culture that comes with that—[is another necessity]. Putting a team together and developing a culture [is essential, especially] when you're in the fun business. Baseball is the vehicle, but I always looked at it as we were in the fun business. Nobody *needed* any of this stuff, so we had to find ways to present it and sell it [like] we're fun. I realize we're not saving lives here or discovering the cure for any diseases.

"And think about it. In life, there are really four things people care about: what they do for a living, their family, their faith and religion—and number four, they care about their sports teams. And it's not necessarily in that order. Sometimes people are consumed by sports, and our job is to make it fun for them."

The bottom line, Gallagher continued, is that if you're handling the marketing of the organization, you must maintain a positive attitude and—being in the fun business—continue thinking of entertaining ways to engage with the fans: for example, coming up with family-friendly themes so that people will come to the ballpark. As Giants owner Bob Lurie once told him, when the team loses, the players, the coaching staff, and management—being the competitors they are—aren't going to be in a good mood, which is understandable. But the staff responsible for marketing the club, even as the team is in the midst of a long losing streak, must continue to maintain that positive attitude and bring creativity to the job to make the experience at the ballpark fun for the fans at all times.

BE A PROBLEM SOLVER AND MAKE A GOOD FIRST IMPRESSION

To get hired for any job to begin with, you must be what Gallagher called a "problem solver." "There's really only two kinds of people," he said, "problem solvers and problem creators. It doesn't matter what business you're in. This is an oversimplification, but there's some people that may not be necessarily the most intelligent but they have a passion and also a work ethic that helps them figure out a way to solve problems or to look at problems as opportunities. They can either lead a team or be a part of a team, the kind of people that a boss [would look at and] say, 'I want that person on my team. That's the kind of person that I want to have on my team.' The opposite is what I call problem creators—people who can be very intelligent and attractive but, for whatever reason, tend to get tangled up in personality issues. Or through lack of effort, entitlement, or lack of dedication, they get tangled up with things that have nothing to do with solving the problem. They're the ones that, if you're a manager, you try to weed out before they poison the well. If you're a manager, you don't want to bring in people who will create more problems than they solve."

So it's important to remember why bosses are hiring staff to join their team. Management isn't necessarily looking to hire sports fans or people with fancy degrees, so being a sports fan doesn't mean you'll get the job if you don't have the right attitude. Similarly, being highly educated means nothing if, for instance, you're always making inappropriate comments on social media. "One of my earliest bosses told me, 'The only reason somebody hires somebody else, it's to take a problem off their back!' They're thinking, 'Okay, is this person going to help me solve my problem, or are they going to be a bigger problem?'" Gallagher said. "Also, it's important to separate yourself from the other candidates, meaning what you're trying to do is that when somebody says your name, they associate something with that. What would you like that to be? That's about your personal brand. Particularly in today's digital world, anything you put online, it's like your digital tattoo. Whatever you put out there, it's out there.

"If you're standing in a line with ten people, what is it that's going to separate you from the rest? If you have only a short amount of time [in an interview, for example,] to make an impression, how will you do that? What is it about you that will make them hire you? When you're in an interview, what's your body language like? Are you looking awake? Are you looking interested? You want them to say, 'I want K.P. on my team. I may not know exactly what it is that the task is, but I've got a problem to solve and I believe K.P. is one of the people who's going to help me figure out how to do it. When things go wrong, this is a person who'll step up and solve the problem. He's there in good times and bad. Win or lose, he's fun to be around.'"

On the flip side, when you're interviewing for a job, make sure the culture within that organization is the right fit for you, too. After all, working for a sports franchise means working long hours at the ballpark, stadium, or arena. Are you going to enjoy being around the people in this organization every single day? "When you're interviewing for a job, they're interviewing you—but you're also interviewing *them*," Gallagher advised. "You have to figure out in fifteen or twenty minutes: Is this somebody I can get up every morning and charge ahead with? Or is this somebody that I just don't want to spend a lot of time with? The old saying, 'You don't get a second chance to make a good first impression' is probably true in this context."

KEEP DOING INFORMATIONAL INTERVIEWS AND BE A GOOD CITIZEN

Another piece of advice Gallagher offered is to never stop doing informational interviews. Don't be worried that you're taking up someone's time, he added, because "I think anybody who works in it at any level has an obligation to talk, on an informational basis, to young people who are interested and just want to learn more about it."

What can also help you as a young person wanting to work in sports, Gallagher continued, is to be known as a team player, someone who cares not only about the organization itself but also the community the organization calls home. "You want to be regarded as somebody that, whoever you were associated with, [people] wanted to have on their team. And because you realized that it was a business, you put in the effort to do that.

"[In any organization, front offices] want people who are fun people to be around but are also people who are dedicated, particularly when times are tough. I mean, everybody can get excited when things are going well. It's when things aren't going well, that's when people with character really show up. And if you're in this business for a long time, nobody wins every year. Nobody even is very good every year. So figuring out that sports is the vehicle but what you're really in is the entertainment business, and you're also in a business where you really have an obligation to connect with whatever community you're in. You should be expected to be a good citizen and do things that use whatever visibility that the organization has to do good things in the community. It's the way you should operate, and plus, from a business standpoint, it also gives other people a reason to support what you're doing, even when maybe the team performance isn't so good."

BE OPEN-MINDED WHEN SEEKING OPPORTUNITIES

Gallagher worked for the Giants for thirty-two years, but there are numerous opportunities outside of the realm of professional sports franchises. Just be open-minded and don't ignore other sports-related careers that are available. Don't limit yourself to thinking you're going to work only for the big-name teams in your area, or that you're considering only minor-league professional teams in the area. "Sports is a business [where] there's lots of opportunities," he said. "I try to advise young people to take the blinders off and don't focus so much on just a franchise. Look at all the people around, whether they're in the media business, the radio and television business, all these companies that spend time and energy and investment in sponsoring teams. They're all involved in the sports business, trying to figure out a way to get their product in front of the people who follow the team.

"And sports management has become an accepted path in business. Ohio University was the first sports management program out there four decades ago, but now there's three hundred or four hundred management programs around. And aside from just the big sports, [there are opportunities in] all the participation sports, all the spectator sports, [and] college athletics. College athletics are being marketed in many ways like the professional franchises are being marketed. There's more opportunities now for women than there have ever been before, which, when I started—I hate to say it—but it was all white guys with short-sleeved shirts and ties on. [At the time,] there wasn't much diversity, and I think [today] one of the positive things about business in general—[and] about sports—is [the fact that] the industry has embraced diversity. [There's] still work to do, but it's better, so I'm a cheerleader for young people who are interested in making it their vocation. I advise them all to pay attention to their network of people. Technology allows you to do that, to stay in touch with people along the way. Find mentors."

Internships are crucial, added Gallagher: "[For] most of the people [working in] franchises around the country [or] who are in the elements of the business, many of them started out as interns and had the opportunity to grow. It's almost like the farm system for business is in internships, so I'd advise them to seek those out."

Understand, too, that there are limitations when you work for a franchise. For instance, if you're ambitious and want to continue to grow, some franchises simply aren't big enough to be able to give you that opportunity. "[Just as an example,] there's no way to say this to you when we're talking about a sports franchise: 'K.P., you've done a great job working in our franchise. I want you to go run the Eastern division of our company . . . ' So sometimes, growth with individual franchises can be difficult, particularly if there's not much turnover.

"So with all the other sports that are out there, all the other spectator sports, there's way more opportunities now and it's not just in the traditional roles that people used to have working for a franchise—and the ways that the teams are covered and the ways that the product is distributed.

"The franchises are just one piece of it. You really have to—if you're interested in this business—broaden your view about the events side of the business, about other types of spectator sports. [Let's say you] live on the West Coast; there's lots of participation sports, whether it's running or volleyball. There's other ways to get involved in sports management, other than just working for a franchise."

IV

SPORTS MANAGEMENT/ OWNERSHIP

14

WNBA General Manager

Ann Meyers Drysdale, Broadcaster and Former Basketball Executive

Job title: Vice president, Phoenix Suns and Phoenix Mercury; former general manager, Phoenix Mercury; sportscaster; basketball color analyst, Phoenix Suns and Phoenix Mercury

Key piece of advice: Don't look back in your life and say "what-if" and be that person that says "would've, could've, should've." Go ahead and try, because then you don't have to say that.

Ann Meyers Drysdale, the vice president of the Phoenix Suns and Phoenix Mercury, has been in broadcasting and held executive roles in basketball since her professional playing career ended. She has also served as an analyst for NBC Sports' coverage of women's basketball. While she is the first to admit that she received her opportunities in the broadcast booth and the front office because of her stature within the sport as a Naismith Memorial Basketball Hall of Fame player, Meyers Drysdale also stresses the point that when somebody gives you an opportunity, you should take it—and be confident that you can do the job effectively.

"I'd been asked since day one when the WNBA first existed to go with a franchise whether as a broadcaster, president, or GM," Meyers Drysdale explained. "Phoenix was persistent, and I was fortunate to step into the role as a GM. I think that I do have a sense of the game, not just the women's game but the game of basketball. I'm not always going to be right. I have made some bad choices in my position. But if you don't take chances, you'll never know. If someone gives you an opportunity, don't worry about failing. You have to have the courage to do it, whether you fail or succeed. The position that I've been with the Mercury as the president and GM and now vice president, I've learned that you have to make choices and they're not always going to be good ones."

For young women looking to become sports broadcasters or work in the front office of a sports organization, Meyers Drysdale suggested getting involved with athletics as early as possible: "I think the fact that we have the opportunity for young girls because of sports being available to them—whether it's basketball, soccer, volleyball, track and field, swimming, golf, and tennis—we're seeing more and more parents having their young daughters get involved with athletics at a very early age. Because of that, the sports world has become so huge, not just as far as a competitor, but whether you become a trainer, a broadcaster, a physical therapist, a coach. . . . And there's so many avenues that you can break into. Also, in TV, there's so many different outlets, whether it be social media, certainly the internet, and we'll see kids shows pop up all the time. You see young boys and girls as broadcasters, whether they're doing newscasts or whether they're doing sports, whether they're doing interviews. So there are outlets out there where a lot of young children can get involved right away. Certainly, you have to have the passion. You've got to want it. If you have a dream, if you have the imagination to do what you want to do—whether it's as an athlete or through sports [or] whether it's broadcasting or anything else, to be a producer, to be a director to be working behind the camera, to be a writer writing stories, or to be an illustrator and so forth—there's just so many opportunities.

"But one, you have to have the passion, and two, you have to have the ability to work hard. If you want something bad enough, you make the sacrifices—but you got to put in the work. Sometimes things get tough when people turn you down and you might have obstacles that come your way, but if you want something bad enough, you got to put in the work and you've got to be willing to be able to change direction sometimes. Sometimes things don't always work out the way we want them to, but, again, it's that work ethic."

As for high school and college students looking to work in sports, Meyers Drysdale said building relationships is key to landing opportunities: "Today, it's not like when I was growing up because, at the time, you didn't have networks such as ESPN, which has opened up so many doors. You didn't have the internet and social media, which have opened up so many doors. So whether you're in high school or college, obviously it's about relationships. It's about doing internships or meeting somebody or having somebody that you know open the door for you, for an introduction, to have an internship, or to get a job. Even if it's at the low level. If you want to get into TV, and if you're pulling cable or if you're pulling copy, you take the job. You get your foot in the door. Anything to get your foot in the door. And you move up and you take advantage, whether you have experience or not. But it's about relationships. It's about you going out and putting yourself out there and introducing yourself to people and doing job interviews."

It's important to realize, too, that failures are often part of the process and that you can treat those failures as learning opportunities. "Lots of times, job interviews are so competitive that [you end up not getting the position], but you've got to take that as an experience and a learning experience on what to do on your next interview," said Meyers Drysdale. "But certainly having internships opens up the door. You have to be willing to get your foot in the door and not get paid sometimes. But again, that's all about developing new relationships. And people see your work ethic and they see that you're passionate about what you want to do, and they can give you guidance—once you get yourself in a situation where you're meeting people all the time and you're able to talk to people."

Meyers Drysdale also suggested looking into getting a sports management degree. If you're in high school, it's not too early to start planning ahead and finding out which colleges offer such programs: "Whether you're in high school or college—and now a lot of the universities, whether you're in a junior college or an NAIA school or a Division II or Division III school or a lower Division I school—a lot of these schools, colleges and universities, have programs or majors in sports broadcasting or sports communications, sports administration, sports this, sports that. So there's a lot of avenues to be able to choose from."

Social media has become more important than ever, but Meyers Drysdale had an important message for job seekers—and it's not restricted to just careers in the sports industry: Be careful what you post online. Universities and organizations do look at your social media posts. "I'm not as into [social media] as some people are," she said, "but I do realize and understand that this is a different generation that they are so consumed by their phones and their iPads and so forth and getting themselves recognized and posting themselves online. Certainly, with regard to some of the things that they post, I will say the majority of companies understand that, and the majority of companies—it doesn't matter what business it's in, whether it's banking or flower shops or grocery stores or whatever, and even universities—do have people where part of their job is to go online and look to see what young people are posting.

"So, for example, if I'm still in college and I apply for a job, certainly they'll take my résumé and they're going to go online and see what I post. What is my social media like? If I use curse words or if I use crude things that I'm saying about people, or if I'm angry about things, I could be at a disadvantage because a lot of companies and businesses today have people whose job it is to check potential candidates' social media for these things.

"On the college level, they have somebody in the athletic department look at their athletes. But that's all they do: They look at all their athletes. It doesn't matter whether it's football or tennis or swimming or water polo, whatever the sport is—and they have the list of all their athletes and they see what those athletes are posting. If it's derogatory toward that university or if it's derogatory or bullying to other people or other athletes, that's all looked at, and there are repercussions. There are consequences in the sense of: Does that athlete keep their scholarship? Does that athlete just come in and get a slap on the hand or talking to? I don't know [the repercussions], but I do know that companies are very aware of social media. So if you go in and apply for a job, they'll get your name and they'll look at what you post. And when you're in junior high and high school, you're posting a lot of stuff that you probably wouldn't post ten years down the road in your life. So if you're with a bunch of friends and you're sitting around smoking pot and drinking alcohol and you're posting that online, companies will look at that."

When asked to share lessons she learned from sports that apply to working within the industry, Meyers Drysdale went back to the basics: Take a chance. Don't be afraid of failure. "You might fail all the time, but you can succeed the next time," she said. "That's what's so great about sports. I mean, you strike out, and you get a hit. You miss a shot at the end of the buzzer, and you make a free throw. You fall short of the touchdown, and you make a great catch. You gotta take the good with the bad, and not every opportunity works out the way you want it to. You have to take that failure. You have to take that loss that people say you're not good enough and you have to turn it around. I've always said, 'Don't look back in life and say what if.' If you don't have the confidence enough in yourself and you say, 'Well, I'm not going to get that job. Why should I apply for it?' then that's how your life is going to be. Or, 'I'm not good enough. I shouldn't go try out for the team because I'm not very fast.' If you think that way, then that's exactly how your life is going to be. But when you have that opportunity, you've gotta try. If you don't try, you'll never know, because that opportunity is [waiting] there for you. It doesn't mean you're always going to get it. But you have the opportunity to try. And whether you fail or succeed, the fact that you attempted, that's what counts because we don't win all the time. I mean, Michael Jordan didn't hit 100 percent of his shots. Wayne Gretzky didn't score on every one of his shots. If you don't try, you'll never know, but there's always that one chance that'll happen.

"There's a famous saying that goes, 'Success is not final; failure is not fatal: it is the courage to continue that counts.' So what kind of courage do you have to go and try something? If it doesn't work out, it doesn't work out. But you can't look at yourself as a failure. You have to look at the situation and say, 'Well, it didn't work out this time.' As an athlete, you mess up. If you're a basketball player, it's, 'Hey, I got beat on defense. Somebody out-rebounded me. Somebody blocked my shot.' Well, what are you going to do next time to make the adjustment? That's what life is. Life is exactly that, whether you're trying for a job or you're in a relationship. You get into disagreements with your loved ones. As parents, you don't always agree with your children. They don't like you today. It's just, like, 'Okay. Well, why?' What do you have to do to make communication better? But I've always said, 'Don't look back in your life and say what if and be that person that says would've, could've, should've.' Go ahead and try because then you don't have to say, 'Well, I could've done that. I should've done that. I would've done that.' And you know what? When you do it, you don't have to say that."

Even in her role as the general manager of the Phoenix Mercury, Meyers Drysdale followed her own advice: Take a shot, even if it means making a decision that might be unpopular with the fan base. The perfect example came when the Mercury had the first pick in the 2007 WNBA Draft.

"We had the number one pick, but I knew the league," Meyers Drysdale said. "I knew our coaches. I knew what they wanted. Sometimes you have to make tough decisions. They may not always turn out the way you hope they do, and we were fortunate that it did. But I've made a lot of bad decisions in my life that I felt was the right decision at the time and didn't work out the way I'd hoped, but it's like, 'Okay what am I going to do to change? What am I going to do to make a better decision next time? Do I get more information? Do I do a better job homework-wise? Do I talk to more people to help me understand certain things with salaries and so forth?' And you can draft a really talented kid, but if they don't have the right character or if they're not the right piece that fits into your team or that position that you're looking for, then it might not work out. Then you got to move on. What are you going to do to move on?

"When we had the number-one pick, our coach was looking for a certain type [of] player and we talked a lot, and I said, 'I think this kid is going to help you.' We felt, too, that the draft wasn't as strong. The number-one pick [Duke point guard Lindsey Harding] was a really, really talented kid, but we already have that position taken on our team. So our coach was not going to pick a player that was going to sit on the bench behind this other kid that was a veteran player and the kind of the guard that he wanted.

"We ended up making that trade [sending Harding to Minnesota for Tangela Smith] and our fans were not happy with me, to say the least. And I appreciated and respected their voices, and certainly I have to listen to that, too. But I walked in—I had to go in right after we did the trade and we did the draft—and I could just feel it when I walked in the room and I thought, 'You know what? This is not a funeral. You're going to be okay. We're going to be okay. The Phoenix Mercury are going to be okay. This is a good trade.' And I explained why and I talked about the kid that we did get."

Incidentally, the Mercury, who hadn't finished above fourth place in the West Conference since 1998, won their first WNBA title that summer and their second two years later, with Smith playing a vital role in both championships. In 2012, *SB Nation* called the Smith-for-Harding deal the best trade in Mercury franchise history.

"It was just very positive," Meyers Drysdale continued, "and a lot of that, too, with all these things about opportunities and you have to try, and yes, you're go-ing to fail—but a lot of it has to do with your attitude. You can be that person and say, 'I've got the little black cloud over my head. Nothing works out my way. It was somebody else's fault.' Or you can be the person who says, 'Okay, it didn't work out. What am I going to do to change?' A lot of times, you have to have a positive attitude. It's not always easy. But having a positive attitude really does help in things that don't go your way."

Although she learned a lot of leadership skills during her own playing ca-reer, Meyers Drysdale also credits legendary UCLA head basketball coach John Wooden: "What I learned from Coach Wooden is that a good leader is a good follower, and, again, you have to be in charge and you have to be willing to make the tough decisions. They may not always be the ones that everybody is hoping for, but [you have to make those decisions]." At the same time, Meyers Drysdale added, as a front office executive you have to listen to your fan base, too. You have to let them know you care about their feedback. "It doesn't matter what walk of life you're in, it's about people. You have to get along with people. You get along with people that are invested in what you're doing, and so you have to listen to them. You may not always agree, but you need to understand where they're com-ing from. [It's crucial that] you listen and they know that you're really interested and take ownership of them being a part of what you're trying to accomplish. They're out there spending their money and they're cheering for your team and so forth, and we need to listen to them. Maybe they don't like the music that's being played before the game or maybe they feel that in the past your organization did things that they don't do today as far as giving out programs or giving out certain T-shirts or whatever, and you need to listen. You're going to have those few that really are always going to complain about something.

"But if you give them the time, if you give them the courtesy to at least listen—and you may not agree with them or be able to do what they want you to do—and people feel that they are valued, that's important. To me, I don't think enough people put themselves out there to say hello to somebody or make them feel good about themselves that you recognize them and that they're important. And in professional sports, your fan base is important. Your sponsors are important. You have to make them feel like they're part of the team and, like I said, you may not do the things that they always want you to do as an organization. But when you sit and talk to them, you listen to them, you say hello to them, and you engage with them, they feel it like, 'Oh, you really care.' It's more important for people to know that you care, rather than what you know."

Sports Executive

Andy Dolich, Sports Executive for All Seasons

Job title: Sports consultant; former team executive in the NFL, NBA, MLB, and NHL

Education/training: Degree in sports administration (Ohio University)

Key pieces of advice: Find out what you want to do. Seek mentors. Do informational interviews. Work on your people skills.

Andy Dolich has more than five decades of leadership in the sports industry, including executive positions on teams in the four major North American sports—the NFL, NBA, MLB, and NHL. Dolich, who has run Dolich Consulting, a sports business consulting practice in Northern California, since 2010, was executive vice president of the Oakland Athletics during their run of success in the 1980s and early 1990s, president of business operations for the Golden State Warriors and Vancouver/Memphis Grizzlies, and chief operating officer of the San Francisco 49ers. In addition, he has held business operations positions with the NHL's

Washington Capitals as well as in the North American Soccer League, National Lacrosse League, and collegiate sports marketing with IMG College.

Dolich also teaches sports business at Stanford's School of Continuing Studies and previously taught at the University of San Francisco, the University of Oregon, and Menlo College in Atherton, California.

BACKGROUND IN THE SPORTS BUSINESS WORLD

Dolich calls himself "one of the lucky people who's turned dreams into reality without any sort of brilliance." The way he remembers it, he didn't even think about entering the sports industry while in college. "My interest in school—although I was not a great student—was politics and government," he said. "When I went to American University in Washington, DC, my major was in government and international relations, with a goal that maybe someday I could work in the state department and have an exciting life in places around the world. Pretty quickly I [abandoned that idea] because, one, I wasn't passionate about it, and two, the level of intellect and quality that I saw at American University was higher than my ability. I was a benchwarmer on the basketball team, nonscholarship, but it wasn't really doing anything for the rest of my career."

But when he stopped playing in his junior year, Dolich started volunteering for the school sports information director and the intramural program: "That gave me the spark, like, 'Wow, I enjoy this, the opportunity to present sport on a college campus . . .' At the same time, I was very lucky to hear about the first sports management program in the country. I was an early graduate of that program at Ohio University, and before you got your master's degree in sports management—this was in 1970—you had to do an internship with a professional sports organization. I was lucky enough at that time to get a job with the Philadelphia 76ers."

Fast-forwarding his career timeline, Dolich spent three seasons with the 76ers, two with the Maryland Arrows of the National Lacrosse League, two with the Washington Capitals of the National Hockey League, and two seasons as the general manager of the Washington Diplomats in the North American Soccer League before he received what he calls "the biggest break" of his career in Oakland. Recruited to work for the A's, Dolich helped turn around a franchise that ranked last in league attendance, increasing season ticket sales from 326 to 16,000 and attendance from 850,000 to 2.9 million in his first thirteen years. During his time with the Vancouver/Memphis Grizzlies from 2000 to 2007, he was part of the team that planned the franchise's move to Memphis and built FedExForum.

ANDY DOLICH. *COURTESY OF ANDY DOLICH*

ADVICE FOR THOSE WANTING TO GET INTO THE SPORTS INDUSTRY

For decades, Dolich has mentored young people seeking careers in sports, and he shared his insights in our interview. "My advice for students and others thinking about getting into the sports business world is to talk to themselves," he said. "At least, in my view, talking to yourself and trying to understand what makes you enthusiastic, what makes you scared, what makes you thoughtful, what makes you happy—I don't see enough people doing that. And they, to a certain extent, get directed toward careers or areas that maybe other people believe they should be in: family, friends, educators, etc. So, if you're thinking, 'What should I do? I seem to have an interest in sport,' have that conversation [with yourself]."

Then, as you're compiling a list of areas which you are interested in within sports, seek out mentors in the industry. You can reach out to Dolich himself for an informational interview. Speak to other executives in the business. Speak to as many of them as you can. Dive deep and find out what these people are all about. How did they get involved? What were their keys to success?

"And then literally go do it. Be aggressive, but not obnoxious. Find that internship. Find that opportunity. Find that team or event that you have your hands around. You're actually there and you're going, 'This is even better than I thought,' or, 'Wow, I don't want to do this. It's boring as heck,' or, 'I don't want to be in *this* part of it; I might want to be in *that* part of it'—for example, college versus pro, broadcast versus analytics, etc."

DO YOUR RESEARCH AND EDUCATE YOURSELF

Dolich is a big believer in the importance of institutional knowledge, which can be defined as the combination of experiences, processes, data, expertise, values, and information possessed by company employees. It can span decades and comprise crucial trends, projects, and perspectives that define a company's history—or, in this case, the sports industry's history. Institutional knowledge can be further classified as tangible knowledge (for instance, records and reports that can be passed between people) and intangible knowledge (namely, skills that can be transferred through trainings and mentorships).

"I do believe that institutional knowledge is very important for young people today," Dolich said. "Although they can do a number of things brilliantly at the same time, meaning they have incredible multitask capability, it's also important to have that [institutional knowledge]. That means [being aware of different areas of knowledge and wisdom like] the scopes of leadership, the do's and don'ts of interviewing, [and] it's important to understand that today's world didn't just come about last week. I mean, it was created over time. Things like salaries and massive rights fees for TV. Things like the history of video boards in the big four sports, with the first one being introduced by the Dodgers in 1980, which wasn't that long ago. And can you imagine going to any sporting event today without multiple HD LED video boards all over the stadium? So having some institutional knowledge of where promotions came from, why analytics and metrics are important on the team side, how they are becoming that much more important on the business side . . . again, it goes back to doing some level of research or self-education. And to me, the simple challenge is that the pool of qualified candidates in today's world is so much larger than when I went into the front office of the 76ers. There's just a massive pool of talent available to teams, leagues, events, colleges, broadcasters, media organizations, and esports leagues than there ever were. So the challenge is, how do you distinguish yourself? If there's a school of one thousand herring, how do I look like a neon herring that pops out in that school? So the analogy is how do I stand out to somebody who's trying to catch me or eat me?

"And I would add to that. I am not a numbers person. And I'll make jokes about analytics and metrics, but I also understand their value in sports. And up until a few years ago, analytics was focused on the team side, player development side, and scouting. Now, it's expanding to the business side of sport. And something that concerns me as I look back, is that the human skills that the potential job applicant has, the presentation, look, sense of humor, ability to have eye contact, quality handshake. . . . You'll have people that could write code at 3:00 in the morning backwards with their left hand—they're geniuses. But when they're sitting in an interview and have to present themselves to the director of human resources or the director of IT at a team, they could be lost at sea. Like, 'Hey dude, how ya doin'?' Oops, sorry, wrong question. I'm not your 'dude.' So spending time [to truly understand] who your audience is, as a job seeker, is really important. The good news is that in today's world, if want to find out about Andy Dolich, as an example, you don't have to go very far. A few clicks, and you got it.

"Now, when [I'm invited do] some teaching—where I'll show up in a class that knows I'm coming—I'll say, 'Excuse me, how many of you actually took ten minutes to find out who the hell I am?' And it's not a lot of hands that go up." Dolich said he cringes when he hears the typical excuses such as, "I'm busy," or, "I didn't do it." In his words, "That's a horribly lost opportunity." The good news, Dolich added, is that you can pretty much find out anything, and his advice is to take the time to do it. "And although this might sound a bit hokey, work on your people skills as much as—if not more than—your education, intellect, or incredible MVP skills in some particular area."

REAL EXAMPLES OF SUCCESS STORIES

Over the years, Dolich has seen many examples of interns and others who worked for him who have gone on to have successful careers. "But I'll go way back to the Oakland A's," he said. "This is 1981. The A's, up until that point, were owned by Charlie Finley. They won three consecutive World Series from 1972 to 1974 with Catfish Hunter, Reggie Jackson, and Rollie Fingers. Finley was very well known and he was quirky, but he was an absentee owner. He was always in the media, but the A's, even though they had a great team, weren't drawing many fans. Finley was a terrific self-promoter but just didn't focus much on marketing the team, and their attendance lagged. And there was literally just one or two people in the front office on the business side."

When the Haas family bought the team in August 1980, Dolich was attracted because he knew that just by putting a sales group together, the A's could be successful: "Because nobody ever asked for it. It's like selling Girl Scout cookies; if nobody asked you to buy a box of cookies, you're not going to buy any. And they're not going to sell anything. In 1981, I was given the opportunity to come to Oakland as the VP of business ops. One of the first things we did was put together a sales force of young men and women whose job was to sell Oakland A's season tickets.

"One was a guy named Steve Page. Steve was doing some work for a congress-man in San Jose, but he wanted to work in sports. He came in, and we hired a bunch of these salespeople. They had no sports experience. They just came from all kinds of backgrounds. Steve, you could just tell, had the right stuff. Today, he's the president of Sonoma Raceway, which is one of the more successful NASCAR tracks in the country and, I think, one of the only road courses that NASCAR runs on, along with many, many other races in the Sonoma and Napa valleys.

"Another guy came to the first group interview that we had. He walks in, he's got blood on his shirt, his tie is ripped to shreds, and it's like, 'Excuse me, what are you doing? Who are you?' He introduces himself as Tom Cordova. We didn't know any of these people and we were doing a mass interview. He was in a car accident coming to the interview. Luckily, nobody was *hurt* hurt. But he definitely shouldn't have come to the interview."

Dolich saw the young man's dedication and hired him immediately: "Right then and there, I could just say, 'That guy's working for us.' And Tom became one of our best salespeople. Stayed with the A's and then opened his own corporate consulting business, and he's done great work over time, selling global corporate sponsorships. That's a long way from being in a car crash coming to the Oakland Coliseum.

"One more was a gentleman named Alan Ledford. Ledford came in when we decided that we were getting a Diamond Vision board. We had to have people running the electronics and doing all that. And Ledford was out of Cal Berkeley—he was a super-bright, terrific, team-oriented person—and he just kept moving up the ladder. He worked for our Diamond Vision group and then he came inside and worked with the business group, eventually becoming VP of business ops for the A's. Then he became president of the Sacramento River Cats, the Triple-A team that came into creation in 2000 and became one of the highest-drawing Triple-A teams in the country. And then moved from that and is now president of the El Paso Chihuahuas Triple-A team and they have a United Soccer League team, the Locomotive.

"Those three just jump out as individuals that didn't come from sports man-agement schools—just thought it'd be cool to work for the A's to sell season tick-ets door-to-door, and all became incredibly successful and have mentored many, many more people over time."

Dolich's message is to just find a way to get your foot in the door. Make that good first impression and get hired, work hard, and you can write your own suc-cess story, too.

From Batboy to Potential Owner

Ben Hwang, Former Batboy and Biotech CEO Who Made a Bid to Own the Dodgers

Job title: Former batboy, Los Angeles Dodgers

Education/training: Ph.D. in biology (Johns Hopkins University)

Key pieces of advice: Raise your hand, talk to as many people as you possibly can, and just get started.

Ben Hwang began working for the LA Dodgers as a batboy as a teenager in 1984—when the ball club was owned by the O'Malley family—and he wound up being in the organization for six seasons before leaving to pursue his college education. Three decades later, when the Dodgers—then owned by Frank McCourt, who'd purchased the team from Fox Entertainment Group in 2004—were put up for sale in 2012, Hwang put together a group to make a bid to purchase the club.

Today, Hwang is the chairman and CEO of Profusa, a company leading the development of injectable biosensors with the goal of transforming personal and societal health and wellness by making our body's chemistry easily accessible.

"My time with the Dodgers was such an amazing experience," Hwang said when reflecting on his days working for one of the most iconic franchises in sports. "It was a bit surreal, [going from being] a Dodger fan as a kid, and then all of a sudden being able to be in the clubhouse and being in the front office."

Although he's now an entrepreneur in biotech and no longer working in sports, the skills he picked up in baseball are "absolutely" applicable to his current role with Profusa. One of the things he tells people, in fact, is that everything that's good in his life, he can directly connect to his time at Dodger Stadium: "My professional experiences grew because on my résumé there's a line that says I was with the Dodgers. It created interest. Every job interview in grad school, every grad school interview, when I showed up for the interview [that led to my first job], they looked at me and said, 'Oh, you're the Dodgers guy,' or, 'You're the guy with the Dodgers.' So I think just the connection with the Dodgers created a degree of novelty as well. I think that opened doors for me quite significantly.

"But more importantly, when I started at Dodger Stadium, I started as a batboy. I was a seventeen-year-old kid with very little experience in the professional world. And all of a sudden, I'm thrown in the midst of incredibly accomplished people with a lot of fame [and] great accomplishments [who] are world class in what they do—both in the front office as well as on the field with the athletes. I realized very quickly that what I learned from my time at Dodger Stadium that's really served me well for the rest of my life is the ability . . . to build relationships and . . . navigate and build those relationships across the vast spectrum of individuals, from the most famous—with the Orel Hershisers and Kirk Gibsons—all the way down to folks that people may not have heard of with very different backgrounds. That ability to create connections—that ability to actually create meaningful working relationships across a variety of personality styles—has served me incredibly well.

"A third thing that I would actually say is the Dodgers are a world-class organization. Everything that we did at the stadium was done incredibly well. Steve Brener, the head of publicity, was the best at what he did. Fred Claire, the general manager and executive vice president, was the best in his field." And working with the best, explained Hwang, created a standard of performance and expectations that was instilled in him at a very young age: "That commitment of getting to the ballpark at 7:00 in the morning and [not getting] home until 1:00 in the morning after midnight when the game's over, being fully dedicated without looking at the clock, being fully dedicated to understanding day in, day out what world class [means], how high do you actually set the standards—and those are the standards that are unwavering and nonnegotiable . . . for a seventeen-year-old kid, that was a great lesson to learn, and that's stayed with me for a long, long time."

DON'T BE AFRAID TO PUT YOUR NAME IN THE HAT

In the late 1980s, Hwang became involved with marketing and promotions with the Dodgers. But, as he noted, he did not land that role by design: "I started as a batboy, as mentioned, managing all the bats in the clubhouse. One of the lessons learned, too—and I tell that to my team and I tell that to young folks who are working in my company as well when they ask, 'What can I do to further my career? What can I do to actually be successful?'—the advice that I give is, 'Don't be afraid to put your name in the hat.' If you already have enthusiasm and a degree of intelligence, you back that up with willingness to actually put in the work, to not be afraid of the task in front of you [and] what the job gives you. Raise your hand when the job [has opened] up and say, 'I may not know how to do it today, but I'll be the hardest-working guy to learn as fast as I can. And I'm not afraid of the work that I have to put in to learn the job and perform well.'

"And you say, 'Don't worry about how much you pay me. I know you're gonna treat me fairly. Just give me the opportunity to show you that I could learn and do the job well.' Listen, if you want to be a doctor, you got to go to medical school. But in many cases, though, in the business world, you really don't need a marketing degree, per se, to be a marketer. You just gotta be willing to work and learn from the best and be able to put in the hard work and the hours. That willingness to raise your hand, put yourself at risk, and be able to dedicate yourself and to learn and not be afraid and intimidated by the task, is the advice that I give to folks.

"Basically, that's what happened. I was a batboy, but as a batboy on the field, before every game there are all these publicity activities going on, community relations activities. There's the first pitch [and] reporters are always around. And because I was a batboy there, what happened is I started to get tangentially involved with the publicity department to help out. [When] they needed to track down a player for an interview, I'd run and help them out and get the player for the interview. So I got to know the publicity director, Steve Brener, and the director of marketing, Barry Stockhamer."

Then, in 1987, after having been a batboy for three years, Hwang decided to leave the Dodgers because he was getting a little older. "After leaving Dodger Stadium as a batboy," he said, "I reached out to Peter O'Malley and asked for a quick meeting just to say, 'Thanks for the opportunity to work with you.' And that's probably one of the few times in Peter's career, my guess is, that a batboy wrote him a letter and asked for a meeting. He was gracious enough to give me his time, and we chatted a little bit."

In that conversation, O'Malley learned that Hwang was an immigrant from Taiwan who'd come to the United States at a young age and still spoke his native language. The following spring, O'Malley invited a group of baseball coaches from China for a sports exchange program. "They needed an interpreter when the team landed in Los Angeles to interpret for them, for that night, during a welcome meeting [with] Peter's right-hand person at the time, a gentleman named [Akihiro] 'Ike' Ikuhara," said Hwang, picking up the threads of the story. "I said, 'Sure, of course I'm happy to do that!' I showed up [and] did the translation that night. [When] they went to spring training, they realized they needed another translator. I went down to spring training for a few weeks to serve as a translator. Next thing you know, I got a call from Steve Brener from the publicity department saying, 'We need some help during the All-Star break. Can you come and help us out for just a weekend? I can't pay you but come and help out.' I said, 'Of course.' And it just snowballed into additional jobs." That one weekend in publicity turned into a homestand. That one homestand turned into a month. That one month turned into a season. "Next thing you know, I was an employee of the Dodgers.

"Every chance that I got, I raised my hand," Hwang emphasized. "If there's a job that opened up—[for example, when] somebody needed help in publicity—I raised my hand. [When] somebody needed help in promotions, I raised my hand. When a job in the promotions and marketing department opened up within Barry's group, I raised my hand [and] asked him to consider me. And they did. And that's how it happened. It started with just a simple phone call and raising my hand—and [asking] to be selected—and it just evolved from a day to a weekend to a homestand, and the rest is history."

SOMETIMES, IT HELPS TO HAVE LUCK . . . BUT MAKE THE MOST OF YOUR OPPORTUNITY

Let's backtrack and talk about how Hwang initially became involved with the Dodgers as a batboy. In his own words, he was "lucky and fortunate": His father's friend Terry owned a camera shop at Echo Park, right down the street from Dodger Stadium on Sunset Boulevard.

"One summer, when I was helping out at the camera shop," he said, "I found a bunch of boxes in the back with negatives and prints of Dodger players and Dodger Stadium. So I asked Terry, 'Hey, what's this?' He says, 'Oh, that stuff belongs to the former owner of the store.' And the former store owner happened to be a longtime Dodger photographer named Andy Castle.

"Being a young kid who's not afraid to just be stupid and aggressive, I asked Terry, 'Oh, great! So, the Dodgers are involved in the store?' And he says, 'Yeah.

There are some people in the front office that still come into the store to get their cameras fixed and get their film developed.'

"So I asked, 'Well, can I get an autographed baseball?' And Terry said, 'Sure, next time they come in, I'll ask and see if you can.' So sure enough, I got an autographed baseball! And I thought, 'Well, if you can get me an autographed baseball, can you get me a job?' I didn't even think about [being] a batboy. I didn't know anything about the business world at the time, and when I asked about getting a job, what I thought was they must've had office boy jobs, like emptying trash cans and vacuuming and running errands. I'm happy to do that. Get people lunch, right? Is there an office boy job there?"

When Terry asked, it turned out there wasn't such a job available—but there was a batboy opening. Hwang's response: "Well, sign me up! I'll do that!"

"So I met the longtime equipment manager at Dodger Stadium, Nobe Kawano. Nobe says, 'Yeah, come! Freeway Series! Come on [board]! We could use your help!' And once again, no guarantees. Just those two games at Dodger Stadium when the Angels came to visit [just before] the beginning of the season. I went, and that turned into a homestand, and that homestand turned into a full-time position as a batboy for a few years. I was just really lucky. But every so often, it's better to be lucky than good."

ADVICE TO THOSE WANTING TO WORK IN SPORTS TODAY

Obviously, times are different now than they were when Hwang first got started with the Dodgers, but what worked for him then can still work for students today. "Thirty-plus years ago when I started, it was a lot more informal," he said. "Nowadays the business of baseball and professional sports has gotten bigger and more structured. So the approach might be different, although I would say that the general premise remains the same.

"The general premise is if you're interested in something, raise your hand, ask for a meeting, ask for a conversation, ask to learn about the individual that you want to meet with, and find out about what they do. And create opportunities for those interactions to be able to demonstrate your talents to that person across the desk from you. Don't be afraid to raise your hand and ask. Don't be afraid to actually put in the work. Don't be afraid to tell somebody that you put in the work.

"I've never asked for a job without having the confidence to know that I could outwork the next person who may be after the same job as I am. I've never asked for a job by asking, 'How much does this job pay?' [Instead, I've always asked,] 'What can I do to actually help the organization? What can I do to contribute positively to what it is that you're doing?' I've never asked for a job without making absolutely certain that the other person knows that it's not lip service when I say, 'I will outwork anybody, and I'll do anything that you actually want me to do. No job is too small for my ego and no job is actually beneath the work that I'm willing to put in.'

"That's true, even today. I have a fancy title. I have a set of responsibilities. But nothing is beneath that title or that responsibility for me to make my company a little better. If it means I have to run to Costco and pick up a [case] of water, I'm happy to do it. If that means that I'm unpacking boxes after a move, I'm happy to do it—because at the end of the day, that degree of [willingness] to do something is infectious, and people see it. And it's a great differentiator. There are a lot of folks out there with great résumés. There are lots of folks out there with great degrees. But to come across with a smile on your face and say, 'I'm willing to pitch in however I can,' I think it's a great starting point to break into any organization. And once you get that opportunity, make sure you shine. Once you get that opportunity, follow up. Make sure you work as hard as you possibly can and create value as much as you can. Everything else is going to fall into place."

TRANSITIONING FROM BASEBALL TO BIOTECH

Hwang left the Dodgers at age twenty-three and has never worked in sports since. For him, leaving pro sports was a purposeful personal decision: "I had not gone to college. I was still working at Dodger Stadium after my high-school experience. I was twenty-three and I thought, 'I need to go back to school. I don't want to go through life without a college degree.' And so I left Dodger Stadium in 1990, really, to go back to school. And when I decided to go back to school, then it's just a conscious choice. I've always enjoyed biology. I've always enjoyed medicine.

"So I started my academic career as a premed and took a bunch of science classes. And then my career became pretty standard, if you will. I went to school. I transferred a couple of times and started at community college, transferred to the University of Southern California for a semester, and then worked at Caltech for a summer in the sciences and transferred to Johns Hopkins—and, really, just ended up getting my PhD at Hopkins in cell biology and biochemistry. And it became natural to actually get into my current field, just because of my academic background."

When the opportunity to own the Dodgers came up years later, though, Hwang decided to get involved. He made a bid to purchase the franchise, working with former Dodgers general manager Fred Claire and former Oakland A's president Andy Dolich to put that bid together.

"It was actually more fun than I had in a long, long time," he said. "Going into it, I'd always known that the task was daunting. I don't have that kind of personal wealth to be able to say, 'I will be the financial backer for the deal and be able to write a check.' However, I did know enough in the business world to understand that putting a group together—and getting the financial backing and such—is not something that you can't do. People do it all the time in the private equity world. So it was a project that I took on because I felt—and realized—that the experience itself would be a lot of fun, and if we worked hard at it and had a reasonable chance of success and it actually did happen, it would've been a really neat thing to be involved in.

"And, really, we're the sum of all our experiences. Whether the experiences are successes, whether the experiences are failures, they're all successes in one way or another. We may have fallen short of our goal in being able to actually own the team—and I realize that that goal was daunting—[but] I knew that the experience itself would be worth having.

"The people that I'd meet along the way and going through the process would be a neat thing for me to learn a lot from. And so we went into it with that mentality. If you go in with that attitude of 'this experience is meaningful' and 'chasing after the goal, the chase itself is meaningful even if we fall short on the goal,' [then it's a worthwhile experience]. Am I disappointed that we weren't successful? Of course. [When] you put two years into a project and you invest into that project with your financial resources and your time, of course you want to be successful. But I think we found success in many other ways."

In terms of working in sports and outside of sports, there are similarities, as Hwang mentioned—for example, putting up your hand and being committed to getting the job done from beginning to end. As for the differences between working inside and outside of sports, Hwang said, "I think working with the glare of the spotlight—even if the spotlight is not on you—I think it's different. I think working with individuals and athletes who are incredibly accomplished and when somebody has the talent to do something that nobody else can do and working with individuals like that, I think it forces you to develop a very different set of interpersonal skills that you may not have to develop in a very strict, structured business environment. But I think the similarities outweigh the differences.

"Because no matter where you actually go, in a business setting or in professional sports, I think that ultimately [you have goals that are meaningful to you]. Your purpose might be different, but I hope anybody who wants to dedicate their time away from their families to create some professional value, I hope that those professional experiences have goals that are worthy and meaningful to that individual. In sports, it was fun, but you also realize [that you actually make a difference in people's lives].

"I was talking to Andy Dolich a few years back, and Andy's brother is a physician. Andy used to say to his brother, 'You're saving lives, and I'm just selling tickets.' And his brother said something that was meaningful: 'Yeah, but you bring joy to 3 million people every single year that I can't do.' [I also remember talking to] the late Mike Heisley, who owned the Memphis Grizzlies for a while. I remember Mike saying the same thing. He said, 'I've seen firsthand how a professional sports franchise that's successful, how it changes the culture of the city. I've seen firsthand how it unites people in a city that may have very disparate backgrounds, and how much joy it brings to a city and to a municipality, and that's a very worthy accomplishment.'

"What we do today in my current company, our goal is to influence the health of the world, and tens of millions of people are going to benefit from this and live healthier lives. That's not dissimilar [from what] sports is, but it's just [a different] arena, right?

"Dodger Stadium, and working for a team like the Dodgers, you bring joy to millions of people's lives every single day. And that's quite satisfying. So I think that there are a lot more similarities than there are differences. I think, ultimately, those similarities drive people's decisions and choices, and those similarities also create successes that you find across the world.

"The things that I talked about earlier: a common goal, raising your hand, and not being afraid to work hard—whether it's sports or outside of sports—if the goal is worthwhile, if the mission is worthwhile, you should definitely do it."

FINAL PIECES OF ADVICE FOR THOSE WANTING TO WORK IN SPORTS
As for final pieces of advice for students looking to work in sports, Hwang suggested getting as many informational interviews as you can and raising your hand. But first, don't be overwhelmed when you're starting out.

"I think it's really easy to be intimidated in the sports environment," he said. "I think it's easy for young folks to look at it and say, 'Gosh, I'd love to do that, but I don't know how or where to start. And why would they want me anyways—because for every job that they have openings, there are hundreds of [applicants]?'

"While it's understandable that that level of intimidation actually exists and it might seem really daunting, my advice would be: 'Listen. Have as many conversations as you can with people working tangentially or directly in professional sports. Get in. Raise your hand. Be willing to sacrifice your time and energy to get started. And once you get started, you just don't know what the future's going to hold. The bad news in professional sports is that it's a small industry, relatively speaking, and it's a small fraternity of people and [a small number of] available opportunities. On the other hand, that's actually the good news. The fact that it's a small community, a small fraternity of professionals in professional sports; the fact that it's actually a relatively small industry, once you get in—no matter where you get in—and [if] you excel and perform and do well, the connections within the industry are actually quite strong. And you just never know when the next opportunity is going to come to ultimately land you where you want to land.'

"And so my advice is if you're committed to doing that, [if] that's something you're passionate about, raise your hand, talk to as many people as you possibly can, and just get started. Don't worry about the paycheck. Don't worry about what the job is. Don't worry about how tough it actually seems. Start somewhere. Start at a minor-league team. Start from the broadcasting angle. Start from the marketing angle. Start from selling tickets . . . because the next opportunity around the corner may be just exactly the one that you want. And in professional sports, I think that's a lot more likely than not because the fraternity is so small."

Baseball Executive

Charlie Blaney, Former Baseball League President

Job title: Former league president, California League (Minor League Baseball)

Education/training: Degree in philosophy (St. John's Seminary, Camarillo, California)

Key pieces of advice: Don't give up. Even if you're offered a job that's not quite a fit with your training, grab it. Once you're in the door, other opportunities will emerge.

Charlie Blaney is the former president of the California League, an eight-team Class A-Advanced league that operated throughout California between 1941 and 2020. The league was replaced by the Low-A West League in 2021 in conjunction with Major League Baseball's reorganization of Minor League Baseball.

At the time of his retirement from the game in 2021, Blaney had been involved in baseball for fifty-five years, including the first thirty-two in the LA Dodgers organization from 1966 to 1998. His time with the Dodgers ended in 1998, when

Rupert Murdoch and Fox bought the club and let go of most of former owner Peter O'Malley's staff, including Blaney.

An eleven-year run of putting together schedules for different minor leagues followed before the California League came calling in 2009 and offered him the position of league president, a role he held for the next eleven years until his retirement in 2021. With MLB taking over and restructuring MiLB during the 2020 off-season, league presidents were being phased out and replaced by regional supervisors. Blaney remained in his post through the end of May 2021 to help in the transition.

In our interview, Blaney talked about his life in baseball and offered advice to students wanting to get into the game.

When asked to describe how he got into sports, he acknowledged that he was "very fortunate and also persistent" when he first landed a job in baseball. "I had come back from serving in the Marine Corps and traveling around the world, and I wanted a job in sports. I'm from Southern California, so the Dodgers were my team. This was in 1965, but I didn't know anyone with the Dodgers, and my degree in college was philosophy. Nobody at that time was hiring any philosophers or machine gunners, and I wanted a job with the Dodgers but didn't know anyone."

Blaney's brother, however, happened to belong to the same Catholic parish as Vin Scully in Pacific Palisades. "My brother never knew Vin or met him," he said, "so my brother asked the parish priest to ask Vin, 'How does a young guy get into baseball with the Dodgers?' Vin Scully, being the first-class gentleman that he is, talked to Buzzie Bavasi, who at the time was the Dodgers' general manager. Buzzie said—this was in August of 1965—'Tell the kid when the team goes on the road to come and see me.' Vin Scully passed that message on to the parish priest, who passed it on to my brother, who passed it on to me."

The following week, when the team was on the road, Blaney drove up to Dodger Stadium to meet Bavasi: "But I didn't have an appointment. I sat around for about an hour because Mr. Bavasi was busy. Finally, he called me in and said, 'Okay, kid. Give me your pitch.' I said, 'Mr. Bavasi, I'll type. I'll empty the trash. I'll sweep the floors. I'll do whatever you want. I just want to work for the Dodgers.' He said, 'No, we don't have anything now, but here's a phone number. You call this number every month. Who knows? Maybe something will come up someday.'"

Blaney went home, found a temporary job working in a rubber factory, and hung on to that phone number. Every month, he called. September, no. October, no. November, no. December? He was told there was an opening in Albuquerque,

New Mexico, with the Dodgers' Double-A farm club in the Texas League. Although he didn't even know where Albuquerque was, he took the job right away.

"I was hired to be business manager," he said, "and it was a three-person office. There was a general manager, myself, and the secretary. I couldn't believe that I was actually working for the Dodgers, and that was the beginning of a thirty-two-year career [with the organization]."

Blaney acknowledges that persistence was one of the key things that worked for him, but there's more to it than that: "Yes, that's something I would suggest to students and others who might be interested in a career in sports business today. But more importantly, I would say [what organizations look for is] someone who'd love to work for your team. When I interviewed young people, something I looked for was their desire. I didn't expect them to come with a lot of experience, because I could teach them and train them what I wanted them to do. But I was always impressed with someone who loved the team and loved coming to work every day. We're fortunate to be in a business where it's exciting, it's fun, it's hard work, and you're with people who are dedicated to the job. And that's infectious.

"Yes, persistence is important, but drive, desire, and a love for the job and the team would be the most important thing. I didn't care so much about their pedigrees or education, because I could teach them and mold them in the way that I needed them to be."

Being in the game with the Dodgers for thirty-two years, Blaney certainly had his fair share of challenges and difficulties along the way. "But in terms of advice for those wanting to get into the sports business world, the first thing I'd say is you have to be available and ready to do whatever the company wants you to do, whatever the boss asks you to do. I was fortunate in my thirty-two years to basically have three different jobs. In the first year, I was in their minor-league system as business manager. The seven years after that, I was a general manager at three levels: Class A, Class Double-A, and Class Triple-A. During that time, I got married and was starting a family. In my first year in Albuquerque, I got married to a wonderful gal from Australia that I'd met in my travels. The next year, [I was] promoted to be a general manager in Daytona Beach [in Class A]. And my wife was pregnant, so we went there for one year and had our child, and then I was asked to come back and be the general manager in Albuquerque. I was there, and during that time we had three other children. Then, when the [Albuquerque] Dodgers went [from Double-A] to Triple-A—[and El Paso became the Double-A farm team in 1972]—we were transferred down to El Paso just for six weeks and then bought a house there and were called back. So we moved a total of six times during the first eight years, so you have to be flexible and available to go where the boss wants you to go."

Blaney's message: If you're looking for an opportunity with a franchise, be ready to go when they want you to go.

After eight years in the minor leagues, Blaney received a call from team owner Peter O'Malley, who asked him to go to Vero Beach to oversee the Dodgers' spring-training complex. Blaney immediately accepted the assignment. "I always took the attitude that when the boss calls and asks you to do something, you better do it or he's not going to call you again," he said. "And after thirteen years in Vero Beach, the boss called again. I had an opportunity to come home to Los Angeles to be the farm director. But for the first twenty-one years with the Dodgers, I was out either in Albuquerque or El Paso or Florida. So that's part of it. If you want to be in the game and work for a company, you have to be prepared to make adjustments in your personal life. Fortunately, I had a great wife who was very understanding not only with the hours that I would spend at the ballpark but also the willingness to move six times during our career until we finally got settled in Los Angeles for the last eleven years when I was the farm director.

"So flexibility is key; if you love the company you work for, you never work a day in your life again. That's what I always told my children and grandchildren, and anyone that I talk to—and I love to meet with young people and try to help them get in the game. The first thing I say is, 'If you find a job you love, you never work a day in your life again!' And that's one of the things baseball offers. Those who are sports or baseball fans, having the opportunity to work in the game, especially for your home team, that's a dream come true, and I was fortunate to realize that dream."

As far as how young people can go about realizing that dream today, Blaney stressed the importance of education. For students who are in college, he recommended they try to choose a major subject or discipline that could be useful in sports: "Obviously, times have changed since I first got involved in the game of baseball. Today it's a little bit more specialized than when I started. First of all, I think education is important. Get a sports management degree at university or a major in sports management and a minor in a field that you might be interested in. For example, it may be marketing or business or finance or analytics or food and beverage." A math degree, Blaney added, is also helpful in baseball because analytics has become such an important part of the sport. As for finding out what your interests are, there are so many aspects of the game within the realm of baseball. Let's say you want to be as close to the action as possible; "if you want to be on the field and obviously aren't good enough to play, you can always look at umpiring." Plus, there are so many other front-office and stadium-type jobs available, including sales and marketing, concessions, operations, stadium work, and accounting. So ask yourself: What is the type of work you'd like to do if you got a job in sports?

"In other words," Blaney said, "if you're interested in baseball, as long as you're getting your education—which is so important—you can be thinking, 'What is it that I like doing? What am I good at? What would I like to do for my career?' So start with getting an education that can prepare you for that. And a good way to get your foot in the door is as an intern. If you can get an internship with your favorite team, that's excellent because here you've got some background education, and a lot of the programs—especially in sports management—will try to get you internships with a team in various sports. If we're talking about baseball, if you were going to USC or UCLA or one of the Southern California schools and getting a major in what I mentioned and getting an internship with the Dodgers, then you get a chance to be seen. People get to see your work habits and get to know you, which is important.

"One other thing that Minor League Baseball has which is excellent for youth who are trying to get in the game is called the PBEO, the Professional Baseball Employment Opportunities. Every year at the Winter Meetings, there are several hundreds of applicants—people and young folks who come to the Winter Meetings—who fill out applications. Then they have lectures during the Winter Meetings about various aspects of the game, but the most important thing is minor-league and major-league teams who have openings post them on the bulletin board at the Winter Meetings, and so all of the young applicants can see the job opportunities, [like,] 'We need an assistant general manager in Visalia,' or, 'We need a field operations assistant in Lake Elsinore,' or San Jose might need a food and beverage assistant, or whatever.

"So you see those job opportunities and then you set up an appointment at the Winter Meetings to meet with the teams making these offers, and that's how several hundred people get hired every year: through the Professional Baseball Employment Opportunities arm of Minor League Baseball. It's very organized and very effective."

If there are sports teams in your area, Blaney added, contact them and try to get an appointment to go meet with human resources or whomever is in charge of internships. "Let's say you're still in college. Say, you're from San Jose, or San Francisco, or Los Angeles, or whatever city—start knocking on the door. Call the Dodgers and say, 'How can I give you my application? I really want to get into marketing,' or, 'I want to get into baseball operations. I've got a degree in analytics.'

Get an appointment, talk to them, and if they don't have anything then, [ask them,] 'Okay, who can I call? When will you have openings?' If you can get an internship, you can get your foot in the door. And while the pay might not be very much, they get to know you. They get to see what kind of work habits you have and what kind of person you are. Getting them to see you physically and getting them to experience your work habits is a big, big plus."

Going back to the idea of "being ready to go when they want you to go," be sure you're flexible and available when the internship or job opportunities come, advised Blaney. If a team offers an opportunity and says it starts next Tuesday but you reply that you can't make it because of other commitments, the job will likely go to another candidate. In baseball specifically, Blaney said, most of the opportunities take place after the season is over, when teams start looking to restaff for the upcoming season because some staffers have either been promoted or moved on to other organizations or occupations: "That's the time they're hiring, but it goes back to the persistence that I mentioned. Get to be seen. Dress nicely. Make an impression, so that when there is a job available, the person can say, 'Oh yeah, I met Charlie. Yeah, he made a good impression. I'll call him and see if he's still available.' You need to work it. If you just do everything by e-mail and let it go, your chances are not as good as the person who met with them, which I think is so important."

With regard to getting to be seen and making an impression, Blaney offered a few suggestions to make inroads: "You've got to get to know [people working in sports]. The only way to do that is to try to meet them, for example, by going to baseball games in your area, by trying to get to know people. Say you're interested in player development or baseball operations and you live in San Diego. Find out who the farm director is and who the assistant farm director is. Get their names and go to a game. Make an appointment to meet them. You may not be ready to look for a job, but you could introduce yourself: 'Hey, Mr. Jones. I'm Charlie Blaney. I'd love to work for the Dodgers someday. How could I get a job? What do I need to do? What do I need to prepare?' I always looked for someone who had the love, the enthusiasm, the drive. You can't teach drive and desire and work habits. Those come naturally. Networking is an art. There are a lot of books on it. It's your own personality. You need to learn how to sell yourself to someone that you're looking to give you a job. Show them that you really want it."

Baseball Executive

Rick White, Baseball League President

Job title: League president, Atlantic League of Professional Baseball

Education/training: Master of business administration (Purdue University); bachelor's degree in psychology (Chapman University)

Key pieces of advice: Think outside the box when reaching out to sports executives. Be the person who wants to go that extra mile, do the things needed to be done, to show desire and passion for that career. Once you get your foot in the door, there are other possible opportunities that might come up later on.

Rick White has been president of the Atlantic League of Professional Baseball (ALPB)—an eight-team circuit of unaffiliated clubs with franchises mostly based in the northeastern United States—since 2014.

Under his leadership, the ALPB has made headlines for its innovations, use of technology, and rule implementations. For starters, the league uses a pitch clock and limits the time between innings in an effort to speed up the game. In July

2019, the ALPB also became the first American professional baseball league to let a computer call balls and strikes when so-called robot umpires were used at its All-Star Game.

But perhaps the developments that have been more significant for the ALPB involve its growing relationship with Major League Baseball, which White had previously worked for. In 2015, the league signed a formal agreement with MLB that put into writing the rules the ALPB would follow in selling its players' contracts to major-league clubs and their affiliates, marking the first time MLB had made any formal agreement with or acknowledgment of an independent baseball league. Four years later, the league began a three-year partnership with Major League Baseball allowing MLB to implement changes to Atlantic League playing rules to observe the effects of potential future rule changes and equipment.

Prior to joining the ALPB, White worked in the American League office at MLB's central offices between 1983 and 1994 and was at one point considered a candidate for commissioner of baseball. After leaving MLB in 1994, White worked at Nike, where he headed subsidiary brands. He also was president and CEO of Reed Exhibitions, Phoenix Footwear, and Imperial Headwear.

When asked how he got his start in sports business, White acknowledged he was lucky. "When I was contemplating my master's degree, I elected to go to a school that allowed me to finish my classwork within one year as long as I composed a master's thesis. Even in those days, that was rare." But he did it, writing his thesis on a baseball topic. "And [my master's adviser] happened to be a baseball fan, was interested in the work, and assigned me to another professor to be my thesis adviser, who was doing research in the same field. So I enjoyed the lucky coincidence of having a very receptive university and receptive master's adviser, and then, ultimately, enjoyed the shift to a different thesis adviser who actively supported what I was doing throughout my master's program.

"Through the research associated with that thesis, I became aware of an opportunity in the American League of baseball. I applied for the job and was fortunate enough to get it, and began working in a public relations capacity at the American League."

When White was in grad school, there weren't sports marketing programs at any colleges around the country. "But today there's a variety of educational ways to prepare for a sports career," he said, "with numerous colleges and universities around the country offering sports management curriculums. But there are alternative curricula that people can pursue that also prepare them for jobs in professional sports, including economics, law, applied mathematics, and so forth, which thirty or forty years ago just didn't exist. But if you look at front offices and league offices, positions are checkered with people who took that route to prepare for a career in sports."

UNDERSTAND A SPORTS JOB REQUIRES HARD WORK

Like many people in the industry, a major challenge White encountered in his first sports job was compensation: "I was moving across the country to New York, where the American League office was located, and New York is an expensive place to live. I did so at an extreme discount compared to my colleagues who were graduating with master's degrees in business. And for the first few years of my career, I could barely afford an apartment or something to eat—and I certainly wasn't being extravagant. Well, that still applies today to people just entering a career in sports, and I'd characterize it as 'normal lifestyle.' A lot of entry-level positions in sport are either unpaid internships or very low-paid seasonal jobs. And this is where passion has to take the place of compensation, and hard work needs to replace aspirational hopes."

But, as White said, if you stick it out, almost universally, good things will ultimately happen. "It requires perseverance, hard work, learning as you go, and applied methodologies, meaning they have to apply themselves to their work." Also, it's important to understand what you're signing up for: "A lot of people, I think, enter sports thinking it's glamorous and fun, and they get to watch games and be a part of something bigger than themselves. And they realize very shortly after they join an organization that they're embarking upon a career—and it requires a lot of hard work."

CONSIDER ALTERNATE MEANS WHEN SEEKING THAT FIRST SPORTS JOB

White added that whenever he talks to young people interested in working in sports, he encourages them to be innovative when seeking that first job. "We all know about job fairs," he said, "and sending résumés and putting together a loose-leaf network of people who might know someone in sports, and looking for informational interviews. We also know about job boards and digital avenues that help us get into sports. That's all become the convention and the norm. To find the job, one must go through those exercises.

"But I'd encourage young people looking for that opportunity to think more broadly and more innovatively around opportunity. I'll give a couple of examples with baseball, but these apply to other sports as well. Number one, I'll guarantee there's a baseball scout in virtually every community in North America, even in the days of TrackMan and analytics. Seldom does someone who wants to work within a business discipline (as opposed to a player discipline) think about scouts as a way in.

"Second, we all have access to information that provides directories. All you gotta do is spend $35 on *Baseball America*, and you get a directory of everybody who works at every club throughout professional baseball. Everybody focuses on the top five or six executives in the organization. And if they're going to contact somebody, they usually do so electronically, and they usually do something with people at a certain level of the hierarchy. Nothing wrong with that. But I encourage those same people to look lower in the organization and to think about whether or not a contact there might lead to a contact with a hiring manager—or more opportunity in the lower level of the organization, where they're going to join anyway!—as opposed to aiming high, where the chances are their résumé or their CV is going to be shuffled off to a hiring manager.

"Third, we're governed now by digital technologies. It has disrupted all of the things that I thought I knew forty years ago. But something that's universal that many young people either disavow or neglect is that people still open the mail. In fact, a letter in an envelope delivered by the U.S. Post [Office] has become so unusual that people are delighted when they get a letter in the mail—because nobody sends them anymore! Young people today normally don't send letters or postcards; they send e-mails, texts, and Snapchat. But sometimes, they need to get a little outside their comfort zone, be a little vintage in terms of their thinking and say, 'Hey! People will read a letter!' Now, a letter with a résumé inside, by definition, stands out. It may still get shuffled off to the hiring manager, but you can cover that with your digital coverage that you already [use, through the job boards and digital avenues].

"So those are a couple of illustrations within the baseball community—but they're not unique [in that they] can work in any type of sports management position.

"Moreover, we sometimes fail to exercise common sense if we really want to get through to someone. If you send somebody, let's say, a box of Cracker Jack, and it's a sealed box or something like that, chances are somebody's gonna open it! So why not think about the novelty of delivery to get your CV in front of somebody instead of only posting your profile on an online job board, where a computer ninety-nine times out of one hundred is going to eliminate your CV because your cover letter didn't adequately cover all of the criteria they listed in the job description. However, you may be a perfect or an ideal applicant. But [maybe due to the way the] computer [is programmed], you aren't getting through to the hiring manager.

"So I always encourage people to network extensively, to network aggressively, and to utilize means with people they don't know or can't get to through the network that are as obvious as the nose on their face but they no longer are on trend. And, again, the U.S. Postal Service, for 58 cents, is a heck of a way to get to somebody. And think about that: Nobody does that anymore, right? If I get a letter or a box, I open it every time. There's some incentive in that if people just think through it a little bit.

"I'll give you one other thing. If people think broadly, there are opportunities. And I don't care where you live, where you're from, who your parents are, etc. You make enough inquiries, and sooner or later you'll find somebody connected to sport. And my experience with people is they want to help, if it all possible. There's no reason to not try to leverage that."

THE IMPORTANCE OF HARD WORK AND DEDICATION

Whenever White is asked to discuss the importance of hard work and dedication, two things jump to mind. One is personal initiative: "When faced with the CV of a person, you have a short amount of time to read it. But it's pretty straightforward to see those folks who have initiative and go beyond classwork or outside of discipline to try to do things that stand out. And it isn't just one or two things, it isn't just charity, it isn't just teamwork. It isn't just being around your team. It's initiative that's honest, that's genuine, and that shows you have the ability to do several different things before and even while you're at an entry-level position and employed. And I can't stress that enough. People notice it. And in many ways, it counts more than just about anything else you do."

Second, not everybody going to a university will have the marquee value of an elite college to dwell upon. "That doesn't mean anything other than the fact that where you do go to school—and what you do when you're there—is far more important than attending an elite college," White said. "That means you have to excel at your classwork, you have to multitask, and you have to show that you've shown initiative along the way. And you want to find some relevant things to the career path you wish to pursue.

"The other big thing I always counsel people on, is it's important to have a discipline that you want to aim for, whether it's marketing or player development or baseball analytics or a whole host of other things. And it's important to prepare for that as best you can. But it's more important to get into an organization than it is to get into an organization in the discipline you wish to pursue. Once you get a job, it's far easier to navigate internally than it is to find a job in your preferred discipline."

Essentially, the point White wants to make is that once you get your foot in the door, there are other possible opportunities that might come up later on.

"And one of the things that happens in any organization—not just in sports—is you have people there who are there for the long term, but you also encounter people who may be here today but not around tomorrow. Usually they leave to take another job, or they learn that this job wasn't for them, or sometimes folks are let go. But there's quite a bit more turnover in sport organizations than most people think.

"So if you were inside and you're getting to know people in the department where you have a preference and you're taking on projects on an extraordinary basis—while still getting your normal work done—when an opening occurs, that's when you have the opportunity to let your interest in that opening be known. And with a little bit of luck, [assuming] you're aiming at the right level, [you might be given strong consideration for that position].

"[However,] if you were a recently hired college graduate and you're within the first couple of years of employment, and all of a sudden a director-level position opens up in another department for which you aspire, you're probably not going to get that job. But that's not a bad time to tell somebody in the hiring role in that organization that you really would like to be in that department. You know that position isn't for you, but if an opening at an appropriate level opens up, you'd be certainly interested in that transition. Nobody's going to hold your interest in a discipline against you."

What they'll hold against you, however, is a failure to ultimately satisfy the obligations and responsibilities in your job description, warned White.

The bottom line once you have your foot in the door: "You have a lot of opportunities to navigate within an organization, as opposed to get[ting] lucky enough to have a job offer in an organization in the discipline you prefer."

PUT YOUR FANDOM ASIDE AND LEARN NEW CONCEPTS

White advised that when people are evaluating opportunities in sports, they dig into the dynamics behind the scenes and not go into any job interview being just a sports fan.

"For the folks who really are going to get the leg up," he said, "they're going to develop insights around the trends governing the sports themselves. And it's usually the business of sports that provides the opportunity, not the visceral representation of sports. So, if, once again, we're looking for an opportunity in baseball, one really has to understand what's going on behind the scenes in terms of labor and player evaluation, in terms of the business of baseball, both locally and nationally, within the broadcasting and rights communities, within different media and those business models and how they relate to your sport of choice.

That's where most people fail, and they come to their application as a fan as opposed to an informed job applicant."

One such example in sports business is the salary cap, which, in North American sports, is used by the NBA, NFL, and NHL, along with leagues such as the WNBA, Canadian Football League, and National Lacrosse League. "Understanding how the salary cap works if you're looking for a career in sports is definitely important," explained White. "What you want to do is two things. One, understand the dynamics of that cap. You can find it. You just gotta work harder to find it. But then the inside part of that is understand[ing] there are people working within the cap to put together teams. And you combine those two things—[and] that should lead to opportunity because insights around that, in many cases, are undiscovered. And if you can bring to the discussion insights around how a cap can be properly managed and can be leveraged to the benefit of the employer or the employee, now you've got something that's a little bit more interesting than saying, 'Yeah, I'd really like a job in player development.' The fact that you thought critically about it makes you more valuable than a guy who's aspirational. The fact that you've thought critically about it, you understand that there's opportunities—both on the team's side but also on the labor side—makes you more valuable and more likely to get a job than somebody else.

"The fact that you thought critically about it but maybe you accepted a job in the mailroom gives you an opportunity to display that insight once you get inside, as opposed to knocking on the door to try it otherwise."

CONSIDER THOSE OVERLOOKED ENTRY-LEVEL JOBS
White added that if you're looking to get your foot in the door, you should consider all options. "I'll give you one where there's always a job. There's 100 percent always a job in the concession operations of any major-league team. They're part-time jobs and not very glamorous. But you're working inside, albeit on the margins. Or you're wistfully saying, 'I'm unemployed. I wonder what I'm gonna watch on television tonight. I think I'll turn on the Dodger game.' Well, is working for their concessionaire glamorous? No. Is it complex to navigate that to get into the right person at the Dodgers? Yes, but [at least] you're inside. And here's another one: I daresay there are probably parking attendant jobs at Dodger Stadium. Again, I'm going back to the lessons I'm trying to throw out there: Have you shown initiative in terms of your desire to get in and take *anything* so you can get in? Yes."

With these examples, White illustrated the fact that there are readily available jobs for those who show the initiative: "And if a college graduate came to me and said, 'I'm unemployed. I'm looking for a job. It's taking longer than I thought.' I understand that. And if you then add to that, 'In the interim, I want in so much I took a job in the parking garage'—or 'I took a job working for Aramark because I want to be close to it and I want to have access to people, and I'm looking for networking opportunities'—now all of a sudden, I think that person's got initiative, and he or she is the one I want to be looking at. As opposed to the person who's sitting on the couch watching the game tonight. And it really doesn't matter where you went to school or even what your grades are. One is proactive. The other is passive. Who do you want to have on your team?

"And again, I do believe that it's hard. There's lots of competition for limited numbers of jobs, but the people who take that extra step, do the research, take a look at alternative means to develop a network, don't just rely on digital technologies—which they have to do anyway—are the ones I want to talk to. And I daresay most people in this world want to talk to them. The people who really stand out are the ones who want to take that extra mile, do the things they need to do, to display their desire and their passion for a career.

"Maybe others might give different advice. That's fine. I don't think most people think granularly. I think most people say, 'Yeah, go out and get your sports management degree from Ohio University.' And that's a great start. But that's not the be all and end all. What do they graduate every year in that program? A hundred and fifty young people? Now you've got 149 other competitors for the same job. So I just think you gotta go that extra mile."

Major League Baseball Team Co-Owner

Peter Seidler, San Diego Padres Majority Co-Owner

Job title: Team co-owner, San Diego Padres

Education/training: Bachelor's degree in finance (University of Virginia); master of business administration (UCLA's Anderson Graduate School of Management)

Key pieces of advice: If you're interested in working in sports, get inside the ballpark, stadium, or arena. Have somebody give you a tour and ask questions, just so you know how things operate within a sports franchise. Also, get the idea of working in sports being glamorous out of your head because it's a lot of work.

Peter Seidler, one of the majority owners of the San Diego Padres, comes from one of baseball's most famous families. Although the name Seidler isn't necessarily a household name among casual fans, Peter Seidler is a grandson of former Dodgers owner Walter O'Malley. He worked for the team in various capacities while Peter O'Malley, his uncle, owned the Dodgers, from ushering at Dodger

Stadium to interning in the PR department to stuffing programs for spring training contests at Vero Beach to later working at minor-league affiliates.

The O'Malley family sold the Dodgers in 1998, and Seidler returned to baseball in 2012 as part of a group (which included members of the O'Malley family
along with civic leader Ron Fowler and golfer Phil Mickelson) that purchased the
Padres. He's also a partner and founder of Seidler Equity Partners, whose investments have included LA Fitness, Sportsman's Warehouse, cable manufacturer
Windy City Wire, Paragon Medical orthopedic instruments manufacturing, and
Allied Oilfield production equipment.

Seidler was gracious enough to take some time out of his hectic schedule in late
October 2019 to contribute to this book with advice and insights for students. He
was, in fact, preparing to fly to Houston the following day for the World Series
(between the Astros and Washington Nationals), and he and his staff had just
hired a new field manager and were looking to round out their coaching staff
leading up to a press conference scheduled later that week.

A natural question to ask Seidler is how one becomes—or develops the qualities to be—a great leader, particularly for a sports franchise. "When I was in my
early thirties," he said, "I started my own firm. I got into the private equity business, and one thing that I learned is if you really think you want to be a leader, you
gotta do a gut check. You gotta look in the mirror and see the reality, not what
you wanna see, not what your friends and family tell you, but what's reality? What
do you do well? What do you need to get better? And be unafraid of criticism.

"Then, the other thing that comes to mind is you really have to have an iron
gut if you're at the top of an organization. You have to deal with unexpected *anything*. I was in the private equity business, so every month I would get financial
statements on the companies that I either owned or owned a significant part of,
and that's a roller coaster."

That means great leaders must realize they need a great team around them. This
is a key ingredient in terms of building a successful—or winning—culture: "So I
decided, as the company founder, it's working but it would work best for me to
have partners and to put them all in one room. This is my vision for Seidler Equity
Partners: Put them all in one room and let the best idea win, whether it's mine
as the older guy and founder or whether it's an intern's or anybody's in between.
The best way to do that, for me, is that you have a real partnership. So my second
partner was my younger brother. Trust obviously matters. My third was a guy that
we'd known and worked with for a long time. Fourth, I wanted a lawyer because
there's a lot of legal stuff that goes on in the industry, so we hired a lawyer that we
knew well. Ultimately, now in that business, I've got eight partners and—I'm down

in San Diego now, but before I moved down here—we all sat in the same room and that's how we went about our business. We knew who we are, we knew what focus we're going to go after, recognizing that it's not the only way to do it, but this is the way *we're* going to do it. You can't be wishy-washy when you're a leader. You gotta know how you're going about it, and then if you're good at it, success follows.

"I think it's the same thing with baseball. In sports, people generally talk a lot about winning. But if you do the right things and the smart things and just basic fundamentally sound things over and over and over again, the winning comes. If you chase winning too much, sometimes you chase it away. And that's what we're building with the Padres: Trying to do the smart thing and the right thing for our organization. At this point, we know what kind of animal we are. We go about it in a way that makes the most sense for us and we decided a few years ago to take a step back before we can, hopefully, really have a sustained period of success. And it's interesting we're having this conversation now because we said, at that time, the decade of the 2020s is gonna be our decade in a franchise that in fifty years had been to the playoffs five times. I honestly and frankly tell our fans or anybody in our organization or the media, what I believe is going to happen—and hold me to it—is we're going to be in the playoffs five times in this decade. And every time we go in, we're gonna expect to win the trophy. That plays out as it plays out, but we were five-for-fifty [and our goal moving forward is] we're going to be five-for-ten starting next year.

"In this case, you have an owner, a president in the business, a president of baseball, and you've got key people in the organization. But I know my style: Let's get everybody in the same room, let's talk through the important stuff, and again, whether it's an intern or the president or whoever, it's 'the best idea wins.' That's not going to happen instantly, but I think at this point it's really happening here [with the Padres], and we'll see if that happens. I'm just super confident that [we'll see over] the next several years—and we talk about it here in terms of the next ten—it's going to really shift this kind of dismal-performing franchise over its history into one that's really special."

Seidler then used an analogy pointing to franchises in other sports that lacked a winning tradition but were rebuilt under strong leadership and ultimately became powerhouses: "Nobody saw San Antonio coming in basketball before [Gregg] Popovich brought them an elite level of results. Nobody saw that happening in New England in football until Bill Belichick made it happen. That's what I hope: ten years from now, people look back to today and say, 'Where did this come from? They've been to the playoffs six times. They've won the World Series. And now they're positioned to do more of it.'"

Of course, a great leader also knows that while stability on a team is essential, changes must also be made when individuals within the team are underperforming. "A lot of layers go into it," Seidler said, "and in my view, there's a lot of turmoil in sports. Every time you look at ESPN, you see the scrolling down the page this time of year [in October] of who got fired and who got hired. We fired our manager and brought in a new one, but I hope we get to a point where we have as much stability as you can possibly have—but not lazy stability, not the same people over and over just keeping their jobs, but that level of stability where everyone top to bottom in the organization is passionate to be best in class. And if everybody around you is best in class, you're going to know if you're not going to get to that level in whatever you do, you're probably not going to be around here, so there's a self-governing factor that goes into it also."

In any successful organization, part of striving to be the best involves the ability to effectively identify and solve problems. When hiring coaches in sports, for example, this includes being able to help players perform better: "To me, the fundamentals always matter: Honesty, transparency, putting the right incentives in place for people. We're interviewing coaches in here now to add to the manager that we just hired, and one of [the] things is just making people be accountable for what they do, and, in some way, shape, or form, be rewarded for it. If we want this player to go from five stolen bases to twenty-five, now's the time to work on it to get prepared to do it. In certain cases, it's really clear how to make that happen. Or if another player should focus on home runs, which is what a lot of people in the game are [focusing on] now, how do we go from fifteen home runs to twenty-five with our player? Part of it is playing time, but as I say those things, I think about attention to detail. I think that's a big separator in greatness. We can all talk strategically about what needs to be done, but the attention to detail, like passion by the coaches to do the extra work with the players, or from a personality standpoint to be able to reach the players—all those things come into play."

When asked specifically to provide tips for youngsters who aspire to land that dream job in sports—one that's fulfilling and rewarding—Seidler shared a few pieces of advice. "A couple of things: People from the outside view working in the sports world as glamorous—and, frankly, it's not. When I was in the private equity world, people thought, 'Oh, wow! You're flying to a new city every day. You're staying in nice hotels . . .' But that's not anything glamorous. It's a whole lot of long days. Everybody in our building loves baseball, and it's not work to them. Often during the season, people come in here at 9:00, and they're here through the end of the game, which might be 11:00. Some of them have work to do with the media after the game. I mean, some of these days are *really* long! And what I found is people that thought it would be glamorous, they typically don't last long. People that love baseball, it feels like a four-hour day, not a fourteen-hour day sometimes.

"The advice I frequently give people who want to get into the sports business is get your foot in the door. That's all you need to do. Get an internship somewhere. If you want to be a general manager one day, start selling tickets if that's the only [position available]. Get inside the building. [With the Padres] we only have two hundred full-time employees, which is about average for a baseball team. Some have a lot less. Some of the big markets have a lot more. But two hundred is good, and everybody knows everybody. And if you're really competent at what you do and really good to work around, those people get on a fast track right away. If you're expecting glamorous and hanging out with Manny Machado and becoming a general manager at the age of twenty-three or something, [that's not realistic].

"So the first step I'd say is really look into what's inside the building. Have somebody give you a tour and ask questions, just so you know how it operates. Then, if you think that's where you want to go, have a career in sports, there's a lot of ways to do it other than working for a major-league franchise. You can start with a minor-league team. You can [explore other areas; for example,] there's so much media around sports. There's so many ways to get in, and it seems like I hear a new story every other day about somebody that started as an intern in the sales office or something who's now an assistant general manager at the age of thirty-two. So, when you're great at what you do and good to work around, it happens fast. But this idea of it being glamorous, it's probably good to get it out of your head because it's a lot of work. But if you love it, it doesn't feel like work."

Of course, as Seidler mentioned, working in sports isn't glamorous. There will be times when you need to step in and deal with a difficult situation or even make an important decision or handle a crisis. Seidler's advice for these situations: Stay calm. "First of all, think about it. Does it help to be hysterical or to freak out in any way? The best leaders are the most calm person in the room when there's a crisis or a tough decision, because it doesn't help you to rush or to panic. I've seen it in a lot of [great leaders] who have a natural ability just to be calm when things are flying all over the place and you don't know up from down. They have a natural ability to get into a space of, 'Hey, these are our core principles. This is an unexpected bit of chaos, but our core principles, or my core principles, that's what we're going to do.'

"I've never seen a great leader that freaks out when everybody else is freaking out. Usually, their face tightens up, their eyes get serious, and they're talking the way we're talking [in this interview]: 'Okay I think we need to do this and this and this.' Probably the few other people in the room that aren't yes men: 'What do you think? Is this the best way to go?' And pretty quickly, they come to a decision: 'All right, this is what we're gonna do.'

"Look, we're human beings. None of us control outcomes. But we *can* control our emotions. And there are times when you gotta think through quickly what to do. It happens in sports a lot. You [might] get a phone call that your player sent out a dumb tweet—or, worse, an offensive tweet—on social media. That happens more these days all the time. Or somebody took a picture of your coach—your married coach—getting drunk with a couple of young girls last night. It's remarkable how much really unexpected stuff happens, but experience helps with those things. But I think there's an innate quality in leaders, like, when things are tough, you get more calm and more clear-minded."

With his background in making transactions in business and in sports, Seidler ended by giving some pointers on the art of making successful deals. The cheatsheet version: Surround yourself with other leaders you trust—experts in their respective areas—and collaborate on decision-making. Do a lot of research, leaving no stone unturned, to make sure it's going to be the right deal. "You gotta look in the mirror and see reality," Seidler said. "I'm not an overly analytical person, so I surround myself with really analytical people. What I try to do and what I've come to believe is if you get in business with the right kind of person—and, to me, that means a person who has a passion to succeed and has a low ego, and it's somebody you can trust—almost always you're going to win. If somebody's lazy, you're not going to win. If somebody's an egomaniac, it's probably not going to work out well for very long.

"And I've always had partners [in business]. When I buy a company, the CEO is running it, not me. In a lot of areas in an organization, the best leaders hire people that are smarter than they are, or experts in their area where they'll never be. That's something which has served me well. I know what I'm good at, and I know what I'm terrible at. I don't like numbers and stats, but I like people. If I'm hiring a manager or spending big money on a player—[I] spend a lot of time with them, getting to know the personal side. Our scouting department has two sides to their scouting card. One is all about the baseball player and the skills and the speed and the power and the defense. The other is all about the personal quality. What was his relationship with his parents? Who were his friends when he started playing competitive baseball? We go deep. We find teammates, former teammates that we can talk to, certainly former coaches, and that tells you a lot about the person you're signing.

"Even in the amateur drafts, the first-round picks cost several million dollars. You want to make sure that's not just a guy that looks good on videos, but actually is a decent guy that you can trust in the context of a clubhouse and with the team. Of course, the same thing goes when you're signing more experienced players to much bigger contracts, and whether it's the players or coaches in the sports world, it's similar to me."

Seidler's philosophy here is similar to when he does deals outside of sports: "For me, when I would fly to look at a new company and decide if we're really gonna take a run at putting a deal together, it was always all about the people. Then I had a partner or two who'd slice and dice the analytics every which way possible and really study this company and study their industry. [Together as a team] we can tell it's relevant today because you know that's a quick screen that we have, but if it's relevant today, the big question for us is: Is it going to get more, more, and more relevant over the course, if we're going to own it forever or we have a five-year time horizon?"

His point is that in successful businesses and organizations, CEOs and other leaders at the top are often skilled executives who are honest, trustworthy, and collaborative, but not necessarily the smartest people IQ-wise. But they're wise enough to surround themselves with a strong management team of other honest, trustworthy, and collaborative leaders who each have their own areas of expertise. "For me in my private equity world," he said, "[what makes successful deals happen is] having the experts that slice and dice the analytical side of things. If [the analytics and numbers lead us to the decision], we're probably pretty good to go. It's similar in baseball; you let your experts do your thing and make sure you got the right experts."

As for final words of wisdom for students looking to work in sports, Seidler offered the following: "Find a couple of mentors that can open some doors for you—and they're not hard to find. There are, at all levels of all the major sports, people that want to pay back or pay forward what they got at some point. Like I said, get a tour through a sports organization and see all the departments, whether it's baseball operations or marketing or accounting or sales or whatever it is. It's instructive to see it. Then, if you have a friend in that organization, he has people that he knows and others. Again, when you get that first job, I really found that people kind of see, 'Wow, it's not what I expected.' Maybe it's the organization. Maybe it's not. But when people start with the Padres, almost within a couple of weeks, I can tell if they're gonna last here. Just finding a mentor that can help you open doors is probably as good a way to go as any."

Sports Management

Jason Takefman, Sports Consultant

Job title: Sports consultant; former general manager, Vancouver Canadians (Minor League Baseball); former content marketing manager, UFC Canada; former director of corporate partnerships, Vancouver Canucks

Education/training: Bachelor's degree in psychology, minor in economics (McGill University, Montreal); executive MBA (University of Washington)

Key pieces of advice: There's no substitute for actually learning by doing. You can see things firsthand, and then you can also make a decision about what exactly you like to do. Because by learning, you can say, "Oh, I *do* like X, Y, Z, or I don't like X, Y, Z." That's just as important as anything you'll learn in school. [And whether it's] internships and volunteering, I always encourage people to get as much experience as possible. Try and get involved with as many departments as possible, to learn what you like.

Originally intending to be a sports psychologist, Jason Takefman attended McGill University in Montreal, considered one of the most prestigious universities in the world. But he changed his focus midway through his university studies, deciding he wanted to work in sports management instead. After doing some research, he realized that path was very much a possibility for individuals like him who never played professionally.

"I Googled a bunch of people who'd been in sports," he said, "and with the exception of, obviously, former players, there were a lot of non–former players who worked their way up through [various avenues], whether it's scouting or internships, and they got their foot in the door. And this was in 2005, at the beginning of the industry, [when] there were not that many sports management programs. Now almost every school has a sports management program. And that doesn't even include some of the digital marketing, sports branding, sports law, and all the different spokes in the wheel about sports.

"And I didn't really have a route to take. I was in Montreal at the time and I didn't really know anyone, so I just applied everywhere, and I ended up getting an internship.

"What happened was a friend of mine, who was a really good hockey player, was moving to Israel and he was trying out for their national hockey team. They mentioned they were looking for some help, so he actually was the one who gave me the contacts—it was on a piece of paper in the dressing room—and I ended up volunteering for the Israeli national hockey team for five or six months while I was finishing my last semester in school in December 2005. This was the International Ice Hockey Federation, Division III. They were very far behind in the IIHF rankings just because they were a new country to hockey compared to Canada, the United States, Czech Republic, Sweden, Finland, and all the main hockey countries.

"That experience benefited me. It benefited a lot of players who obviously wouldn't have gotten a chance to play internationally, wouldn't have gotten a chance to play at that high level had it been a little bit more developed country. Not to mention, there's a lot of people working very hard to turn it into a hockey developed country to get rinks built, and I was able to be there at that time, which was very exciting."

Although the internship was for the Israeli hockey team, the position was in Montreal, which allowed Takefman to finish up his final semester at McGill. "The fundraising was headquartered in Montreal, which was really helpful. As for the team itself, they were based out of Israel, but they would do these fundraising tours. So they played the Nepean Raiders in Ottawa. They went to New Jersey to play against a high school team there, to Montreal to play against the Midget Double-B team, to Philadelphia to play a team, and a few other cities."

While that experience in his last semester in university helped Takefman get a taste of what it was like to work in sports, he still didn't have connections. Upon graduation from McGill, he compiled a list of sports teams across Canada and attempted to contact each and every one of them. Unfortunately, none of those organizations gave him an opportunity. It took an unexpected twist for him to land an internship with Minor League Baseball's Vancouver Canadians: "When I graduated, I just sent out a bunch of letters and e-mails, and made phone calls to anybody. I made a point to reach every single sports entity in Canada: amateur, professional, everybody, and it was very difficult. I ended up securing an internship through a friend of a friend of a friend, who introduced me to the assistant general manager of the Colorado Springs Sky Sox. I was going to drive there from Montreal."

Due to unforeseen circumstances, though, Takefman never made it to Colorado Springs: He wasn't even allowed to cross the border. This was a little over four years removed from the 9/11 terrorist attacks and increased border security was still in place. At the border, he was told he wasn't given proper work documentation and was therefore denied entry to the United States. When the Sky Sox assistant general manager heard about the situation, he felt so bad that he personally contacted the Triple-A Ottawa Lynx and Single-A Vancouver Canadians—the only two remaining affiliated minor-league baseball clubs based in Canada at the time—to see if any job openings were available.

"These two teams didn't get back to me when I originally reached out to them. [But when the Sky Sox's assistant GM] made the introduction for me, that obviously went a lot farther than me making cold calls or writing letters to try and get my foot in the door with them."

Thanks to that personal introduction, Takefman was offered a job in the ticket office for the Lynx in early 2006. But he realized it wasn't a good fit for him. For starters, the Ottawa franchise, he learned, was on its way out of town—the Triple-A International League team was ultimately sold to new owners just five months later and would relocate to Allentown, Pennsylvania, beginning in 2008, to become the Lehigh Valley IronPigs. He also learned the Lynx drew about one thousand fans per game, meaning there wouldn't be enough meaningful work for him. Thus, he turned the Lynx down, drove nearly three thousand miles out west, and took an internship job with the Vancouver Canadians in March 2006.

Vancouver proved to be a good fit. Takefman's work ethic was quickly noticed by the Canadians organization, and he was promoted from intern to ticket office manager to director in seventeen months. When the team changed ownership in 2007, he was the only member of the former management team to be retained, and in October 2009 he was named the club's general manager.

One lesson to learn from Takefman's story is that when you're new in an organization, you should try your best to learn from the best. In his case, with the Canadians, he learned about sponsorship sales, an important skill that helped him land a role with the NHL Vancouver Canucks less than a decade later. "I had two great teachers," he said. "[One was] Graham Wall, the director of sales and marketing with the Canadians. He took over that in my first year. He was part of the new ownership group. He was amazing. And he taught me some of the structure, pricing, and meetings, and all [the relevant details]. The second person was the GM who initially hired me, Delany Dunn. He taught me a lot about the value of sponsorships and how it frames the brand of an organization—and I would never have truly thought that, or at the very least, I wouldn't have thought like that. And when you're new, that's very important to be able to have people to reach in and help you out."

When asked what a GM on a minor-league baseball team does, Takefman said, "It's completely different than that of a major-league team. On a minor-league team, it's about the business and operations. The general manager looks over the business operations, revenue generation, game-day presentation, where the players live, and things like that." A big part of his focus was on sales. "I like to have all the sponsorships sold by about a month before the season. You want to have your barbeque area and suites sold out long before that. You want to have a waiting list. The best thing you can do in the off-season is to say, 'Listen, unfortunately, we're sold out. But we can get you into another date.'" As for seats to the general public, Takefman and his sales team focused on trying to sell out days in advance, and eventually weeks in advance.

He stayed on as the Canadians' GM for four years before deciding to move on. At the time, he was in his early thirties and felt he needed a new challenge. Wanting to explore other opportunities the sports world had to offer, he found his answer: a position with UFC (Ultimate Fighting Championship) Canada in Toronto.

"I was in a very steady [position with the Canadians], and I was doing my executive MBA at the University of Washington, with the team helping me out. But the thing with the Canadians is that, as fun as it is, it's finite. It's thirty-eight home games [at the time with the team's Short Season Single-A designation]. There's only so much you can do, and we'd done everything. [Attendance-wise] we were at 98 percent capacity. I wanted to do something that was totally different, learn a different part of the business. And a friend of mine in the business told me, 'I just saw on a job board that there's an opening in the UFC Canada office and you should apply.'"

Takefman applied, met with the hiring director, and was hired for the position of content marketing manager for the UFC Operations for Canada, Australia, and New Zealand. "I did event marketing, content marketing, and pay-per-view marketing," he said. "I was also part of the internal negotiation team [dealing with TV contracts]—we'd moved from Rogers to TSN, and we moved from TVA Sports to RDS. [Rogers is a regional sports network in Canada and TSN is the Canadian equivalent of ESPN. TVA and RDS are French-Canadian sports channels.] That was very exciting, and I'm very grateful and appreciative that I was a part of it."

As for students interested in such a job in sports, Takefman offered the following advice: "I'd say a business background [is essential] because [in an area such as] content and media, it changes every six months. I always tell people like right now and then—I do a little bit of sports representation, [where] I do contracts for a few people and sponsorships—and I say, 'No one knows anything about the future, and we know it's going to be on a different platform. We know it's going to be accessible, and it's going to be user-driven. It's going to be as easy as possible to consume. But other than that, we don't know.' And had you told me eighteen months ago that Mike Tyson was going to fight Roy Jones Jr. with Snoop Dogg smoking a blunt eight feet away from them while there's a pregame concert going on, on a platform named Triller that nobody's ever heard of before, I would've said you're crazy. And not only did that happen, but they actually sold over a million pay-per-views. So that's just proof to stay flexible.

"And the contracts that we renegotiated, their usefulness expired after eight months. I know this because [I was told by my former colleagues], 'You did good work, but it's February now, and that happened [the previous] May, and it's expired.' Business moves around so much. I think to be able to understand that, you want to be as flexible as possible, but also offer the most amount of value [to build that relationship with them and have them later renew], which is very important. You need to be able to think of what's best for both sides, especially when business moves very fast. The last thing you want to do is kind of anchor people down to assets and contracts that are expired or that aren't relevant anymore."

Takefman found that the UFC job offered the type of challenge he was seeking. No two days were the same: "It changes all the time. In fact, I'll tell you a funny story. My first day at the UFC was on November 25th, and November 16th was [the event in which] Georges St-Pierre and Johny Hendricks fought. And part of the reason why my job existed was because the business in Canada was growing

exponentially and they needed more people to handle the duties related to growing the business. Among them was someone to manage the business while the
person above me was going to focus on larger marketing and branding positions
throughout Canada, Australia, and New Zealand.

"And November 16th, Georges St-Pierre essentially retires in the Octagon, and
that was very unfortunate, because he was the most popular fighter at the UFC
and he was Canadian, and he was even French-Canadian, which obviously helped
those rights quite a bit.

"And then November 25th was my first day. The very next day, our TV rights
holders and partners, Rogers and TVA Sports, announced that they were going to
do NHL. Not only that, but they were going to broadcast it on Wednesdays, Sat-
urdays, and Sundays. Well, Wednesdays we broadcast the Ultimate Fighter and
studio programming, and Saturday is a live event and they replay it on Sunday,
and the replays do really, really well also. The whole business changed. So no two
days are the same." An important lesson here: Remain flexible, learn to pivot, and
have an open mind as to your job duties. When you encounter a problem, throw
out everything you know and start over.

Takefman left the UFC twenty months later when he landed a role with the
NHL Vancouver Canucks as director of corporate partnerships. "The UFC was
slimming down their front office because they were going through a sale at the
time. A lot of my peers were either let go or they left, or their jobs were dissolved.
Six months after that, they closed three offices, including the Canadian one and
half of the UK office. So they were trimming down ahead of their sale.

"The other reason I left the UFC was I wanted to move back to Vancouver.
I'd been on the board of a few charities, particularly JCC Sports Dinner, and the
Canucks' business wasn't doing super well at the time, and I embraced that. That
intrigued me." For Takefman, the Canucks opportunity felt like a "fun rebuilding
project." As it turned out, though, "It wasn't. I was wrong about that—and that's
another lesson: you can be wrong about something—but that's what attracted me
to [the Canucks' job]."

Takefman left the Canucks after one season and started his own sports consulting business, collaborating with local businesses in the Vancouver area, which
he was, at the time of our interview, still doing. He's also been a project adviser/
teacher assistant at California State University, Sacramento since 2020 for a Business Analytics class.

Going back to how he got his start in sports, Takefman noted that he was persistent. "Reach out to as many people as possible. There's a time and place for a
little persistence and to be able to show someone your value. I also think you want

to be realistic about what you're doing. Let's say you don't have writing experience and wanted to be an editor. That wouldn't necessarily be helpful. But if you went to your school newspaper and volunteered or if you had relevant journalism experience, I think that is very helpful, realistic, and doable.

As for final pieces of advice for students, Takefman shared some of the principles that have served him well in the industry: "We used to have two rules: One, you don't make fun of your own players—even if it's just in jest—just like you don't make fun of your own team or people you work with, and two, don't gossip. You're going to pick up a little bit of information and knowledge, and you don't want to gossip. There's no shortage of people looking to get information, whether it's the local media, national media—they're celebrities. Them asking you for information and developing a relationship, that's very intoxicating, or at the very least, palpable, that somebody wants to talk to you."

Finally, he said, keep learning and stay current. "There's lots of good content out there. A very good daily [e-newsletter] is JohnWallStreet from *Sportico*. [The writer's actual name is Corey Leff, but he goes by the name JohnWallStreet in his e-newsletters.] He has a very good daily e-mail where he summarizes everything very succinctly about what's going on with sports [business]."

V

FINDING AND WORKING WITH ATHLETES

Sports Agent

Ronald M. Shapiro, Sports Agent
"Life by Accident"

Job title: Sports agent

Education/training: Law degree (Harvard Law School)

Key piece of advice: Do whatever you're doing well, even if it's not exactly what you think you want to do, because you don't know when opportunities will come.

Ronald M. Shapiro, named one of the one hundred most powerful people in sports by the *Sporting News* in 1999, is a well-known figure in the world of sports agency for his work in the business spanning more than four decades.

Shapiro represented professional athletes for forty-three years in a sports agency career that began in 1975, when he was hired to represent future Hall of Famer Brooks Robinson of the Baltimore Orioles, and ended following the 2018 season when the last active player he represented, Joe Mauer of the Minnesota Twins, announced his retirement from Major League Baseball. His list of professional athlete clients—according to his profile page on the website of his Baltimore-based law firm, Shapiro Sher—includes more Hall of Famers than any other agent, as he represented some of baseball's biggest names, including Robinson, Jim Palmer, Cal Ripken Jr., Kirby Puckett, and Eddie Murray during their playing careers.

Although he no longer represents professional athletes—and no longer practices law—Shapiro was still active in the world of sports business at the time of our interview. A *New York Times* best-selling author, attorney, educator, and world-renowned expert in the field of dispute resolution, Shapiro still serves as a special adviser to Steve Bisciotti, the owner of the NFL Baltimore Ravens, and has also served as an adviser to the general managers of the NBA San Antonio Spurs, Oklahoma City Thunder, and Brooklyn Nets.

Shapiro, whom *USA Today* once called "one of baseball's most respected agent-attorneys," has authored several best-selling books, including *The Power of Nice: How to Negotiate So Everyone Wins—Especially You!* which explains his philosophy of mutual benefit negotiations. Originally published in 1998, *The Power of Nice*, was excerpted in *Fortune* magazine and named one of the "Top 10 'On the Job' Business Books of the Year" by *Library Journal*. A revised edition was released in 2015.

RONALD SHAPIRO. *COURTESY OF RONALD SHAPIRO*

In 2013, Shapiro was named as a member of "The Champions: Pioneers and Innovators in Sports Business" by *Sports Business Journal* and *Sports Business Daily.*

And while Ronald Shapiro's career as a sports agent has ended, the Shapiro name remains relevant in the world of Major League Baseball. At the time of our interview, Ronald's son, Mark Shapiro, was president and CEO of the Toronto Blue Jays, a position he has held since the end of the 2015 season.

Although Shapiro has had a long and active career in the sporting world, he said that career path wasn't by design: "First of all, [with regard to] my life, I call it 'a life by accident,' meaning things happened that I didn't plan. I even frequently say to young people, 'Do whatever you're doing well, even if it's not exactly what you think you want to do, because you don't know when opportunities will come.' When I went to law school, my plan was to join my father and his small business that he had. He was an immigrant who was an amazing person who didn't have a lot of education but made a lot of himself. He inspired me but he passed when I was relatively young. So I went to law school, graduated, and didn't know really what I wanted to do—didn't have the first thought about sports, by the way—and I went into civil rights law initially. And then, because that didn't earn any money for my law firm, they asked me also to be a securities lawyer, which is investment law."

From 1972 to 1974, Shapiro served as Maryland's securities commissioner. And believe it or not, he said, because he was in civil rights law and securities law, he ended up in baseball. How did that happen? "I graduated from law school in 1968, I started my career path in '69 and '70, and in 1975 I got a call from the owner of the Baltimore Orioles baseball team [Jerold Hoffberger]. He said, 'Could you help our legend?' And I said, 'What's that about?' He said, 'Well, we have this guy named Brooks Robinson . . .' [Robinson, of course,] ultimately ended up in the Hall of Fame. [He was] a great third baseman, but at the time he was finishing his career and he was about to go bankrupt because of bad investments."

Hoffberger explained in the call that he knew of Shapiro's work as securities commissioner. "He knew I had become a regulator in the local securities world and wondered if I could use that expertise to help Brooks work out of those bad investments," Shapiro said. "He also wanted me to know that he called me because he also knew of my work in civil rights law, helping young people who didn't want to get involved in the Vietnam War avoid leaving for Canada and losing their citizenship." Unbeknownst to Shapiro, one of those young people he helped was a member of Hoffberger's family. "I didn't know it was his nephew— but I helped a nephew of his—until he wanted to repay the favor by asking me to help Brooks. So, quite circumstantially, I ended up in the world of baseball and, ultimately, professional sports. When I did that, I continued to be a corporate lawyer, a business lawyer, a civil rights lawyer. I continued to do other things, but the bottom line is, that's how I ended up in [sports]."

Shapiro's path was unique because he never intended to work within the sports industry. But for those who prefer not to go the "life by accident" route like Shapiro and whose goal is to become a sports agent as soon as possible, a bachelor's degree in sports management is highly recommended given how competitive the industry has become. In addition to a degree, top agents typically hold a master's degree and many even have a law degree.

Of course, becoming a sports agent may not be for everybody, but many different careers exist for students and young people passionate about sports. Whatever career in sports it is, for those still in college looking to pursue a job in the industry upon graduation, Shapiro said the first step is to recognize that the field is full of people who want to be in it: "If you're a general manager or you run an agency, you could expect to get hundreds of letters in a month, or a series of months, [from people] looking to be in the field. So I always say to students, 'Get the best grades you can because that distinguishes you right away. Network as much as you can into relationships. Use whatever network your school has, but it's going to be somewhat circumstantial that you end up in it—because so many people aspire to be in the field, for good reasons and bad reasons.'"

With the sports business world changing dramatically over the years, Shapiro believes students can further prepare themselves by continuously staying abreast of the latest trends in sports. In the case of baseball, with the sport's heavy reliance on technology and analytics in recent times, it's crucial for anybody interested in landing a job in the industry to keep up to date. "Analytics and understanding the dimensions of the collective bargaining agreement in sports are probably the two most important skills you can develop," said Shapiro, "because it's a lot more complex than when I got started. So I would urge you to really do everything you can to absorb analytics and to do everything you can to understand the collective bargaining agreement that guides the various sports you're in. It's more and more complicated. If I went back into the agency business, which I started to wind down twelve years ago, I'd have to do a lot of learning of the CBA to be effective."

For those wanting to work in the front office of a sports organization, Shapiro added, it's also essential to be an effective leader while developing strong business acumen. He used his son as an example: "I have a son who's rebuilding the Toronto Blue Jays and built the Cleveland Indians into what they are. And he built his business skills, his baseball skills, his analytical skills, and as he rose the ranks of the Indians and ultimately tore them down to build them up—which he's now doing in Toronto—he developed a lot of different skills, from astute business skills to the skills of understanding baseball and an array of some other things. I was writing some notes about him because I'm giving a talk in the not-too-distant future. I remarked that not only was he good at the baseball end of things, but in Cleveland, he was great at building an organization of great people and giving them the opportunities to develop and build themselves. So when he left Cleveland, it was going to be as good as or better than when he was there, because he'd built such good people under him that they could sort of take over. That is the mark of a good leader in any kind of business enterprise, let alone a baseball team. So I'm very proud of him, [not only] for all the 'Executive of the Year' awards he got in baseball, but more importantly, for the executive that he became and the leader he became."

If he were hiring young people for his own firm, Shapiro said, he'd be looking at a few important characteristics, just as any other executive would. "I'm not hiring people anymore, but if I were, the first thing I'd look for in people is their empathy, their ability to be empathetic, and some humility. Obviously, I have the statistics on them. I want them to be intellectually strong, obviously. But humility and empathy are really, really important to me. As is their experience. If I'm looking to fill a particular role and they have experience in that role, that plays into it as well. But human qualities—having strong character—are really important."

SKILLS LEARNED OUTSIDE THE CLASSROOM

Some things, such as those strong human qualities, aren't learned in the classroom. To be successful in any field, it's essential to learn skills and knowledge from sources outside of the classroom.

It's no different for Shapiro. Although he graduated from Harvard Law School, he learned many valuable skills from various mentors outside of college, lessons that have had an influence in the success of his career. "My father, who passed when I was very young, established in me a view of the importance of all people, that the chairman of the board is no more important than the maintenance man in the boiler room of a building," he said. "That every human being is worth something. Respecting them and enjoying them—and doing what you can for them—is important. Also, my father gave me a 'glass-half-full' philosophy, which is important for negotiations: Even when things don't look good, you can make them good. So my father was a big person in that. There were also some teachers along the way.

"But I'd say that in sports, the first man I negotiated with was a general manager of the Orioles named Hank Peters—Henry Peters—who's now deceased. I did Brooks Robinson's last contract with him, and I did a couple hundred other contracts. And Hank was quiet, not an extrovert [but] more of an introvert. He was a good listener. And [from Hank] I learned that it was really important [to follow this philosophy]: The less said, the better; the more you learn, the better; dumb is smart, and smart is dumb. The first time I negotiated with him, I wanted to show him how smart I was and how much I knew, and he just listened. I gave him all my stuff but he didn't give me a thing. Then, when I said, 'Let's do a deal,' he said, 'Ron, I'll get back to you.' And I learned that negotiation is about patience, process, listening, learning, and then, ultimately, crafting something on the basis of that.

"So Hank was a great influence on me, and my dad was a great influence on me, in a professional sense. I think those were the two major influences."

Obviously, education in the classroom is just as important. One valuable skill Shapiro acquired in law school was how to write more effectively: "[Other than Hank and my father, there was also] some writing teacher that I had in a remedial writing program when I was in law school, because I never really developed good writing skills until I was in law school. He was a major influence on me, because he just ripped up everything that I ever wrote. And I finally learned to be a writer as well as a good speaker, and that was life-changing for me."

THE POWER OF NICE: THE KEY TO SUCCESSFUL NEGOTIATIONS

Those who have been associated with Shapiro have said that one of his strengths as an agent was the credibility he established with both the teams he dealt with and the players he represented. When asked to identify the key parts to maintaining those types of relationships, Shapiro says he keeps it simple: Just practice the Power of Nice.

"With me," he said, "the cornerstone of being a negotiator, both in terms of the people you represent and the people you deal with, is embodied in a book I wrote called *The Power of Nice: How to Negotiate So Everyone Wins—Especially You!* Now, it wasn't called, 'Be Nice and Roll Over and Make People Like You!' It was based on the principle that if you empower yourself with a systematic approach to negotiation, which the book lays out, that you don't have to be overly aggressive, you don't have to feel inferior, you can go to the table as an equal or better, you can accomplish much of what you want to accomplish, but you don't have to destroy the other side. And if you approach negotiations that way—rather than a battle or you're gotta bang them on their head and look like the victor, beat them up in the press—over time, you build credibility, because you act with integrity but you still seek to achieve what you want. You don't sell your clients out. They feel good about you. And they like to be associated with you."

As Shapiro explained, the concept of being nice applies even when the side you represent wants you to be tough. "Sometimes you get a client who says, 'That's not the way I want to be. I want to be a tough son of a gun.' You know, I'm being tough and powerful but I'm doing it in a way that doesn't aggressively negate the feelings on the other side. And I think that's all about relationships, whether it be in sports or whether it be in the corporate world that I work in or the nonprofit world that I do a lot of work in. The same principles apply. So you ought to at least read about the book—if you don't get the book—and understand that that is the cornerstone of making good deals and building great relationships, which is so important."

PREPARE, PROBE, PROPOSE: THE THREE Ps

Shapiro is a firm believer that people from all walks of life can make deals that achieve their goals if they embrace the systematic approach built on his philosophy the Power of Nice. He shared a few more pointers on how to obtain the desired result in a negotiation, whether it's a business type of contract or a deal involving an athlete: "In terms of what I've written about negotiations, I'd always tell young people, keep in mind that being systematic allows you to gather information, which is so important to negotiations, so that you can ultimately build a strategy that involves accomplishing your goals that doesn't seek to diminish the other side's feeling about itself or its position. So that's the essence of the Power of Nice, and the system that I created."

Shapiro breaks that system down into what he calls the three Ps:

Prepare: Research. Study. Stockpile knowledge. "Get all the information you can and strategize as much as you can. That's the first P, and there's a preparation checklist that goes with that." Essentially, added Shapiro, the idea is that you should not go into a meeting until you know everything you can about your position, evidence for and against you, comparable situations in the past and present, what you are aiming for, and what you are willing to settle for. Also, know about the other side, its position, and views. In other words, the more you know before the dealing begins, the better your position.

Probe: "Even when you think you're prepared, don't just go to them with a proposal. Go to them with questions. Find out what they're all about. Find out what their interests are. And 'Probe' is all about asking questions and listening." Many people think that asking questions is a sign of weakness, but that belief, said Shapiro, is a myth. Instead, what you should be doing is to approach the other side and ask them questions.

Ask direct questions. What does the other side really want? What are their short-term goals? Long-range plans? From the direct questions, explained Shapiro, you might find that you can enable them to attain their long-range goals even if you aren't able to meet their short-term ones. Ask indirect questions, too: Where the other person lives and went to school, and what they do when they are not working. From these indirect questions, you will learn what to talk about—and what to avoid—when taking a break from negotiating. Listen for clues as to how the other side thinks, acts, and feels.

Propose: "There are some principles that guide you in how you propose; aim a little bit high or low depending on where you're going. Don't immediately accept the offers." The Cliffs Notes version of Shapiro's third P: A proposal is a starting point, not final. Give the other side something to think about. Don't just give them something to accept or reject, to take or leave. A good proposal, instead, should lead to conversation: swapping of needs and wants. Also, try not to make the first offer. When you do make an offer, make it strong, solid, and reasonable. Be open to change it as the process unfolds.

In addition to the three Ps, added Shapiro, don't forget to practice scripting: "[That's] the subject of another book I wrote, *Perfecting Your Pitch* [published in 2013], so that you deliver messages with confidence—and the other side doesn't see weakness in what you're saying and push you back but, rather, understand that you have some conviction about what you say."

Shapiro continued, "Now, I'm summarizing hundreds of pages and years of thought, but it's all about being systematic, and I emphasize that the three Ps are not linear. You don't prepare, then probe, and then you propose. You might prepare, probe, prepare some more, probe, prepare some more, propose, and start probing again—because the key word to understanding negotiations is that it's a process and not an event. It's not a matter of going to the other side and saying, 'This is what I want'—and they say, 'This is what I want.' You're working through a process to get you what you want to get. And in trying to get it, you have to embrace the principle that to get what you want, you're going to help them get some of what they want. And I'd say those are the guiding principles, focused on gathering enough information to really be effective. And then using that information to hatch a strategy, and then ultimately doing a deal. And you end up doing a deal that leaves you with a relationship—because even when the deal is done, you're going to have to work with them."

For example, even after a deal was completed in baseball negotiations, as a sports agent he had to work with those same general managers again later on: "When I represented real estate transactions, I've had to work with landlords and tenants again. I mean, finishing a document doesn't mean you've finished the deal, because you're going to have to work some things out over time."

For more about the kinds of skills that make a successful agent, check out Ronald M. Shapiro, with Jeff Barker, *Perfecting Your Pitch: How to Succeed in Business and in Life by Finding Words That Work* (New York: Hudson Street Press, 2013), and Ronald M. Shapiro, with James Dale, *The Power of Nice: How to Negotiate So Everyone Wins—Especially You!* (Hoboken, NJ: Wiley, 2015). Shapiro's theory, the Power of Nice, is based on a simple yet savvy business principle: You want to figure out something the other side wants, they want to figure out something you want, and the two sides make the deal based on that. As a result, each party gets a little of what it wants and subsequent deals will follow. This book is recommended for those who would like to learn how to use Shapiro's systematic approach to empower themselves in negotiations.

Wealth Management

Brandon Averill, Athlete Wealth Management Partner

Job title: Managing partner, Athlete Wealth Management

Education/training: Certified financial planner (Chartered Financial Analyst Institute) and certified private wealth adviser (University of Chicago Booth School of Business); former minor-league baseball player

Key pieces of advice: Having the right designations is crucial to get into wealth management. Make sure the client's best interests are taken care of. Always deliver on what you promise.

Like many athletes who didn't reach the big leagues, Brandon Averill wanted to stay in the game when he realized he wasn't going to make it to Major League Baseball. Drafted by the Houston Astros out of UCLA in 2004, Averill played two seasons of professional baseball as a third baseman, not advancing past Single-A, before retiring from the game at the age of twenty-three.

Today, Averill is still very much involved in the world of sports. A certified financial planner (CFP), he's the managing partner at Athlete Wealth Management (AWM), a company offering a wide range of wealth management services to professional athletes and their families, with offices in Phoenix, Arizona, and Pasadena, California. In 2016, he was named by *Investment News* as one of the top forty financial advisers in the industry under age forty.

When Averill established AWM with his younger brother Erik, who also pitched in minor-league baseball with two organizations, it wasn't just out of a desire to stay in the game; it was their passion to help athletes they'd played with and competed against both in college and in the minor leagues.

"We founded the company about ten years ago," Averill explained in a 2019 interview with the *Life in the Front Office* podcast. "My brother and I are the founding partners. We have a third partner as well, Robert McConchie. We got into this business, really, to change the culture of how and why athletes use their wealth. The reason we got into this business was I'd played in college at UCLA, and my brother Erik had played at Arizona State. Through those experiences, we had the opportunity to play with some really great players, some guys that had the opportunity to play in the big leagues [and] earn some money.

"We also both had short pro careers as well. But those experiences [showed us] what clearly had become an epidemic of athletes just not doing great things with their money. And so we developed a passion for helping those players. . . . We've been really fortunate in that we've been able to build a model that, we think, serves the athlete really well, and [we've] kind of just built the relationships over the years that have led us to be successful."

One might think that the original concept of AWM was Averill's idea, but he actually credits Erik, who's two years younger, for the idea of starting the company. "When I got done with my playing career, I went into corporate banking," Averill continued. "That's where I got my first finance education. Four or five years after I'd gone into the corporate finance world, Erik's playing career came to an end. He had an opportunity to intern at Morgan Stanley [the investment bank and financial services company and] just fell in love with the idea of helping athletes with their finances. At that same time, he was that bug in my ear: 'Hey, let's go build this thing together.'"

At that time, several of Averill's UCLA roommates were just entering the major leagues, and having heard many horror stories over the years of high-profile professional athletes in various sports going broke following their playing careers, he decided he wanted to get into business with Erik to help his friends and other athletes avoid mishandling their own finances. (In March 2009, *Sports Illustrated* reported that an estimated 78 percent of retired NFL players were either bankrupt or under financial stress within two years of hanging up the cleats and 60 percent of former NBA players were broke within five years of retirement, adding that numerous retired MLB players had been similarly ruined.)

"It's really often a guy that has an adviser but just didn't have the skills or the knowledge to pick the qualified advisers," Averill added, referring to factors such as poor financial literacy, ill-chosen accountants and other financial advisers, high-risk investing, and cultures of lavish spending as among the chief reasons professional athletes run into financial problems upon retirement. "What it really boils down to, they didn't have anyone that they felt comfortable going to for advice, and they just didn't know how to pick qualified advisers.

"So that was Erik's sales pitch to me. He lured me away [from the corporate banking world]. We spent a short period of time at the wire house at Morgan Stanley and really figured out quickly that, while that's a good model for the majority of Americans, for those with complex needs, such as professional athletes, that multifamily office model is the key. So we split from there and ended up founding a company under that multifamily model."

And what exactly is the "multifamily model"? In Averill's words, "the whole gamut of services that a professional athlete would need," which specifically means AWM "can give advice [from] taxes—tax planning, [and] certainly investments—[all the way] through estate planning and insurance as well."

The range of services AWM offers is more than simply tax planning, investment management, and estate planning. "In the simplest way, when we explain it to potential clients, . . . [anything] that's going to happen around baseball, you know, baseball business, an agent is going to deal with," explained Averill, who figured that as of June 2019, the firm was serving the needs of approximately 120 full-service clients, 70 of whom have had major-league service time. "Anything that money touches, is something that our team is going to deal with, and that's quite a bit. . . . If they're going to purchase a car [or] a house, we're going to be involved . . . down to the mortgage. We're going to be involved with the realtor, all the way down to nannies. We make sure they're set up on the payroll, they're properly insured, background checks are made."

Then there are "fun" services that AWM helps with, too. "We have engagement ring conversations all the time—how much to spend on one," Averill added with a laugh, before bringing up the service of educating the kids of pro athletes. "Some of our clients have signed $100 million contracts, and they're raising children. How do you raise children that are raised in an environment that they still respect money and still respect the people around them? How do you pass your values on to your kids? So we do a lot of education through that, which is a whole lot of fun. We've developed extremely close relationships with the majority of our clients. So it's a lot of fun to be in this business."

In terms of the services player agents offer versus the types of services Averill offers, those are two different things, as he explained: "From an agent standpoint, your primarily responsibility is negotiating with the team. So you're going to represent the player in contract negotiations with the team. You're also going to represent the player in contract negotiations with endorsement companies, whether they're equipment companies, etc. That's the agent world. Of course, they do other services as well. On the financial side, we don't handle any of the agent responsibilities. That being said, we do work very closely with a number of agents . . . most often [in terms of] structuring contracts. So an agent will negotiate the total dollar amount, that top-level amount." Let's say that the agent negotiates a six-year, $140 million contract for the player. What does Averill and his team do? "We'll come in and say, 'Okay, based upon that, here's an ideal structure from a tax perspective.' So we come alongside them and provide the best outcome for our clients."

As far as Averill is concerned, there's another difference between the two roles: "The other distinction is that for an agent, their work comes during the player's playing career. When the playing career is over, sure, they stay in their lives, or many of the good agents stay in those players' lives . . . whereas we have the opportunity [to see our impact beyond the player's playing career], which Erik and I and our team really love. That is, when we bring a client on, it's for life. We really get to see an impact, not only in their playing days, but in their retirement years and beyond that as well."

What advice would Averill give to those who want to do what he and his brother are doing? Having the right designations is crucial for anybody serious about getting into the wealth management business. And be ready for the competition in the industry: "There's a lot of former athletes that get into our business because the financial business is a competitive business. It's an area that, if you're willing to put some hard work in and compete, generally you can start off being pretty successful.

"But, to us, we didn't just want to be former athletes in the financial space. We knew that if we were really going to make an impact, we had to be at the top of our game, from a financial expertise standpoint. So when we decided to get into the business, we picked the model that we felt was the best, which was the multifamily office model. . . . Then, early on, we dedicated ourselves to getting the certified financial planning, the CFP designation. To us, really, that's just table steaks.

That's something that, if you really want to be in this business, in our opinion, you've really got to get that designation at a minimum. And we didn't stop there. We both hold designations called the certified private wealth adviser designation, which is really a designation that gives you the education to deal with clients that have a net worth of $5 million or greater. With the earnings that professional athletes have throughout their careers, that certainly vaults them into that category.

"That's Erik and I personally on the general advice side. And we built up our team with expert CPAs to handle the tax side and accounting side, we built up our team with CFAs, which in the investment field is the absolute cream of the crop, one of the most difficult designations to get in all fields. Oftentimes, [when] we're sitting down with families, it's great that we understand the lives of the player, when to call, when not to call, what it's like to go 0-for-4 with four punchouts, what it's like to hit a game-winning home run. All that stuff is great; we can relate on that level. But at the end of the day, you're hiring financial experts, so I'd say anybody that has a real passion for that financial expertise and can marry that with a playing background or even just sports in general, and tie into a team that maybe has some playing background. I think to be successful in sports, that's really what it takes."

One might think that being in wealth management, Averill logs long hours in the office. But that isn't the case at all. He spends a lot of time on the road: "Technology is amazing now that we've pretty much got an office anywhere I'm sitting. Chase Ballpark right now in Arizona is fully functional from a work standpoint. We have a great support team in the office as well that take care of some things. On a typical day, it's a lot of communication with our clients, a lot of texting, phone calls, FaceTime, so, just really, that consultative relationship with a lot of our clients. We've got a lot of tax planning conversations with our CPAs. I wish there was a typical day. But it's also what keeps it exciting. We're not a suit-and-tie shop that is staring at fourteen monitors and thinking we can trade the market. It's a little different than that."

And, fittingly, coming from a sports background, Averill said trust and teamwork are keys to everyone's success. A perfect example is the working relationships with player agents. Although the services that he and AWM offer are different from the roles that player agents perform, Averill stresses that it's important for them to work together. After all, they have a common goal: Make sure the client's best interests are taken care of.

"You understand it from the agent perspective," he said. "It's a very, very competitive landscape. Anybody that's considering getting into the agent business, I'd highly encourage you to spend a lot of time talking to agents and what their experience is. It's a very, very difficult business. They're protective, and rightfully so. It took us a long time to build our credibility. We work with, at last count, twenty different agencies. Our clients are represented by twenty different agencies, and to pull that off, it's a difficult thing, because to get them to trust you in an industry that's worried about different people in their lives potentially flipping them to different agents, it takes quite a bit of time and trust. Really, just continuing to show up and doing what you say you're going to do, and not violate the trust of the agents, yeah, they're very important all the way round.

"If you can continually provide good work for your clients, [because] at the end of the day these agents want their clients to be taken care of, it definitely helps to build that trust. We've found the agents that represent our clients to be really good people that want to make good impacts on their lives, [and] it's happened to work very well."

Scouting in Football

Neil Stratton, Adviser for Aspiring Football Agents and Scouts

Job title: Inside the League founder; adviser in college football; adviser for agents and scouts

Education/training: Degree in journalism (Marshall University); networking

Key pieces of advice: Scouting isn't the "fantasy football" dream that many people might think. Passion and sacrifice are inevitable in the industry. The pay is small and the hours are long. You're up against deadlines, often lonely and unwelcome at the school you're visiting.

Neil Stratton has loved the game of football since his youth, playing high school football in West Virginia, followed by a brief stint as a walk-on outside linebacker at the U.S. Naval Academy in the 1980s. Not good enough to reach the pros—he was, in his own words, "perhaps the worst player on the worst team in America" while at Navy—he decided he wanted to help people succeed and build connections in college and pro football. In 1997, he helped start a small draft-oriented publication, *Lone Star Football (LSF)*, publishing four editions annually with a partner over the next four years. In 2002, Stratton launched the website Inside the League (ITL), which published one report daily Monday through Friday from September through the end of the NFL draft in April. Today, ITL publishes several times weekly on a twelve-month news cycle, with the goal of helping people in the football world (whether they're agents, financial planners, wealth managers, scouts, and others across the industry) succeed in the business of the sport.

Although he's never been an agent, Stratton has served as an adviser to schools from the Big Ten, ACC, WAC, Conference USA, and Pac-12, and he knows as much about agencies and agent recruiting as anyone in football.

In 2018, Stratton published *Moving the Chains: A Parent's Guide to the NFL Draft Process*, sharing valuable information he learned in his two decades working with scouts, agents, financial advisers, and others associated with the NFL draft process. Two years later, he published *Scout Speak: Thinking & Talking about Being an NFL Evaluator*, with a foreword written by New Orleans Saints assistant general manager Jeff Ireland.

In our interview, Stratton offered valuable perspectives and advice for aspiring football agents and scouts.

HOW INSIDE THE LEAGUE HELPS ASPIRING NATIONAL FOOTBALL LEAGUE AGENTS

One way Stratton and Inside the League help people progress in the industry is preparing aspiring National Football League agents for the examination run by the NFL Players Association (NFLPA), a mandatory exam that covers topics such as the CBA, salary cap, player benefits, and other issues relevant to player representation. (In addition to successful completion of the multiple-choice proctored exam, requirements for becoming an NFLPA agent, as of this writing, include a nonrefundable application fee of $2,500, undergraduate and postgraduate master's or law degree from an accredited college, authorization to perform a background investigation, mandatory attendance for a two-day seminar, and a valid e-mail address.)

"When I first launched ITL in the early 2000s, there was no exam for being an agent," Stratton recalled. "I think you registered and you paid a fee, and you had to have a certain amount of schooling, a degree, and they did a background check. If you checked all those boxes and your check cleared, congratulations. You're an agent. Then they went to a test some time after that, it went like that for a few years.

"Then I think it was in 2014 or 2015 that they made the test significantly harder. It went from where there's about a 75 percent passing rate to about a 45 percent passing rate. [Just a couple of years prior to that], we'd launched our first exam and it's a multiple-choice exam that very closely mirrors what agents actually see when they go to take their certification exam in July. [In 2019,] we added a second exam. So now we have two forty-question multiple-choice tests that an aspiring agent can take that allows them to see the questions that they'll see on the exam. They're obviously not the same exact questions, but they're very similar in structure. Typically, the NFLPA will give you a scenario and then ask several questions based on that scenario. So it's rather involved and you have to know what information is relevant and what's not.

"We also partnered with a group that sells a comprehensive study guide, which really cuts the CBA down to a more manageable size and gives people a better idea of what it is they need to study for the exam, rather than the entire CBA, which is pretty voluminous. We also have a newsletter series that goes out to everyone who's going to be taking the exam. It gives tips on the exam and the industry. It gives them an idea of what they need to be studying, what they need to be doing, and what the industry is going to look like."

WHERE NFL SCOUTS COME FROM

For those aspiring to become a scout in the NFL, the road is difficult if you didn't play the sport, but Stratton said it's not the end of the world if you never played in the league: "Scouts come from a lot of places. Some—not as many as you'd think—are ex-NFL players. Most played at least some college ball, though this is less common than it used to be. Many are ex-college coaches that knew someone and got their break that way." Others, Stratton added, are family members of somebody in team ownership and get their foot in the door that way.

"But the thing to understand," he continued, "is that scouts are getting younger and younger, and often making less money, because teams see scouts as replaceable." The trend in today's game is centralized decision-making, with teams asking their low-level scouts to gather information such as 40-yard dash times at the NFL Scouting Combine, stats, and criminal histories, and then letting the general manager and his personnel form opinions and make evaluations.

Does that mean poor job security for NFL scouts? Many teams see scouts as "almost dispensable," confirmed Stratton, and that's why a team normally brings in new scouts on a sort of three-year probationary period. "If he doesn't seem to get it, or maybe isn't thorough enough, or doesn't click with his boss, he may be tossed aside." Furthermore, regime changes—which are the norm in modern pro football—also cost scouts their jobs; for instance, when a general manager leaves an organization to go to another one, he might bring in his scouts from his former team because he perhaps is more comfortable working with them. "That's why," Stratton explained, "every May, right after the draft, there are dozens of changes to teams' scouting staffs. For example, we tracked 142 changes in staffs that took place in the NFL between the start of May and the end of July in 2013." That number seems high, but Stratton estimated the over/under on front-office changes is usually around one hundred terminations, promotions, transitions, and other moves among scouts.

NFL scouting staffs are also impacted when new owners come into the game and try to put their mark on the league, added Stratton. "In the old days, you found that the scouts were easy to pick out at an all-star game because typically, they had no hair or gray hair, they were ex-college coaches who lived in a certain area, knew everyone in that area, and could get good analysis and good answers to their questions because they'd either coached against or with virtually everyone they were driving around and seeing in their region of the country. It has evolved now into where, when you go to an all-star game, it's hard to tell the players from the scouts because they're more often than not very young. They're ex-players. They're still in shape. They're people who have a lot more energy but not as many contacts and not as much experience."

A scout's role also differs depending on organization; some are information gatherers while others are talent evaluators. "The New England model—and New England's been the model franchise for the last ten or fifteen years or so—is they just send young guys out, and they don't pay them much," said Stratton. "Primarily, they gather information. I don't mean to make harsh generalizations but, for the most part, they're not asking their scouts to come back with opinions, so much as hard facts: arrests, height, weight, injury history. Those kinds of things. And then asking the brass to make the decisions. In the old days, you had spirited arguments among scouts because the guys had coached, they had played in many cases, they knew what teams were looking for. They were used to teams doing a certain thing. They were cut from a different cloth. But as the 'Moneyball' idea has come into the game and the new breed of owners have come in and want to run NFL teams like they ran their businesses, they're looking more toward analytics and more toward math. They're looking to spend less money in their scouting departments. And we've seen that across the league. We're going to find out if that trend holds."

Additionally, where scouting is heading in a postpandemic world—where priorities and contacts may bear more or less importance—is still an unknown:

"Now that people aren't going on the road as much and they're relying on their contacts more to gather information, other than what's on an open Zoom call where everyone's in at the same time listening, you better have guys that have connections to those people that they're speaking to. It'll be interesting to see, whenever new general managers are hired, when these GMs populate their staffs, if they start looking for older, more experienced scouts because they want someone who's going to be able to have the relationship with someone that can give them information rather than just someone who goes out and brings back hard facts and does nothing more than that. There has definitely been a change over my twenty years in the way scouting and evaluations are looked at. I think in some ways we're about to see that change back. We just don't know yet."

All of this means that if you're an aspiring NFL scout, you should understand that job security isn't high and you're not going to make a lot of money. So even if you've ever won a fantasy football league and think it's a glamorous job evaluating talent for a living, understand that you're not going to be well-compensated in real life as a scout.

Stratton elaborated: "The difficulty with scouting that I think a lot of people don't recognize is you're certainly not getting rich. It's an industry where you've got to pay your dues and work your way up. The salaries are better than they used to be, and there are even some first- and second-year scouts that are approaching $100,000 a year. But that's certainly not the standard. You're usually gonna start out at around $40,000 or $50,000, and that's not a lot of money. And teams are growing younger because they're seeking to get cheaper in the scouting room, and that's a whole 'nother conversation. The pay is small, the hours are long, and—under normal circumstances, in a non-COVID year—you tend to be out for a week sometimes at a time, and that varies depending on the team and how they run things. But you're up against deadlines. You're very often working by yourself. You're not always welcomed to a school, because what the scout does has no bearing on whether or not a school wins on Saturday, and that's ultimately the number-one priority for a school, obviously. There are a lot of long hours. It can be lonely at times. The work is very tough.

"Your rank-and-file fan thinks scouting is like fantasy football, times a million. Well, it's not quite that. It's a lot more of drudgery and driving late nights and getting up early, sitting in a scouting room all day and talking to people who may not want to give you the information that you seek. There's a little bit of detective work there. Scouts don't have as much power as maybe people think they do. There's a perception out there that they're the ones calling the shots. What they have is a piece of the puzzle. Depending on the team they work for, they may get to see the whole puzzle when it's completed, or they never get to see more than just the one little piece they built and the one they put together. It varies by team.

"There's a camaraderie to it, there's a fraternity to it that, I think, is appealing to a lot of people. But that's such a small part of it that, you'd better be coming into it for a passion about the game and about doing your job, because it's not nearly as glamorous as people think it's going to be. Again, just the chance to work with other people and talk football, and be a part of the industry, isn't something that you're always living. There's just a lot more times, especially during a non-COVID year, when you're working by yourself, you're off on your own, and you're a lone wolf. If you're going to pursue this industry, you need to understand all those things going in."

HOW TO GET ACCESS

Whereas baseball has the Winter Meetings, where young professionals can network with team executives and others in the industry, there aren't such events in football.

"There are two events in a nonpandemic year, two places that everyone goes, when it comes to football," Stratton explained. "That's the Senior Bowl in Mobile, Alabama, which is held in January every year, and also the [NFL Scouting] Combine, which happens at the end of February and early March.

"The difference between the two, or at least it has been in the past, is that the Senior Bowl is what I call the NFL's backyard barbeque; the barrier to entry is pretty low. You don't even have to have a badge or credential to go to the Senior Bowl. You can get into the stadium and watch what's going on, and you can come to the hotel and hang around the lobby. You can go to the restaurants and go to the bars, and you can have an insider Senior Bowl experience very easily. You don't have to be a scout or an agent, and you can still feel like you're part of all that."

The Combine, however, is more like a closed-door meeting. "It's like a private party," continued Stratton. "Everyone goes to Indianapolis thinking, 'I'm just gonna hang out where everybody is.' It's not that easy because the players are working out at Lucas Oil Stadium, and you gotta have a badge to get in there. They're housed at a hotel where if you walk into the lobby without the proper credentials, you're going to have a security guard in your face immediately. The media have their own room that, again, you can't go into unless you have the proper credentials.

"The NFLPA hosts a large conference for all agents, but you can't walk in there unless you've got the proper credentials. And you're probably detecting a theme here. But that's how the Combine is. Now, you can go out at night to St. Elmo's or Prime and get a steak and a martini and be among the people, and you're going to make some relationships and meet some people there, but by and large it's a lot harder at the Combine."

Stratton, however, offered some words of advice—and concrete tactics—for those aspiring to get access, network, and find their way onto the first rung in this highly competitive industry: "[Inside the League] partnered with the College Gridiron Showcase, which is in Fort Worth, Texas, every year. I had a chance to speak at a symposium about three years ago. There were probably five hundred people from the college personnel community. A lot of those people aspired to be NFL scouts. I said, 'How many of you all knew about the College Gridiron Showcase when you're going to the NCAA seminar in San Antonio?' There are all these people that aspired to be scouts and are in San Antonio drinking beer with their buddies. About three hours away, we were having an event where we had one hundred NFL scouts and lots of need for volunteers, and great chances to network and meet people. But people weren't in tuned with that because they were used to doing things in a certain way. And I get that.

"But the point is if you want to work in football, you've got to be very intentional about looking for opportunities to go meet people, to go work for people, to prove yourself to people. And if you aren't doing that—and your hope is that you can just stay in your lane and just stay within your own network and make your own friends—your chances aren't very good. And there are people who aren't working for colleges, and they want to get on Twitter and talk about their opinions and about the draft. And that's a lot of fun—and there are a lot of people who are really good at that.

"But football is one of the most network-oriented industries that you're going to find out there. If you don't go out and meet people—and, more importantly, have a mentor or champion who'll go to bat for you and help you find the opportunities, it's almost impossible to break in, because you just have to have kind of that invitation to come in, and then you have to work hard. If you don't, and you're just watching and hoping that someone calls you or waiting for the phone to ring, it's probably not going to ring. So I always recommend to people, 'Listen, go find a camp that a player's putting on, or go volunteer at a stadium, or go do whatever you can, to start building these relationships and meeting people.' That's how I approached it as well when I first was starting out. It's so important to go out and make those relationships so that someone will pull you into the industry rather than [just] hoping for an invitation, because it's probably not going to come."

Certainly, developmental leagues are good places to meet people and build relationships. "Presuming the XFL returns in a timely fashion," Stratton said, "that's an outstanding place to go and learn and volunteer and put your skills to work. More often than not, especially the XFL and the CFL [Canadian Football League], which have much smaller staffs and budgets, you've got a much better opportunity to find someone that wants to let you have real responsibility and develop your skills and learn. It may be a situation where you're not getting paid. I know there have been a lot of people pushing back on the idea of an unpaid internship, but the facts are that if you want to work in this industry, you better have something that's your currency. And for most people, your currency is your time and your willingness to work hard for minimal or no pay. And if that's something you can't do, I'm sure you can find an internship somewhere that will pay you, but it's probably not going to be in pro or college football, because despite the fact that there are a lot of people really getting rich in these industries, the fact is that there are hundreds of people that want to do this kind of work, you've gotta be willing to go in and do the things that other people don't want to do. That's how you separate yourself from everybody else, and that's how you become a commodity that people need."

The point is that if you're looking for a place to put your skills to work and make important connections and access opportunities, you should take advantage of leagues such as the XFL and CFL. "Sometimes taking advantage just means showing up at the offices and saying, 'Hey, can I staple something for you or run errands for you?' It's just going in and finding a way to work your way into the mix and become invaluable, and one thing leads to another, and then you're doing it. These leagues will provide opportunities for people who are hard workers and hustlers and interested in the industry."

ANALYTICS IN FOOTBALL

While analytics is becoming more common in sports—and has changed scouting standards and approaches—it's still not an exact science, said Stratton. There are differing ways people interpret what all this quantitative data means, with a perfect example being how analytics is used to evaluate quarterbacks.

"The difficulty with analytics is you ask two different people and they have a different answer on what analytics really is," Stratton said. "Some people see it as, 'Here's what I'm gonna do in this down and distance on this kind of a game, at this time, on this surface,' etc. Others see it as, 'This is the kind of player we're gonna draft.' Others see it as any number of things. But when it comes to quarterbacks, I think what we've seen especially is the rise of accuracy as a real determinant of future NFL success. And even within accuracy, how accurate is he [from] one to five yards, how accurate is he [from] six to fifteen yards? How accurate is he [with the] deep ball? What about the patterns as they change? What about against certain defenses? And we've seen quarterbacks be evaluated a lot more so with those kind of numbers because that is something that's a bit more quantifiable. Now, at the end of the day, what you call a good pass may not be what I call a good pass. What you call a drop may not be what I call a drop. What you call 'should've been an interception,' maybe I say, 'probably not.' So there's still a level of subjectivity and I don't think we'll ever get away from that no matter what we do."

The bottom line: "I think there's a certain mix of analytics and traditional scouting that is most effective. The problem is no one really knows what that mix is. So everyone's still trying to figure out what that golden mix of analytics and old-school scouting is. I don't know if we'll ever really know how to crack that code exactly. If we do, we certainly don't know it yet, or at least I don't think anyone's going out there and saying, 'Here's the combination. Here's a formula.'"

EXPLORING OTHER LEAGUES, AND A FINAL WORD

Before the inaugural XFL season came to a screeching halt in March 2020 when pro sports, like the rest of the world, shut down because of the COVID-19 pandemic, Stratton was recommending the league to those seeking an opportunity in scouting in football.

In a blog post titled "Want to Be an NFL Scout? Start with the XFL" published in February 2020 on his blog *Succeed in Football*, Stratton pointed out that Bears assistant director of player personnel Champ Kelly, Browns area scout Gerald McCully, Tampa Bay scouting coordinator Cesar Rivera, Chiefs national scout Cassidy Kaminski, and many other NFL evaluators all got their start in alternative leagues. "This is great news for aspiring NFL scouts," Stratton said. "While the best routes into scouting remain working in college personnel or, even better, having a father who's in the NFL, there's an opportunity here [with the XFL]."

However, he added, you have to know how to take advantage. Here's what he recommends:

1. Reach out. Several XFL scouts and evaluators can be found on Twitter, many of them friends of Stratton's. "If you reach out to them with the right attitude, you've got a great shot at making contact." But first . . .
2. Make it clear you'll do anything. You'll have to prove that you are reliable and hard-working. "That means you might have to run errands, load and unload,

make copies, bring coffee, whatever," Stratton suggested. "Make it clear you are *elated* to do this."

3. Don't send scouting reports. As Stratton said, "the *first thing* most aspiring scouts want to send is a résumé and scouting reports, and the *last thing* most scouts I know want is the same. You need to impress upon them your willingness to do anything before you assert your eye for talent."

4. Be there. If you already live in an XFL city, you have a huge advantage over everyone else, and the same is true if you're trying to volunteer with virtually any team in any league.

Do all these things, Stratton suggested, and "maybe you're the next Will McClay, vice president of player personnel for the Cowboys." Back in 2001, McClay was director of player personnel of the Orlando Rage of the original XFL, a league that lasted just that one season.

Whether the current XFL—which began play in 2020 before being shut down during the COVID-19 pandemic—has a future remains to be seen. As of this writing, the league, under new ownership, is expected to make its return to the field in 2023. But it doesn't have to be the XFL. If there are leagues in your area that can allow you to get your start in the game, reach out.

If you'd like more ideas on how to break into the NFL, it starts with knowing what's going on behind the scenes. For more information and additional tips from Neil Stratton, visit his website, http://insidetheleague.com, and his blog, https://succeedinfootball.com, both of which offer critical tools for anybody aspiring to build a career in college or pro football.

VI

ANALYTICS

Analytics in Baseball

Ari Kaplan, Baseball Analyst

Job title: Global AI evangelist, DataRobot; data science and analytics instructor, Sports Mangement Worldwide; former manager of statistical analysis, Chicago Cubs; special consultant to the GM, Baltimore Orioles

Education/training: Degree in engineering and applied sciences (Caltech)

Key pieces of advice: Find out what skills are needed for the jobs you're interested in and take the necessary steps to acquire those skills. Write to as many organizations as you can to seek opportunities. Focus on being the best you can at the role you're given.

Ari Kaplan is a leading figure in sports analytics, having worked with more than half of all Major League Baseball organizations and many global sports media organizations during his three-plus decades in baseball.

The cofounder of Scoutables (which has provided advance scouting and analytics to broadcast and online media as well as MLB organizations) with Fred Claire, Kaplan was hired by the ownership of the Chicago Cubs in 2010 to create and lead the organization's analytics department. He was later a special assistant to GM with the Baltimore Orioles, which included three postseason appearances in seven years.

"I'm most known for creating the Cubs' analytics department, and I also worked with the Orioles as assistant to the GM," Kaplan explained when asked about his background in baseball. "I've had almost every role you can imagine in the front office, including helping out with every aspect of player decisions and being a major-league scout. Now I teach a couple of courses online, helping people get into the game, with the focus on helping them pick up skills in analytics. Analytics is one of the big focal points. I teach a course on baseball specifically and data science. I teach another course on sports in general, focusing on data science, artificial intelligence, and software programming. For people who pick up these skills, it's a great way to get into the game. That's just one of the ways to get into the game. As a result, I would say there's about thirty people that are now

ARI KAPLAN. *COURTESY OF ARI KAPLAN*

working in professional sports that came from my mentorship, which is great. It's a great satisfaction to help others achieve that."

For anybody interested in working specifically in baseball, Kaplan said for starters it might be worthwhile to check out a book called *Do You Want to Work in Baseball?* by Bill Geivett, who has three decades of experience in professional baseball as a player, scout, and front office executive. "Bill had a nice chart which shows all thirty general managers and how they got *their* start in the game. Most of them actually worked as interns in the front office. That means getting your foot in the door at any opportunity. Unfortunately, it doesn't pay well. But if you're willing to make that sacrifice, you get in and then do hard work, have dedication, try to learn, and be a jack of all trades. Basically, be willing to start at next to no pay to get in, and realize it's a journey. The people that tend to succeed are not the ones that come in and say, 'I'm going to be the next general manager.' Even if that's your belief, focus on the job at hand. If your job is to organize media guides, then do whatever you can to do the best job you can, as opposed to constantly trying to network and look for the next thing. Focus on being the best you can at the role you're given."

That's not to say you shouldn't network. But don't network with an agenda while ignoring the job you've been hired to do. "Talk to people. Communicate. Collaborate," continued Kaplan. "Specifically for sports, [if you're looking to get your foot in the door,] there are always different avenues. Internship is one way. Some people start out in the media and then transition onto a team. There are other people who, like one of my students, worked in the grounds crew to get into the game."

It's also essential to have skills relevant to the positions that teams are hiring for, which is where Kaplan encourages people look at job postings for sports teams: "See what skills they're looking for. A lot of times you don't have that skill, but you do whatever you can to pick it up. For example, speaking Spanish these days is a plus. You could pick that up as a second language. Being able to edit videos is a plus. So start downloading video-editing software. Sometimes you might see that software programming language, like SQL or Python, is a skill that people are looking for. So if you don't know it, take an online course. Watch YouTube videos. Download the software and try it out.

"The bottom line is to look at job listings, see what skills you have, see what skills you need to pick up, and then just write letters to different teams. Be willing to take rejections. I have a lot of stories about people who write letters to all teams. Highlight what you're looking for. Highlight what skills you have that match up with the jobs. Sometimes you write thirty letters and don't hear back. Try again the next year. You might hear something. You might get an interview. You might not get the job after the interview. But if you are persistent and willing to adapt, learn the skills, see what skills are in more demand, then you're in a better position to get that job. But timing is everything. If someone says there are no jobs, just thank them and try again at a later time, saying, 'I'm reaching out to see if anything has changed. I'd love to meet with you or somebody.' Do that in a polite way and people would appreciate that. Be persistent."

Kaplan also suggested checking out a website called TeamWork Online (https://www.teamworkonline.com). "They have a listing of several hundred jobs in and around football, basketball, baseball, and that's really a portal that's fairly new that teams are using. It's much better than it was a few years ago. That's one."

Another website he recommends, for baseball specifically, is PBEO.com, which is Minor League Baseball's official employment service site. "For baseball specific[ally], there's the Winter Meetings, which are every December in different cities. There's something called the PBEO Job Fair, where it's mostly minor leagues. There are a couple hundred job openings and a couple hundred people looking to get jobs. They may not be at the major-league level, but that's a great place to start, too. It's preferable to start in the majors, but it's so competitive that oftentimes just to get a minor-league opportunity is worthwhile. So go to the Winter Meetings for baseball specifically. Just network, meet people, talk, and write letters to the teams before the Winter Meetings and try to set up one-on-ones. These are the basic fundamentals to get into the game."

Kaplan, who now teaches analytics at Sports Management WorldWide (SMWW), explained why the Winter Meetings provide a tremendous opportunity to network with those in the game: "Typically, if you're not yet in the game itself, I always recommend [the] Sports Management Worldwide Conference there, which is a day on Monday where we have, basically every hour, a key speaker, like Dan Duquette or Rick White and many others, presenting in panels. I host the analytics one, but you have Oscar Suarez and others talking about agents, and [others talking about] marketing. I highly recommend that. I used to go before I became involved in the organization.

"But aside from that, you'll find that there's a lobby where people in the industry are just networking and trying to make new friends, and that goes until 2:00 or 3:00 in the morning. So don't be shy. It could be a bit intimidating to walk up to strangers, but try to be prepared by looking at the different websites of all thirty teams and trying to learn the names of not just the GM or assistant GMs, but the directors of baseball operations. [Before you show up at the Winter Meetings,] try to figure out what unique skills you might have—maybe it's just passion and a great work ethic—and then try to meet as many people as you can. A lot of times people judge what skills you have but also how you come across and how you might work with somebody, since when you're with a team, you're working long hours and teams are looking for people that are pleasant to be around as well."

The point, Kaplan explained, is that if you attend the Winter Meetings without any specific intention of getting a job, and all you're doing is to network and meet people, you can come away with fifty new contacts after three or four days. Then you foster those relationships and keep in touch with those people.

Of course, since Kaplan is known for his expertise in analytics, he also offered his thoughts on how students and young people can enter the sports industry via that specific route: "Analytics is a big trend in all of sports. I don't always like to self-promote, but for the courses that I'm teaching at Sports Management Worldwide, students get to talk to me as somebody who's been in the front office, and I'm accessible to them. Since I've been in the game, it's access to myself who could just honestly answer any question. In the past, you pretty much had to play baseball or have some special situation to be able to work in the game. But now it's opened up where if you have a special skill, like in analytics, being able to program, do database, use SQL, program in Python, or do web development, you can get into the game. You may not have that baseball pedigree, but teams need those skills, and in my class I help explain and teach and expose various levels of those skills. Typically, one or two students from each of my classes [end up] working for teams, and that's something I'm very happy about since there's only thirty teams and there's probably realistically a couple hundred job openings every year for a professional or a major-league organization.

"Of course, there are also a ton of online self-guided courses out there. But the big three skills today are Python; R, which is a data science modeling environment; and SQL, which is a database language. So if you could learn one, two, or all three of them, the saying is that if there are two candidates who are otherwise a tie, the [tie-breaker] would go to the people with any of those skills."

Learning these skills doesn't mean you read a book on it, emphasized Kaplan. "It means you've downloaded the software, you've collected some data—and Kaggle is a great source of free baseball, NFL, and NBA data—and you've actually done some mini projects on your laptop. That's how I know before I hire somebody that they know what they're doing. It wasn't just an academic certificate; they're able to actually do the work."

Because analytics has become so popular in sports, there's a tendency to think working in an analytics department of a professional sports franchise is glamorous. As Kaplan cautioned, though, don't expect to get rich quick—and expect tons of competition.

"There are two big challenges," he said. "One is, really, that the entry point is low money, typically. If you have data science skills or analytics skills, you can probably make multiple times [more, in terms of salary,] in the nonsports world. So one challenge is if you need to have a job and you need to have money, at first that might be a challenge. So there's the financial aspect. You have to be willing to put in a couple of years at low pay.

"Then, the other is just that there's so much competition, and the competition isn't always the highest skilled. Teams are mobbed with thousands of people sending in résumés or samples of their work that it's hard to call somebody and get a response."

In regard to the second challenge specifically, what you can do, suggested Kaplan, is be able to explain concisely what you're looking for and how your skills can benefit the organization you're interested in working for: "I just think the second challenge is that there's so many people competing that you just have to be persistent and be able to answer quick questions. Like, 'What are you looking to do? What can you do to help a team?' So, for example, [a good answer might be something like,] 'Hi, I'm looking to join as an analytics intern with your major-league staff. I have two years of experience with Python, and I've done work with baseball data.' Just being able to say that in one or two sentences is helpful.

"So be able to say in one or two sentences who you are and what you're able to help with. 'Hi, I'm Ari. I'm looking to get involved in the analytics for your team. I have two years of Python experience working with baseball TrackMan data.' Just something simple like that. 'Can we talk? Or can I send you some examples?' It's just that thousands of people are also sending e-mails to the team. That being said, each team is looking to bring on a handful of people every year. So it does happen on the analytics side."

Don't be so focused on analytics, though, that you ignore other ways to get into the game, added Kaplan. He gave two examples: scouting and sales. "If you're looking to get into scouting, [that's another avenue, although] all the focus is on analytics these days. But for scouting, there are fewer people competing. So if you're able to evaluate player talent, if you're able to identify whether a pitch is a fastball, curveball, changeup, or splitter, then you also have value to a team. For example, if you know how to identify if a pitch is a slider, curveball, or fastball, there's an opportunity to work in video departments. Or you could go to a team and say, 'I've watched a lot of games, I've evaluated players, and here are some sample reports I wrote. I'm able to identify pitches. I'm looking to be an associate scout for the upcoming season.' That's another avenue. An associate scout is almost like an intern; you get paired with a professional scout to watch games next to them. They get to mentor you.

"I have a huge honor of being a major-league scout for many years. It started on the analytics; it was never really in my background. But being around the game, watching the game, I added on to my job skills of being a minor-league and major-league scout. That's very hard to do to get that credential. But if you're looking to get in the game, all you do is you can go to a high school game or a college game or a minor-league game, or even a major-league game. Start writing observations of a player. There's a whole bunch of websites that have scouting reports that are open to the public for them to just submit their own scouting report. That kind of gives you a template on what language to use, what observations to look out for, how to grade a player. So . . . for a pitcher, you want to start grading the fastballs, what their pitch is like, their command, control, how they throw sliders, how they attack batters, their consistency, and their leg movement. While you may have no clue on anything at the beginning, you could go to MLB. com and just type in 'Scouting report Clayton Kershaw,' and you can read up on what other people talk about, what they write up, and then you just copy what they do but with your own observations. 'Copy what they do' meaning how they organize the reports, how succinct these are, and how they grade players. Then you just watch a high school or college player, come up with a couple of reports, and then start submitting them to teams. 'Here are some examples of players I've evaluated. I'd love to be an associate scout,' which is the entryway. Or you don't need that. You could just say, 'Pick a high school or college or minor-league stadium near me, and I'd be happy to, on a trial basis, be able to work with you.'"

If you like sales, that's another way to get into an organization. "I've also had people get into the game going one of the easier ways, and that is approaching it from a sales perspective," Kaplan said. "I would say 'easy' if you have sales experience. Minor-league teams, especially, make their money by ticket sales and sponsorship sales. If you're willing to work for a local team in the minor leagues or even the majors as someone in sales, it's probably a quicker way to get in. It's like the gateway to other areas. So just call up a team and say, 'I have high energy. I want to help increase your sales. I'd love to get involved with your team.' These are all different ways to get in."

25

Analytics in Basketball

Marshall Payne, Basketball Operations Analyst

Job title: Basketball operations analyst, Sacramento Kings

Education/training: Master of business administration in business analytics and master of sports administration (Ohio University); data science courses; knowledge of computer languages SQL and R; internships

Key pieces of advice: Do informational interviews with people in the industry. Ask, "What are the specific steps I need to take to get good at what I need to get good at?" And do it.

Marshall Payne, who has an MBA in business analytics and a master of sports administration (MSA), is a member of the Sacramento Kings' Basketball Operations and Data Analytics Department, since the start of the 2019–2020 NBA season. Prior to landing the full-time position with Sacramento, Payne was an intern in both the Indiana Pacers' (September 2018 to December 2018) and Kings' (January 2019 to May 2019) basketball analytics departments during the 2018–2019 season. Following the 2020–2021 NBA campaign, he was promoted by the Kings to the role of senior data scientist, basketball operations.

In February 2020, Payne sat down with the *Life in the Front Office* podcast to share insights about his experience in the world of basketball analytics and his journey to get to where he is today. According to Payne, taking night school classes and seeking out the advice of an industry veteran helped pave the way to his career in basketball analytics. "About six or seven years after undergrad, I started to become a little more focused on my career," he explained. "Instead of having what I'd describe as a string of random jobs here and there, I decided I wanted to get more focused. I started taking a few night classes at Stanford University taught by Ohio legend Andy Dolich. He mentioned that if I'm serious about working in sports and if I'm thinking about going to grad school, I should check out Ohio. I did, and fortunately, they accepted me. It's been a great ride since then."

After completing his master of sports administration program in 2018, Payne landed a basketball analytics internship with the Indiana Pacers that September. When he completed that four-month internship, he received another basketball analytics internship opportunity right away, this time with the Sacramento Kings in January 2019. "The main thing I took away from that experience [with the Pacers] was just, in grad school you hear a lot about organizational culture and building a winning culture—and that was certainly true in Indianapolis," he reflected. "Not only did I really enjoy the day-to-day of working as a basketball analytics intern, but just the people in the whole basketball operations and those I met with on the business side as well, they were all just really kind, respectful, and hardworking people. I would say it's less about what you're doing and more about who you're doing it with. I'm really thankful to my boss, Spencer Anderson, who runs the analytics department there. I had a coworker, Nick, who I worked very closely with and learned a lot from, and I was able to transition pretty smoothly once that internship ended right into another internship with the Kings, so it was nice to have another opportunity waiting for me when that first one ended."

But it's not always the case where an individual has other jobs lining up after the first one ends, as Payne himself would find out. As smooth as that transition from the Pacers to the Kings was, it was not smooth once his Kings internship ended in May 2019. "At that time, there wasn't a full-time position available," Payne explained. "I was on the job hunt over the summer in 2019. Fortunately, a position opened up and they brought me back on. The summer right after grad school in 2018, it was also pretty difficult to get that first opportunity, which is part of the reason I was so grateful to the Pacers for giving me my first shot. I think that's something a lot of people pursuing careers in the sports industry come to realize, is that once you have your foot in the door, that's a big deal. But getting your first opportunity is really tricky sometimes. You just got to be patient, stay persistent, and continue to build your network."

In terms of how to receive that first opportunity, Payne had the following piece of advice: "If you do quality work and can build good relationships [with people you] come across, I think inevitably, you do get your first opportunity. Then, hopefully, you do well in that. Eventually, you start getting some momentum and instead of looking at your résumé and seeing this barren landscape, you see one cool opportunity and then it eventually grows and you become a pretty legitimate candidate."

As for what working day-to-day in analytics entails, it's not what many people assume, according to Payne. "Some of my friends will be asking, 'So, you're at the game, tracking stats and stuff?' No, we get our data elsewhere. It varies day to day. No two days are the same, like most jobs. At a very high level, what the department that I work in—our basketball analytics department—does is we try to use objective information to help inform basketball-related decisions as well as we can. So that falls into stuff with roster decisions as well as in-game strategies. We build predictive models. We help build reports for coaches. A lot of it is a coach or someone on the player development side is curious about something, so we'll look up information for them. Then we really just kind of be stewards of high-quality and reliable data, and try and help make sure that the decision makers have the best and as much information as possible when making those decisions."

And unlike what one might assume, analytics isn't just about tracking numbers. Being a strong communicator, Payne emphasized, is also key. Sure, a data analyst spends a huge portion of the day being on the computer. But there are also times when collaboration with other analysts is needed. And at the end of the day, a data analyst has to explain—for example, to a coach—what a piece of data means and how to put it to use, and that requires strong communication. "At the end of the day," he said, "when I was interviewing for a ton of jobs [in 2019], I would always say, 'I have solid skills as a data analyst.' [Let's say] you can build the most accurate predictive model and have all this amazing data, [but] if you can't communicate what's important about it, why that's important, and how that can help, then it's essentially worthless. It's definitely balancing building relationships with other people on the basketball operations side of things with the Kings. I would just say that communication is key.

"Part of it is just trying to foster a culture of open communication and relationship-building. The work we do is pretty technical, but even when we're 'in the zone' on our laptops all cranking up some computer code, the people in our department all sit in an open area, all next to each other. There's chit-chat throughout the day. If I have a question and need help with something, I'm more than comfortable with reaching out to a coworker about it. We have different people within our organization that have different levels of interaction with other parts of the basketball operations department. It's trying to stay in the steady state of getting the work we need to get done, while also being open to questions or requests or collaborations—more of the interpersonal side as well."

As for how someone interested in analytics can follow in his footsteps, Payne acknowledged that his path was unconventional. But after consulting with professionals within the industry, he figured out how to reach his goal—and he took the steps to get there: "I took a unique path because I don't have the educational background that the majority of people in analytics departments have. I'd say the typical educational background is majoring in computer science or math or statistics—these are very technical and highly quantitative educational fields— [whereas for me in undergrad,] I got my major in global studies mostly due to not knowing what to do with my life. Once I realized in grad school, 'This is the path I want to pursue,' I felt a little bit behind the eight ball simply because, while I've always been pretty good with numbers, I didn't know any computer code or anything like that. The first step for me was identifying specifically what skills I needed to get good at. You hear 'analytics,' and that sounds great. But what does that actually mean? Is there a certain computer language or certain software that I needed to get familiar with? What are the specific steps I need to take to get good at what I need to get good at? So I found that information out from doing a lot of informational interviews with people in the industry [and] reaching out to some Ohio alum who are in the sports analytics field. My ending question during those conversations was, 'If you're in my shoes with a year or two left in grad school, you have a lot of educational resources in this awesome university I'm in, and you're trying to get somewhere close to where you're at now, what would be the things you'd focus on? What would be the skills you'd try to develop?' That gave me a pretty good picture of what I needed to get good at. From there, it was 'just do it.' I took a lot of additional electives in addition to our sports administration curriculum, and that provided a good undergrad-level foundation of data science computer skills. From there, it was working as hard as I could using online resources. There are YouTube videos for everything [along with] a lot of computer coding, bootcamp-style websites out there. And then just working on independent projects as well. I find that you can take classes and learn [all the theories], but until you actually crack into a project and realize where the challenges are actually—and figure out ways to solve those challenges—it's tough to put the hypothetical into action. The main things I focused on were SQL and R. These are the two computer languages that are commonly used. From what the people in the industry said, if you get those two languages down pretty well, you'll have a good foundation to build on from there."

The way Payne approached the informational interviews was straightforward but effective. Essentially, it came down to two key elements: "I think for the informational interviews, the two most important things for me when setting up those types of phone calls would be, first, make a connection with this person who's in the field that I ultimately want to get into. That's something I tell undergrads who now reach out to me and are asking for advice. As technical as sports analytics is—and there is a baseline requirement for some technical aptitude—it's still all about the relationships. Maybe it's not as much versus sales, but still, all of the opportunities that have been afforded to me have—maybe not directly—been from relationships I've built and connections I've made. That was the point of making those calls. The next thing was trying to drill down specifically, 'What should I learn?' Those were the two main goals with those calls."

Payne even shared some tips about preparing for job interviews with an organization's analytics department. "I applied for another couple of internships that I did not get before I finally got my opportunity with the Pacers," he said. "What really stood out was a lot of them run you through a project if you make it that far down the interview process, and they ask a lot of technical skills. But they also ask a lot of basketball-related questions. This ties back to earlier what I was talking about with communication. You can do the most in-depth statistical analysis about basketball, but a coach comes up to you and says, 'Hey, how do you think we defended the pick-and-roll last night?' and you go, 'I don't really know what a pick-and-roll is,' then it's not a good look. So knowing the sport and knowing what's going on in the league—if you're applying for a job with a specific team—I would suggest knowing about their current situation, knowing about the players on their roster. That was certainly helpful the summer right after I applied for an internship with another NBA team. Lo and behold, they asked certain questions about the upcoming draft: 'What would you do in the off-season if you were in our shoes?' Fortunately, I've been an NBA fan my whole life [and] did some additional research specifically for that call. I was able to at least give an answer, hopefully without looking too bad—although I didn't get it." He paused for a laugh. "So maybe I didn't give the best answers."

VII

OTHER CAREERS
IN SPORTS

Message Board Operator

Jeff Fellenzer, Former-Baseball-Stadium-Message-Board-Operator-Turned-College-Professor-in-Sports-Business

Job title: Sports business college professor, University of Southern California; former message board operator, Los Angeles Dodgers

Education/training: Bachelor of arts in journalism (USC Annenberg); master of arts (USC Annenberg); writing for school newspapers and the *Los Angeles Times*

Key piece of advice: Most jobs aren't about how much you know. It's about how you can thrive in a team environment and be a good teammate, and have the right work ethic, the right attitude, and your ability to make the company that you work for better.

Jeff Fellenzer, whose first sports job was running the message board at Dodger Stadium, has more than three decades of experience in sports management, news media, and higher education, along with extensive background as an entrepreneur.

An associate professor of professional practice at USC's Annenberg School for Communication and Journalism, Fellenzer's Sports, Business, Media class averages 125 students each semester, one of the university's most sought-after classes. He also runs a Sports and Media Technology course that focuses on the tech sector's impact on sports, as well as a class called The Athlete, Sports Media and Popular Culture, which focuses on the image of the athlete and the media based on how athletes have been portrayed through the years in film and on TV. A Heisman Trophy voter since 2007, he has been a featured speaker on multiple occasions at the Sports Business Classroom program in Las Vegas, held in conjunction with the NBA Summer League, moderating panels and lecturing on the subject of networking, résumé writing, and interviewing.

In our interview, Fellenzer discussed his experiences in the sports industry and offered advice for students looking to get their foot in the door of the competitive field.

For starters, Fellenzer's career and path illustrate a key, yet basic, point: It doesn't matter where you start. You just have to get involved. He started out operating the Dodger Stadium message board before transitioning to media positions with the *LA Times*, CBS Sports, and the NFL, and then into education, enjoying a fulfilling career at USC as associate professor helping students navigate their careers in sports.

"It's been one of the real blessings in my life," Fellenzer said about his time with the Dodgers. "I was the Dodger Stadium message board operator in 1976 and 1977. I was a student at USC, and I'd written a paper for class about the Dodgers and their PR department and community relations. In the course of it, I was offered this position replacing somebody who'd been there for a number of years. It was operating the message boards—before Diamond Vision became a reality. Now the scoreboards are so high tech throughout sports, but at that time, it was still pretty basic.

"Anyway, I worked every home game for those two years, and I did a few home games the following year. I learned so much from Fred Claire—he was the one who'd officially hired me—about treating people and being professional, how to really conduct yourself in the best way, how to always put your best foot and your best face forward, and doing it for the good of the organization. I learned a lot of life lessons there, and the experience opened doors for me I could never have imagined, and it all started with Dodger Stadium."

Twenty years later, Fellenzer and Claire reconnected to share their knowledge with young people interested in a sports career. This was 1998, when Claire had just left the Dodgers and Fellenzer had just agreed to teach Sports, Business, Media, then a new class at USC that focused on the business side of sports and the media. "I had become an adjunct professor at USC in 1990 and taken over the only sports media class offered at the university at the time," recalled Fellenzer. "Fred did the class with me for three spring semesters. Starting in the spring of 2002, I started teaching the class solo. In 2011, we decided to offer the class year-round, and [shortly after that] USC offered me a full-time position, a professorship. I've been doing it on a full-time basis as a member of the faculty at USC since then."

For students serious about getting into sports business, Fellenzer suggested developing a habit of reading the *Sports Business Journal*: "I call it the bible of the sports business industry and always encourage students to start plugging into the *Sports Business Journal*. I don't require them to subscribe, but I always strongly encourage them to, if they're serious about [sports business] as a career, plug into the publication as quickly as they can. It covers the business of sports unlike any other, top to bottom. You need to start learning the language of sports business, becoming aware of what some of the current issues are, and, quite frankly, finding out what kinds of jobs are out there and what your niche might be. Most students have no idea the breadth and the depth of the industry until we start to discuss it. And I use the *Sports Business Journal* a lot to give examples of jobs that are out there. So I'm very bullish on that publication."

To further illustrate the point about students discovering jobs that are out there, when they're reading about the individuals featured in the *Sports Business Journal*, sometimes they might come across positions and companies they haven't heard of before, which makes them stop and think, "Wait—what? This actually exists?" To try to learn more, students can then try to connect with those individuals on LinkedIn and say, "I'd like to learn more about what you're doing in your field. I read about you in the *Sports Business Journal*."

The next example Fellenzer brought up illustrates this point perfectly. Years ago, he brought into his class a guest speaker named Casey Wasserman, a sports agent executive and the CEO of Wasserman, a sports marketing and talent management firm. "I had a student in 2006 by the name of Brendan Meyer," he said. "He didn't know what Wasserman was—or even who Casey was—when I brought Casey in as a guest speaker. That summer, because of finding out about the company, this powerhouse sports agency that just continues to grow in so many areas representing so many athletes worldwide, Brendan landed an internship at Wasserman. He has not left Wasserman, and today he's a vice president. He didn't know the company existed before taking the class. And that's what I'm alluding to when I say that so much is about just finding out, just plugging into resources, something like the *Sports Business Journal*, and finding out about ways you can get involved.

"For me, it was operating the Dodger Stadium message board. It really wasn't even an internship. It was just a job that was available that turned into something pretty close to what internships typically are. But I had a desire to be in sports and I just continued to meet people. Once the door opened at Dodger Stadium, I met somebody else from a class that I took at USC that opened the door to working at the *LA Times*, and so I had a part-time job at the *LA Times* soon after I'd met the person who had come as a guest in my class. I think there's a lot of ways to connect. You have ways now to establish your voice. You can start a blog. You can start a podcast. You can have a YouTube channel. There are ways to get the attention of the right people. The key is to just get started."

The stories of Fellenzer's journey and Meyer's success lead to the next piece of advice for students: Just get involved. Get internships. Volunteer at sports-related events or companies. "They're so willing to take students on in volunteer capacities. Internships are a little harder to get today than they used to be because there are so many students who want to get into the business of sports. But it doesn't mean you can't get them. Most students find them at some point while they're in school. You just need to make a concerted effort to get involved, and I encourage students as soon as they get to campus. Don't wait until your junior year and think, 'Ahh, maybe now's a good time to get an internship.' You can hit the ground running when you get to school as a freshman and start looking at reaching out.

"The students that generally have been the most successful that I've worked with are those that got involved from day one, as soon as they got to campus. So I think just gaining practical experience, now more than ever, because companies have so many choices of students that want to get involved that they could use internships, really, as auditions. You'd find that it's getting to be rare when a company has to hire someone that they have, for a first-time job, an entry-level job. It's getting rare to find a company that doesn't have prior experience with that applicant in the form of an internship—or highly recommended by someone that somebody at the company is close to. So it's a win-win. The company gets to see young talent at work, and the young people get a chance to get practical experience and see if it's something they're good at and enjoy doing."

And when you reach out to organizations, don't forget to consider every single entity. In Southern California alone, said Fellenzer, as an example, there are so many sports teams to check out: "A great thing about being at USC is you're in this vibrant marketplace, where it's the sports and entertainment capital. You've got two pro football teams, two baseball teams, two hockey teams, and three basketball teams (counting the WNBA). You've got minor-league baseball, which is an area I think sometimes students forget about. You've got the Rancho

Cucamonga Quakes, the Dodgers' [Low-A] farm team. There's a team in San Bernardino; the Angels' [Low-A team] is there. There's Lake Elsinore with the [San Diego] Padres. Those are great places to start because you have to wear a lot of hats. You learn about everything. You learn a lot about sales. As almost any sports executive will tell you, 'If you can sell something, then you'll really bring value to an organization.' That's because sports is—like most businesses—about selling something."

As far as developing a blueprint for success in a sports career, Fellenzer shared what he calls his four Ps: "We all have different pathways to get where we have been or are going. In my case, I'm still on a pathway and still want to do a lot of things. But along the way, I wrote down a few of the things that I felt were important in my development as a sports business, sports media professional. And I have my keys to success. I also have my four Ps. They are—and I say these in order—passion, preparation, performance, and persistence.

"I start with passion because that really is what fuels everyone's fire. This doesn't go just for sports. This can go for your career in whatever direction you're going in, whatever field that you're in. You need to have passion.

"I think the next most important thing—I call it my MVP, my most valuable P—is preparation. I know as a professor, if I walk into a classroom feeling in any way not as prepared as I feel like I should be or could be, I just don't feel like I can perform as well as I could have otherwise. Obviously, if you're in sports as a player or a coach, you've got to be very prepared. In fact, I like to go into any kind of a classroom setting overprepared—so that I'm covered no matter what happens during the course of the class, for example, if I have a scheduled guest speaker who all of a sudden can't make it. You've got to be ready to go and still deliver. So preparation is of the utmost importance in the whole process.

"Performance, obviously, in sports, [is crucial]. Sports . . . is a bottom-line business, [whether it's] on the field or in the front office. On the field, . . . there are so many players trying to get to that spot. In the front office, it's exactly the same way. There's so many people wanting to work in sports. There's always people ready to take your place. So performance is essential. You gotta deliver when you get the opportunity.

"Persistence, which is the last P that I added a few years ago, ties everything together. You've gotta be persistent in your approach. You've gotta be persistent when you're trying to get a job. You've gotta be persistent when you're in a job. That's because answers don't come right away sometimes or automatically. They come because you're persistent in getting the answer, to whatever question you have or whatever you're trying to approve for your organization or your company. It usually takes some form of persistence. If you're in sales, it *really* takes persistence, because you're usually not going to get a sale done in the first conversation that you have. So persistence ties everything together in its own way. And those are the things that have really worked for me in my career. I hope they're able to help others that may be just starting out or at an earlier stage in their careers."

Networking is also crucial when it comes to landing a job in sports, Fellenzer said. "Sports is an unconventional business in terms of the pathways in. There's no real pathway. In the law profession, you go to law school, you work for a law firm, and then you hopefully have offers to choose from. With sports, it's so much based on your network of people that you meet along the way, people that you're fortunate enough to meet along the way, people that you start meeting by [doing] internships [and] volunteering. In my case, I met several speakers in classes when I was a student at USC, and that was before e-mail and before the digital world. So you tried to make contacts by just meeting people in person and getting a phone number. You tried to connect in the best ways that you could. And so it's so much about building that network."

But what would the advice be for those who aren't assertive or confident in approaching people? "You could do it in different ways. You don't have to be the person that's a natural salesperson that can stand up in a situation and meet someone and be confident and charismatic. Not everybody is that way. You just have to find different ways to connect. You might be a more subdued person, a little more quiet, but very much of a hard worker and keep your nose to the grindstone. I've talked to people in sports business in different positions that will talk about that kind of person. They like to have a mixture of people when they build a company. You gotta have those people that are out there, that can handle a situation and be comfortable in front of people and just mix right in and hit the ground running. But you also need those people that work hard, people that are a little more on the quiet side but diligent—and they're an essential cog in the operation. So you just have to find other ways to connect. It might be by e-mail [or] by a one-on-one meeting, [such as] informational interviews. You gotta be a little more creative. You gotta get to the person and be upfront, and say, 'Look. I'm not a person that's probably naturally aligned with a sales mindset,' even though, really, when you're working for almost any company, you're kind of always in sales [in one way or another]. But that may not be your greatest asset. And so you're not going to be somebody that's going to be out there on the front lines, necessarily, representing a company. But you're working in the background, doing something that maybe is equally as important. It's just not as visible. So you just have to sell yourself when you get the opportunity to connect with people."

The good news, added Fellenzer, is that organizations realize that each individual is different: "I think people today are very mindful in hiring positions that not everybody is built the same, and you know that when you build a team, not every person on the team is kind of that alpha male or female. Teams work because you've got people filling different roles, and you've got to be able to define what you think your role could be when you get the chance to talk to someone about yourself. So I think it's great having self-awareness and being able to sell what it is that you do well and how you can impact the company."

Another obstacle some students face is their lack of confidence simply because they feel they don't know about sports as much as others. That, Fellenzer said, shouldn't be an issue because sports organizations aren't hiring people strictly because of their knowledge of sports. "I make that a central part of every class that I teach. I usually bring it up the first night of class. These are sports classes filled with kids that are really into sports. And I like to make the point: If you're not as knowledgeable about sports—what a lot of people talk about as sports trivia, that stuff we see and becomes the basis of arguments and discussions and quizzes, trivia quizzes and questions—I always say, 'Look, you don't have to be the person who knows all those answers.' And a lot of times, women get intimidated because they're in the classroom with a lot of guys. They don't have the same base of knowledge and they'll say that. And I always make the point: You don't have to have knowledge of sports at that level to succeed in sports. What you have to have is a passion for wanting to be the best you can be at whatever your role is. You want to be a hard worker. I always say, 'You may not be the most talented at whatever company you're working in. But there's no excuse for not being the hardest worker.' If you have the most talent and you're the hardest worker, then you're Kobe Bryant or LeBron James or Wayne Gretzky.

"Companies in sports today are not going to hire who knows the most about a sport or a team. They want to hire people who are hard workers and great communicators and have a great work ethic, [people who] are good problem solvers and self-starters, [and] people who are motivated and driven for success. In fact, I bring in a couple of women that are former students of mine, one in particular, to address this very topic.

"She's the vice president of operations for Golden Boy Promotions, Oscar De La Hoya's boxing company. She started off working part-time for a sports PR company, and the people at Golden Boy watched her work at an event that she was running. She was handling the PR for this event. They were so impressed with how she carried herself, how she handled her business and ran this press conference, that they got in touch with her and brought her in to interview for a full-time position. And they offered her a job! But she knew absolutely nothing about boxing, which she tells my class every semester that I bring her in [as a guest speaker]. And I mean zero. But they figured what she didn't know about boxing, she could learn. What they knew they didn't have to teach her was how to carry herself, how to work hard, how to communicate well, and how to have poise under fire. Today, she's the vice president of operations for Golden Boy Promotions, and a sport, boxing, that she at one time, when she was hired, knew zero about. That's the best example I can give that you don't have to be the most knowledgeable about a sport to be successful working in sports."

One final piece of advice from Fellenzer: Get involved. Be around. Build relationships. "I have a friend, a retired athletic director, who believes in leadership by walking around. In other words, just by being somewhere and observing, you can learn so much. So I would say, for students who want to break into sports, [you can gain so much by] just volunteering to be part of something, trying to get an internship where you don't even know for sure what you're going to be doing—but just being around and just observing. So much about sports is about relationships. That's part of my keys to success. It's all about relationships and relationship building. You build relationships, many times, just by being around. And it's not just about who you know. I also like to add that it's all about who knows you, as well. Not just who you know, but who knows you. And you have a better chance to get relationships built and for people to know you when you volunteer and when you agree to help out and just get out there, and have people go, 'Hey, who's that person?' Like, 'They're always here. They're always helpful. They really work hard.' And you catch someone's eye. Sometimes you don't even think about these different ways that you can connect. But just volunteering and agreeing to come out and help out, that's usually how you can get noticed and get the opportunity. It's just being around sometimes."

Team Historian

Mark Langill, Baseball Team Historian

Job title: Team historian, Los Angeles Dodgers

Education/training: Degree in journalism (Cal State Northridge); writing and public speaking skills; a passion for sports trivia

Key pieces of advice: Volunteer, do internships, be unafraid to ask questions, and follow your passion. Believe that you can do it. Never, ever say that you can't, and don't let others convince you that you can't.

Mark Langill, who covered baseball as a beat reporter for the *Pasadena Star-News* from 1989 to 1993, is the publications editor and team historian for the LA Dodgers. He has been a member of the Dodgers front office since 1994, originally joining the club's Broadcasting and Publications Department as an assistant.

A huge Dodgers fan since his youth, Langill is an expert when it comes to trivia about his favorite team. His vast knowledge of all things Dodgers was quickly noticed by the organization, and his position as publications editor eventually evolved, incorporating the official title of team historian in 2002. The franchise had gone through two ownership changes, Langill explained, "and they said, 'Look, we don't really know what you're talking about but you know what you're talking about. How would you like to be responsible for every miscellaneous phone call that comes?' I was like, 'Absolutely!'"

Langill added, "I basically spent my youth preparing for a role that didn't exist at the time." That last comment isn't hyperbole. When he was named the Dodgers' team historian, it was a job title no other Major League Baseball organization had. MLB already had its own official historian, and the only other person with a similar title in professional sports had retired from the NFL Green Bay Packers public relations department and was called "team historian emeritus." The Bos-

MARK LANGILL WITH HALL OF FAME MANAGER TOMMY LASORDA. *COURTESY OF THE AUTHOR'S COLLECTION*

ton Red Sox followed a similar route, hiring former sportswriter Gordon Edes as their team historian in 2015.

Langill recognizes how special it is to be first with that "team historian" title, but stressed that the role is to help people understand the organization's rich history through its larger-than-life personalities, on-field heroics, and behind-the-scenes stories that connect generations of Dodgers fans—not to show off all the obscure trivia that he knows about the team. "I never make it about me," he said. "It's not what I think because there are hundreds of thousands of 'Dodger historians.' I'm the one that's blessed and lucky enough to be able to work for the team. I make the analogy that it's kind of like working at Yosemite. I can't take credit for the beautiful scenery and the history and everything like that, but I certainly can appreciate it. And there's not a day that goes by that I don't appreciate what the Dodgers have meant to so many people over the years and what they've meant to me. And just the importance that anybody that works for a ball club, the responsibility that they have to the community, because think about this: What other venue do people look forward to visiting? Everything else, it's, 'I have to go to the store. I have to go to the mechanic. I've got to go to the doctor.' You hear it in their tone of voice. But with a baseball game, it's, 'I'll be there on the 24th against the Cubs.' You can hear it in their voice. That's the best part because sports is such a great way for people to communicate. You can't really do it with politics or religion anymore. We don't know what's going to happen. It is the most wonderful reality show. For every Bobby Thomson heartbreak, there's Kirk Gibson limping around the bases. I've always been fascinated by it."

And the work isn't about rattling off numbers and stats. Langill's title might be specific, but the job comes with many different responsibilities that go beyond historic moments and statistics. For instance, Langill may be tasked with researching uniform designs from the early 1900s, searching for an old photo, or looking for an alumnus or relative from the past. There are also regular speaking engagements involved, whether it's visiting schools to talk to students or moderating Dodger Stadium functions such as alumni breakfast events for fans featuring former players and coaches—roles he's very comfortable in.

When asked his secret when it comes to being a natural speaker, Langill admitted he was lucky to have come from a family that taught him well but added that taking public speaking courses is beneficial. But the first step is to realize that sports is supposed to be fun: "I think the most important thing is to be able to smile and have a sense of humor. Don't take yourself so seriously. If you watch CBS News at night or CNN and you see things around the world, you're like, 'Okay, a bullpen with a 6.00 ERA does not even equate to a problem that somebody else might be having.' If you try to compare a sports problem with a real-life problem, [you have to step back and realize that] sports is an escape. [For me,] I think the personality was always there. I learned from my grandfather in terms of talking to people. I heard this story about the time he had a retirement party working for the LA County Assessor's Office, and my grandmother said that the elevator operators all chipped in for a gift. She couldn't believe how many different people he'd spoken to. I learned that at a young age, and I tried to be nice. And it turned out that the nicest person I've ever met turned out to be my mother. When you have that background as far as that type of example, I had that at an early age.

"As far as public speaking, I took a speech class at Pasadena City College, which really helped me because there's a difference between giving a speech and being conversational. If I was a television host, that would be different. But normally my role is, one, someone asks me a question, or, two, being a moderator. [In those situations] you want to be conversational. A lot of times you want to ask the question that you're not necessarily sure of the answer—because if I'm interested, I'm thinking maybe the audience is interested."

And it does matter the audience you are addressing: "Some of my background as far as public speaking, I was asked to go to elementary schools in the South Pasadena area and talk to kids. What you realize is that you may know everything about the 1927 World Series, but if you don't know the age group and if you're not sure how to relate to certain age groups, you learn real quick. For example, kindergarteners. They love to be able to talk, and you don't want to speak for a long time and make them just be quiet. [To get them involved] right off the bat, [you can ask them]: 'Who's been to the stadium? What do you like on your hot dog? Who's your favorite player?' Get them engaged."

Speaking to teens, on the other hand, might require a different approach—even if they're fans of the sports organization which you're representing. "The thing I learned with high school students is they get to the point where they don't necessarily want to say anything," Langill said. "At that point, with peer pressure, they don't necessarily want to speak in that atmosphere. So what I always do is ask for a volunteer. I'll ask that person five or six questions about him- or herself, and I'll put that information on the board. And I'll say, 'See? Now, I know about so-and-so. You never know down the road who you may meet. Never discount whatever connections you may have down the road.' Then what I also like to do is I'll give [the volunteer] a jersey or something similar: 'Oh, by the way, you never know what's going to happen if you volunteer for something.' Many times I try to give an authentic jersey. You get the gasps from the other classmates. And that's what you really want. In that type of situation for a high school, you don't necessarily want to come off as, 'Look, this is what I know.'"

What Langill wants to accomplish in these school visits is to inspire students—and encourage them to not be afraid to pursue their dreams. "The two things that I really want to emphasize to people: 'How many of you can raise your left hand? No problem? How many of you can raise your right hand? Didn't seem that hard, did it? But sometimes it's the hardest thing in the world if somebody asks for a volunteer and you really want to do something, and you don't want to raise your hand in front of others.' I use myself as an example. I would say, 'I was the only one in my peer group who was into Dodger history, who was into all that trivia. But it was so very interesting to me. And look, all these years later, there's nothing greater than to be able to say I *get* to go to work—instead of I *have* to go to work.' And I'll say, 'Look. You may not be into the Dodgers or baseball. That's fine. But if you can find a little niche that's important to you, let me tell you something: It's been the most wonderful thing for me. Just listen to that inner voice.' That's a different type of public speaking that I do for students."

Although he admitted he is a Dodgers fan, he also said it's easy to maintain that level of professionalism when he is at the ballpark. "I actually don't [separate fandom from professionalism] because the easiest thing in the world is just to treat everybody as you'd want to be treated," he explained. "It doesn't matter as far as if they're a player, a manager, a food vendor, [or] an intern. People are people. That's the easiest thing in the world. As long as you do that, don't worry about the standings, don't worry about somebody's statistics, that's the easiest thing in the world. Just try to be as nice as you can to people, in all walks of life. That's the best thing that you can do. Because if you're working for a baseball team, you should approach your job exactly the same way if you're in fifth place riding a ten-game losing streak or you're on the 1927 Yankees, because your job shouldn't change based on the team, the attendance, the weather, [or] anything like that."

As long as you treat every single person with respect and treat everybody the same way regardless of whom that person is, Langill said, then it isn't hard to remain professional at all times: "[When you see] a great big star player, you just say, 'Good morning. How are you?' As opposed to, 'Hey, big fella. You're gonna hit number fifty today?' I would never do that. We're all going to have different roles in life, and I think the easiest thing to do, especially, let's say if you're a writer, it doesn't matter if you're covering a Little League game or Game 7 of the World Series. Those basics don't change. The game that the person is playing is just as important. Your duty to the reader is just as important. [Ditto] your duty to a customer [and] your duty to a coworker. If you remember people are people, then you should be able to work anywhere and do anything because that's the common denominator."

How can somebody follow Langill's footsteps and do what he does? He believes it's important to have role models in the industry. Learn how those sports professionals made it into the business. Follow the paths of those whom you emulate. Langill, who began his professional career as a beat reporter, listed a few examples of those who started out as sportswriters before transitioning into prominent roles within a professional sports franchise. "You don't look at the finish line. You say, 'What is this person doing? How did he start off?' Whether it's Fred Claire or Steve Brener—both of whom had a writing background—or Red Patterson, who hired Fred. He was a sportswriter, too."

Langill also shared the reason he chose the college he attended: "The only reason I went to Cal State Northridge, I said, 'If it's good enough for Steve Brener, then it's good enough for me.' That school produced him and Dick Enberg [who attended Central Michigan but was an assistant professor and baseball coach at Cal State Northridge]. I kept it real simple. It was the people that were more important than the institution. So-and-so went here? Then I'll go here." The lesson? Higher education is important; college is essential to your success. But as far as which school to pick, just get in the best school you can—or the school where your role models went.

Other than education, having the right mindset is crucial, as is following your passion. "First of all, don't say that you can't do anything," Langill emphasized, "because if you say you can—and you say you can't—chances are you're right. So right off the bat, get that negative stuff out of your head. Don't let people say that you can't do something. Follow that inner voice. Find somebody that's of interest to you, and just ask them questions. You don't have to make it like a job interview. Just say, 'Hey, if you've got a couple minutes, I just want to ask you about how you go about your day.'"

Along the way, Langill tried his best to learn from those already in the industry. One key lesson is to always continue honing your craft, no matter how long you've already been doing it. "I can remember somebody at the *Pasadena Star-News*, a gentleman named Steve Hunt, who said, 'It took a few years before I wrote anything that I liked.' That was a revelation to me, because when you see this person published in the newspaper, you think he's a natural. And suddenly, if he's admitting that he had to work on it, that just sort of humanizes it."

He also said he owes his career trajectory to many individuals who offered to help out along the way, right from a very young age. He recalled being a sophomore at South Pasadena High School, where he'd place a sweater beside his head in English class because he'd sneaked in a radio to listen to the ball game. "I [would also] bring a sports page to class every day, and my English teacher, unbeknownst to me, nominated me for the school newspaper. That's one thing. The first week that very next year when I was on the school paper, there was a notice on the bulletin asking for a volunteer to cover [South Pasadena High School] football games for the local city paper. That's another thing: Volunteering for something. That led to an internship at the *Pasadena Star-News*, where, all of a sudden, I learned behind the scenes what it was like in an office. Anybody that has an interest, whether it's what I do or it's in sports: Internships are so valuable, especially while you're going to school, because it's a chance to see behind the scenes. It's like auditing a career without having to commit to it. It really takes the mystery out. Once you see people in that position, you find out, 'How do they do it?' And everybody has to start at some place. You go about it by actually finding out the mechanics of how things are done, volunteering and internships—and not being afraid to ask somebody a question."

Regarding that last point about not being afraid to ask somebody a question, Langill remembered being at a high school basketball game where he saw a familiar face: Glenn Parsons, a sportswriter from the *Pasadena Star-News*. He approached Parsons and introduced himself: "I said, 'You're Glenn Parsons!' He was the prep [sports] columnist at the time. It turned out I was one of the better correspondents phoning in the games to the paper. Well, a couple weeks later, he asked me if I wanted to work inside the newspaper office taking the scores."

Langill admitted he's been fortunate to get to where he is today. But he also put in the hard work to continue receiving those opportunities. What he's accomplished can be done if you volunteer, do internships, are unafraid to ask questions, and follow your passion. Believe that you can do it. Never, ever say that you can't, and don't let others convince you that you can't. And when mentors are there to help out, it makes it that much easier. "[It took] a handful of people—the English teacher who nominated me for the school paper, the city paper editor that said, 'Sure, we'll give you a chance,' Glenn Parsons from the *Star-News* who said, 'Hey, you wanna take some phone calls?' and all the mentors inside the *Star-News*," he said. "Suddenly, going from a high school junior just starting out to having the Dodger beat at twenty-three. And I didn't do anything special. I was just lucky to be surrounded by mentors and other people who were supportive. If you find people who are supportive of you or who can give you advice, or who can give you a good example, or somebody that you want to emulate, that's the most important thing."

Digital Media and Adviser

Chelsea Heyward, Sports Industry Professional

Job title: Digital media manager, LaChica Sports & Entertainment; adviser, Players Coalition

Education/training: Master's degree in sport management (California State University, Long Beach); doctor of education, organizational change and leadership (USC)

Key pieces of advice: Be realistic with your expectations. Take a sport management program. Take on as much as you can, for example, volunteering—you never know what relationships it will get you.

Chelsea Heyward, a sports industry professional, works as an adviser with the Players Coalition and a branding and digital media manager with LaChica Sports & Entertainment. As if that wasn't already enough, she is also a research associate at Morehouse College in Atlanta, where she teaches Sport, Culture and Power. After earning a bachelor's degree in psychology at Long Beach State, she wasn't sure what to do next. When she learned about the master's degree in sport man-agement, though, she stayed at Long Beach to enroll in the program. That's where it all started, as Heyward then went on to USC for her doctorate in organizational change and leadership.

In our interview for this book, Heyward offered insights about what has worked for her in her career, along with valuable advice on how to become an open-minded learner and get your foot in the door in the sports industry.

First off, with her roles with the Players Coalition, LaChica Sports & Entertain-ment, and Morehouse College, Heyward is living proof that you don't necessarily need to be working for a professional sports team to be involved in sports—and within the industry there are myriad roles and positions available. For instance, with LaChica Sports, she handles branding and digital media. As for what "brand-ing" specifically entails, Heyward explained what that is and how she stays cre-ative and current in the realm of digital media. The short answer: Being a lifelong learner.

"For me, I really enjoy people," she said. "So I enjoy paying attention to and watching people, and so when I look at branding, either branding a business or a company or an initiative is trying to look at it from a person's perspective, so if this initiative were a person, what would it look like? And so then, from the branding perspective, if you're able to hone in on those character traits, then you can help guide the brand in the direction that will make it be most efficient in whatever its mission is.

"[In terms of how I stay current,] I consider myself a lifelong learner, so I'm always tapping into different mediums of downloading information in different categories. Whether it's listening to a podcast or watching a documentary or reading an article, I'm always trying to stay abreast on what's specific to my field, but then also implementing practices in other fields. So whether I'm listening to something on ancient civilizations or something around the neurology behind manifestation, then there are different key components I think when you're in-undated in that much information that you can see a clear overlap for and it helps you get creative around your approach.

"Another way to say that is if you're only siloed into operating within one space and only downloading information from that one space, you'll only ever know what's worked thus far in that space. But creativity comes about through mixing ideas that haven't been mixed before, and I think this happens in archi-tecture, too. You see buildings that are built in ways that reflect how things move or operate in nature. And so like having a spiderweb being a catalyst for how wiring goes into a wall or something like that, that's a really specific example of how emerging ideas can help strengthen a particular industry in ways that people haven't thought about before. So, I try to stay tapped into both what I'm doing, but also what others are doing in other spaces and figure out how to take their best practices and then layer them on to my own."

Heyward acknowledged that although she's found a way to be involved in sports, she didn't know what she wanted to do when she was still in college. But with an open mind, she listened to guest speakers who came into her classes and learned as much as she could about her options before making a decision. The art of listening, she said, is crucial for students as they navigate their own career paths in sports: "I tell my students this all the time: You should listen to listen, not listen to respond. When someone is giving you information, a lot of the times we're thinking about how it is that we want to layer on our own objectives or our own alternative solutions. And I think if you listen to listen, then you can really tap into the essence of where a person's coming from or who they are and figure out deeper ways to connect with them. So, from that influence, it also helps keep you open minded.

"So, for a freshman or a person in high school, I'd probably recommend that they do that when given the opportunity to connect with the person in a position of power or someone that they admire, but also continue to reach out to get in contact with as many people as you can. When I was in the master's program at Long Beach, one of my favorite things to do was informational interviews so that you could just learn what it is that someone did and figure out if that's some-thing you want to do, or if that's something that [makes you say], 'Okay, I know I definitely want to stay away from this.' But if you're listening to listen—not necessarily listening to figure out how to get in with that person, or get a job, or build a relationship, or get free tickets—then you're able to download a lot more information with your lens being wider."

Another piece of advice to students interested in working in sports is under-standing that it is a job and—unless you're a broadcaster or a media member—you're not going to be watching the games. Also, if you're fortunate enough to be interacting with athletes, you can't be acting like a fan around them. "First, especially the professional athletes, it's about treating the athletes like people, but also understanding what their schedule and their world looks like and so not necessarily trying to insert yourself or just have a conversation for fun, like trying to make things very turnkey, be in and out, and make as small of a footprint as possible. Then, from a fan's perspective, I actually have ended up watching games less because I'm just either busy doing something or I missed that start time or I'll have something on in the background, so I don't have as much time to just sit and enjoy a game. But I think also a lot of the athletes that we work with are, from my biased perspective, some of the best humans on the planet. I'm fans of them as humans. If there's an opportunity to catch what they're doing specifically, versus my own personal fandom of the Lakers, for example, if there's something to catch with one of our guys who's on the Lions, I'll keep up to date with what's going on, because I'm interested in supporting that person specifically. But when we're working together, they're a colleague and not someone that I idolize or want to get a picture with."

For any students interested in doing something similar to what she's doing now, Heyward offered the following suggestions: "I'd recommend that they utilize the sport management program at Long Beach State and apply because if nothing else, they get a master's degree. But what it really is, because it's sport management, you understand the business side of sports, so you understand all that goes into it, which becomes really important for understanding how things work. I think one of the things people misunderstand about the sports industry is they think you just start and then you're making all these millions of dollars and then you have all this access—and it really takes a long time to get there. Yes, the players and the head coaches make a lot of money and have a lot of fame and fortune, but the rest of us work behind the scenes a ton and do put in a ton of hours to get the access, or the trust, or the relationships, and that takes time. So for a high school student, first setting that expectation that this isn't something that you're going to be thrust into overnight, so that they're aware and able to stay motivated in doing the work and realizing that, 'I'm not going to meet LeBron James tomorrow.' That's the first thing.

"The second thing, going back to that . . . school piece, is getting educated on all the different aspects of sports. You can't know what you want to do until you have access or exposure to all the other things that exist. When I first started, I knew absolutely I didn't want to work in professional sports. I wanted to work in college. And then I worked in college and I liked it, but I didn't want to spend my time there, and then started doing things more with the Coalition and ended up loving professional sports. But it wasn't until I had that exposure, and that exposure came about through just trying different things.

"After having the education, the third piece would be [to] try as much as you can, take on as much as you can. You don't know what relationships it'll get you. In a lot of cases, to do the really cool things, you'll have to do it for free. An example of that is, for the last several years, because I'm based in LA, I've volunteered for the West Regionals for March Madness, which usually oscillates between Honda Center and Staples Center. In working those events, I've worked for free.

The first time I did it, I was at a marketing table out in the plaza area, just getting people to spin a wheel. The next year, I was a band liaison. Then, because most of the people stay involved there, the year after that I was assigned to be band liaison again, but then something happened with one of the team escorts. Because they knew my character and they knew I'd put in the time and the work, I was brought on to be one of the team escorts. Ever since that time, I've been usually a team escort. But I wouldn't have known if I didn't try, and it was something I had to volunteer for. So sometimes, the coolest opportunities come for free."

It's also during these opportunities that you might find mentors in the business—or, in Heyward's case, in the classroom, where she met a marketing professor named Angela LaChica, who happened to be the founder of LaChica Sports & Entertainment. When it comes to finding mentors, Heyward said, "I usually prefer to move organically. So even in the space where people network, network, network, it's not necessarily about getting to know as many people as you can. It's getting to know as many people as you can, as deeply as you can. With the Angela relationship, [it was,] 'Let me see if there's a way that I can work with her without it being at an expense to her.' I had the social media background and she had her social media account for LaChica Sports at the time, so I asked her if she needed any help running that. She said she did, but she couldn't pay me. [But] Angela's one of my favorite people in the world, and this relationship is priceless. So recognizing that I had a skill that she could utilize, I offered up that skill and then just grew through watching her.

"And one of the things about mentorship for me is that I don't need someone telling me, 'Here's how we do things. This is the list of A, B, and C of how I operate.' I can just watch someone and pick up on their cadence and their sequencing of activities. With her, specifically, I was able to just watch and pick up and she'd still drop in nuggets like, 'Oh no, let's do this because this is my thought process.' So, from her perspective, she'd let me know her train of thought behind why we did something which is really important, so not just like, 'Okay, here, go do it,' but then she'd also put me in situations where I'd have to think, or she'd ask me what I thought.

"So, for young people seeking out mentors, finding someone that doesn't tell you what to think, but gives you a framework of how you should think, becomes really important. So if you have a skill that you can offer someone else, even if it's for free, I'd take that path, but also recognize, too, that people need to eat and need a house over their head. And so balancing that and figuring it out [is important]. For myself, there was actually a period of time where I had to leave the sports industry, so my full-time job ended up being at a corporate food company.

And I still stayed in touch and kept the relationships with the people in the sports industry, and once something became available, then I was able to dive back in because I'd gotten to know those people deeply. So recognizing there's not a one-size-fits-all solution, but if people know themselves well enough, they can figure out what path forward best works for them."

29

International Opportunities

Aggie Dent, International Sports and Sports Media/Sports Marketing

Job title: Global communications coordinator, DAZN Group; podcaster, *Adventures with Aggie*

Education/training: Bachelor's degree in sports management and minor in studio art (NYU); internships

Key pieces of advice: Stay open and try anything and everything. It's okay not to know exactly what you want to do. Internships are a great way to test many different types of careers.

Aggie Dent graduated from New York University in 2021 with a bachelor of science in sports management and a minor in studio art, but her career in the sports industry began well before she finished college. During her time at NYU, Dent gained valuable internship experience in marketing, communications, and media through internships at Formula E, the FC Bayern Munich soccer club (Germany), and the Sydney Sixers cricket team (Australia). She even started a podcast called *Adventures with Aggie* in April 2020, focusing on the stories of athletes and sports executives and on the way sport defines adventures in life.

In August 2021, Dent began working for DAZN Group as the global communications coordinator based in New York City. At the time of our interview, she was also a graduate student at Columbia University, pursuing a master of science in sports management.

Just weeks before landing her position with DAZN Group, Dent spoke with me to provide insights for students interested in a career in the sports industry.

Her first piece of advice: Follow your passion. One of her passions is her podcast. "At the beginning, it was business-oriented," she said. "I was interviewing many sports professionals, front-office employees, talking about how they got to where they are and how people like me could get there one day. Then I found there are lots of athletes that are working in the sports business that also play. They're active players." Wanting to hear from current athletes who are making an impact on the business side of sports, Dent began interviewing some of them. "Then it took a turn when I wanted to dive deeper into storytelling within sport. So right now, I'm focused on delivering the stories of athletes off the field and how their sport has defined what they've done with their lives. We have lots of content planned throughout the rest of the year covering lots of different sports. We have a series on ultimate frisbee and one on goalball. I don't know if many people know what goalball is, but look it up—it's really cool. All kinds of sports, all kinds of athletes from all around the world, and I'm going to take it as far as it can go. There's no finish line in sight."

As of the one-year mark of the podcast launch, *Adventures with Aggie* had thousands of followers and in more than thirty-five countries. As far as Dent is concerned, anybody with passion can start a podcast and become as successful as she has. For her, the free time she had during the COVID-19 pandemic was all she needed: "I was stuck home quarantining. And I figured out that people within the sports world had thirty minutes of time on their hands and they'd talk to me, so I started reaching out to a bunch of different people. I started with people that I knew within my internships or just in my network, and then I started pushing it a little bit more. I was like, 'Oh, I really want to talk to this person,' so then I started growing it. I think just getting started, it was the curiosity of actually wanting to know how these people got there. There are people within the sports industry that I looked up to for the four years that I've been studying the sports industry, and I'd wondered, 'How did they get there?' You can read somebody's LinkedIn bio, but hearing what they went through while getting to all of those stages that are on their bios, it's so different to hear it directly from the person. You don't see all the rejections that person got along their pathway or along their bullet points at different companies on LinkedIn, but they'll share that, and they'll say, 'This rejection helped me get here, or helped me do this.'"

On the topic of rejection, for students and others wanting to start a podcast but are afraid of potential guests not responding, Dent said you've just got to try. Reach out to as many people as you can. "You never know if you don't try. It's cliché, and you hear it all the time. But it's serious. I was sending probably twenty-five messages or e-mails a week just trying to get guests. Maybe it was on Instagram messages, like messaging people who are training for the Olympics. 'Hey, will you talk to me? Will you tell me about your story? I really want to know this and this.' Now I don't have a problem asking people to speak with me because I think it's rewarding for both of us to have them share their story, and then knowing that people are listening to them. Hopefully, it's motivating them to go do something in the world—if it's train for the Olympics, or get up and walk down the street and get some exercise in that day, I don't know. But hopefully it motivates them to do something. And when starting a project like this, I never imagined that my show would have listeners in thirty-six countries. That's not something I was trying to do. It just happened, and it happened naturally. And, obviously, this wouldn't have happened if I didn't try. I was just trying because I was having a good time. I think the second piece of that is have fun with it. Maybe it's because I have that curiosity that I want to know more about my guests that I bring on the show, but . . . I love talking to these people on Zoom. So take that first baby step, have fun, and you never know if you don't try."

That last statement also applies to Dent's willingness to reach out to sports organizations overseas and seek internships with them. And, just like goalball, mentioned earlier, she takes the time to find out about and become involved with nonmainstream sports, such as Formula E. In the spring of 2021, in fact, she was the public engagement coordinator with Formula E, and her duties included seeking local vendors and hiring nearly one hundred staffers to work a racing event in Brooklyn. With the pandemic still going on, Dent also coordinated COVID-19 testing schedules for all staffers.

While the Formula E event took place locally, some of her other internships were with professional sports organizations outside of North America. Dent has interned specifically for the FC Bayern Munich soccer club in Germany and the Sydney Sixers cricket team in Australia. For those opportunities, it was a matter of going onto the team websites to find the contact e-mails of the appropriate people within those clubs. She'd write an e-mail introducing herself and asking if she could help with a project or research, which then evolved into an internship.

That, for her, is the easy part. The time difference is another matter. "On my Google Calendar," she said, "I have all the time zones turned on, so it tells me what time it is everywhere, and what time I'm doing things and what time they're awake or not awake. The remote aspect is incredibly helpful, though, because if we weren't remote right now, I wouldn't be working for these teams across the world. I was bored and I was like, 'Hey, I can help you. Even though I'm across the world, I could help and do some projects, do some research.' And it's been awesome, because with the remote lifestyle that we live, you can work whenever you want, like, whatever hours of the day. Sydney is a fifteen-hour difference [from New York]. I was on a meeting the other day at 10:30 at night. And that's just what it is. I also see it come into play with my podcast. I record at all hours of the day because my guests are from all over the world. So I'll wake up at 5:00 in the morning and record because that's when somebody can do it. But I think the early mornings and late nights are well worth it. The content that I can make for my podcast with athletes from all over the world, it's so valuable and it's worth losing that hour of sleep."

One additional tip Dent offered about podcasting is to be clear to guests that you're interviewing them to allow them to tell their stories: "I always preface my shows with—I say this to every single guest—I'm not trying to ask you hard questions. The point of the show is for you to deliver your story in a way that you want to. I think it's a privilege to be able to hear those stories firsthand. And I think they appreciate having the platform to deliver it themselves, rather than another media outlet covering it for them or something like that, because these words are coming straight from the person."

Dent offered one final piece of advice for students and others thinking about following her path: "I would say try everything. Four years ago, when I was a freshman, I never thought I'd be in sports media. I never thought I'd be any kind of host or recording myself for fun. I never thought I'd be speaking to strangers on Zoom or in person every day. I wanted to work at a desk [doing] office work, administration stuff, business stuff. I put myself in this position of creating content. Never thought I would do that. And that's just because I had the opportunity to try it. Try everything, meaning, I've had internships as well in all different sectors of the sports industry as a whole. Partnerships, research, data, business development, media, and social media as well. I didn't know what I wanted to do and that's okay. You don't have to know what you want to do. Once you try all the things you think you want to try, then you can know what you want to do. I'm happier doing what I am now because I love my show and I love speaking to people. But I think 'try everything' is the most vital piece of advice that I also received as a freshman, was these seniors saying, 'I was in your shoes four years ago. I had no idea what I wanted to do with my career, but just try stuff. If you don't try it, you don't know.' Try everything you can. At a reasonable amount. You don't have to do one hundred internships. But try something because it interests you."

Digital Media Designer

Sydney Noland, Digital Media in Football

Job title: Digital media manager, Seattle Seahawks

Education/training: Bachelor of fine arts in design and visual communications (Ball State University); school projects outside of classes; internships

Key pieces of advice: Establish a personal website featuring your portfolio. Showcase your work on platforms like Behance. net. Network with other sports designers. Post frequently on Instagram, Twitter, LinkedIn, and other social media sites. Don't accept that failure is the end of the road.

Sydney Noland is the digital media manager for the Seattle Seahawks, a role she has held since May 2021. She first started working for the Seahawks as a graphic design intern from July 2017 to January 2018 before she left to work as a graphic designer for the Institute for Health Metrics and Evaluation (IHME) for a year. In January 2019, she returned to the Seahawks as digital media designer, a role she held for the next two and a half years before being promoted to digital media manager.

At the time of our interview, Noland was still in her role as digital media designer, about which she spoke at length. She shared the surprising fact that she never intended to work in sports—the opportunity came because the Seahawks were the only organization that offered her an interview. "I'm originally from Indiana, from the Midwest," Noland explained. "I'm from Indianapolis, and I grew up there and went to school there at Ball State University. I ended up actually moving out to Seattle due to my husband being in the navy. We got stationed out here. That's what started our journey over here to the Pacific Northwest. But my first time to the Pacific Northwest was actually in Portland. I was visiting with a friend because she was just checking out the Portland area for potential internships. I thought, 'You know, I really like it over here. It's really nice! I like the Pacific Northwest!' Things just kind of worked out. My journey started with the Seahawks by accident. When we first [received orders to move] to Seattle, I was looking for a job after college. I applied to probably thirty to fifty jobs, and they were the only ones who got back to me with an interview for their internship position. That's how everything started."

What's unique about Noland's experience is that she didn't have any connections in the sports industry. "I was in Florida with my husband—he was my fiancé at the time—and he was at work for the day, and I thought, 'I'm going to look for some jobs and internships and see if there's anything new up,' because I'd been searching for a while. I believe I saw the job on Glassdoor. I went to the Seahawks website and read up different things about the company, and I thought, 'This could be a cool brand to work for.' It just seemed very energetic and it looked really fun to do. It was different and outside of my comfort zone, obviously, because I knew nothing about football. But in a design sense, the design seemed interesting. It seemed like a good experience and something I could learn from. That's how I found the job. It was all by accident." The lesson here is: Be open to learning about something entirely new.

Noland didn't think the Seahawks were going to call her, but she received an e-mail one month after applying for the internship: The Seahawks wanted to interview her. In the e-mail, she was informed that the organization only did in-person interviews. Although she and her husband didn't have to move to the Pacific Northwest right away—they had a little more time before her husband was required to relocate to Seattle—Noland wanted to attend that interview, so they left Indianapolis about a week after she graduated college. The interview, as it turned out, went well. The interviewing manager called Noland back an hour later to say she was being offered the graphic design internship.

"I'd never planned to work in sports," she continued. "I visited Nike when I made that trip to Portland and I was like, 'Oh, this is awesome. I'd like to design at a place like this.' But I never had a thought about working in football—barely knew anything about football, compared to now. That was definitely not expected or planned at all. In college, I'd thought about working at a design agency or some other company being an in-house designer. I was used to those types of situations. But never in sports. I didn't even know the sports design industry was such a niche within the design industry."

The graphic design internship ended after seven months, at the conclusion of the 2017 NFL season, and Noland found a graphic designer position with the IHME. But she made enough of an impression that the Seahawks brought her back in 2019 as their digital media designer. In terms of what exactly a digital media designer does for a sports organization, Noland says it's what she loves doing: creating templates and graphics. "A lot of my day-to-day—it sounds kind of boring, but it's actually really fun—I'm focused on creating templates for our social media channels on Twitter, Facebook, Instagram, and TikTok, doing a lot of social media templates and posts for our social media channels [along with] a lot of graphics for our website and graphics for our app. That's where my focus is at . . . within all of those digital spaces. It doesn't seem like a lot, but a lot of work goes into designing for those different platforms." Because of the current trend across the majority of industries to move toward more digital content, most of her day-to-day is digital work, and the internship opportunity she had in 2017–2018 taught her many of the skills she needs today. "There's a lot of small areas that require graphics. And nowadays, we're even more into the digital realm because of COVID and pulling back a little bit on print, especially [beginning in 2020], realizing how valuable these digital spaces are. That's a lot of what my day-to-day is. When I was an intern, though, I did a lot more print and had a little bit of taste of the digital realm. I realized I liked this area over here."

Of course, in all sports, fans have the habit of criticizing designs they don't like, whether they are uniforms or, in Noland's case, graphics and templates. She doesn't let negative comments by fans bother her, though. She's also appreciative of the fact that she's given freedom by the organization to show her creativity. "Usually, it's just all me," Noland said when asked if any fan input ever goes into the designs—or if she receives directives from management. She joked: "I'll read the comments left by fans sometimes, and I'll see a comment like, 'There's too much green in this!' And I'll make a wallpaper that's all green." In a more serious tone, she elaborated, "But it's all from me, from my mind and my vision. I'll get some feedback from people within our workspace, but it's mostly me."

Some might think that working in digital media design is a seasonal job, but that's not the case in the big leagues. The way she explained it, Noland works for the Seahawks year-round because there's also work to be done in the NFL off-season. "I'll say that there's just always something to do, for sure. There's time for rest, absolutely. I make sure that is a priority and that there's time for rest and to regenerate, otherwise I'm not going to be able to do my job well. But I always get this question: 'What do you do in the off-season? Are you doing anything?' I'm like, 'I'm doing so much right now!' Sometimes, I feel like there's a little bit more of these little things that pop up here and there in the off-season that I'm not prepared for, which is okay. During the season, it's a little bit more turnkey because I know what to expect. I know there's a game coming up, and I know what to get ready before this upcoming game. So there's a lot more expected day-to-day, whereas in the off-season it's more sporadic. I think we're getting better and getting to the point where things are more planned out throughout the whole year. But I always laugh when I'm asked the question, 'What do you do in the off-season?' I'm doing a lot!"

For Noland, working for the Seahawks organization has been a tremendous experience: "The most fun part about my job is seeing a big campaign come together as expected and looking great. I love the creativity that goes into my job and that my coworkers are so trusting of my abilities. When I feel like I'm doing something crazy, I feel like I get that support, like, 'Yeah, let's try it!' They're always willing to try something new, which makes working there so much more fun, because you're able to experiment and try different things. That's how I feel like the Seahawks [organization] is, [in terms of providing that] type of environment. We're always trying to do something new, do something different, and also involve the community, which I love. That really makes it so fun." Pressed to name her least favorite part of the job, she responded, "The free-agency period is kind of hard because you just never know what's going to happen. It could be a Saturday, and we sign a player and then we need to make a post and get those graphics together. But we've gotten to a place where there are more people who are able to use my templates that are available, so it's not just all put [in] my hands."

If you are interested in digital media design in sports but not truly into business disciplines such as marketing—just to name an example (but more on that later)—Noland said you're not alone: "I honestly know probably nothing about marketing, so I'd say it's definitely not important. But my first love was definitely just drawing. I've always been someone who loves art and drawing, [and I'm always] doodling all the time. Then, my stepdad said, 'Why don't you check out graphic design?' I'm like, 'What's that?' I ended up actually taking a visual communications class in high school. I didn't realize that was graphic design, but I thought, 'I really love this class!' We were building websites and I was photoshopping everything. At the time, I didn't even know Photoshop was a design tool, but we were using Photoshop. I really wasn't the PowerPoint [expert when it comes to] creating these elaborate slides. I was like, 'Is there something to this?' But I've always just loved art and always been very passionate about it." The lesson here is: Follow your passion. It might lead you to that dream career—in sports. And don't worry if you're not an expert in the actual sport or sports business.

Nobody's journey in the world of sports is easy, and Noland's is no exception. She shared one story to emphasize the point that one mustn't feel discouraged if things don't initially work out. "When I first applied to Ball State and applied to their art program, I did not get in. I didn't make it with my portfolio, which was all over a bowl that looked like it was floating. I was so upset and I was crying after the portfolio review. My dad said, 'It's going to be okay. You're going to get in,' because they had a second round, too. But the kicker was I needed to get into the program to apply for the scholarship because I needed that to attend school. I just ended up really working hard on the scholarship piece anyway and applied without even being a part of the school's art [program] yet. Somehow, I made it in and got the scholarship." The lesson learned from this story? Resilience played a crucial role in Noland's dream. Despite initially being rejected by Ball State's Fine Arts Department, she persevered. In her own words: "Failure does not mean it's the end."

On the development of her career skills, Noland acknowledged the actual courses she took at BSU didn't necessarily prepare her fully for her professional life, but the projects she worked on there helped tremendously. "Definitely my classes gave the basics and didn't give the expectation of what the design world is like and what the industry is like. [What helped, though, was the fact that] we had this student- and faculty-run organization called the Digital Corps at Ball State University."

The Digital Corps, in simple terms, is an on-campus agency of problem solvers and creative thinkers at Ball State—and a member of BSU's Office of Information Technology—with students from multiple disciplines working together to create innovative solutions. Participating in the Digital Corps gave her some much-needed hands-on learning. "It was great because you could work and also go to school, but the work was focused on your major," she said. "[For example,] they had [projects relating to] design, video, marketing, UX design, and development. I thought it'd be really cool just to work on [these] projects for the school. There'd be different professors or different schools [making various requests] to the Digital Corps, and [I'd] work on these projects and really apply my skills. That's where I felt like I really built my design skills. I was able to do that early. Upon graduation, I felt like I was ready to really show my stuff in the design industry."

Noland added that the internships she lined up over her college years were key, too, to helping her with some valuable hands-on learning: "And also the internships that I had along with that were really important just to get a feel of what the design industry was like, and really helped me grow those skills for sure."

As far as marketing, although Noland stressed she knows nothing about it, she did offer some marketing tips for aspiring digital designers wishing to raise their profile and cultivate their brand. "For sure, having an online portfolio is super important," she emphasized. "That's, in my opinion, step number one. If you can't get a website up and running, I'd say a second would be [using an online platform like] Behance.net and having your work up there. It's super easy to put projects up there and showcase your work—and network with other designers. And if there's anyone looking to get into the sports industry, there's always tons of sports designers on there, and I'm always seeing their work. It's very active on there. Instagram is another great place. I've also been seeing a lot of design work on Twitter, where I feel like people are more free to repost work that they have—whereas on Instagram, you post it once and it's just there. I encourage people to repost things and just show off those things again and not feel pressured to only share it once. And LinkedIn, too, which is a more professional space. But those different places are definitely great ways to showcase your work and share it."

Networking with other designers is helpful. When looking for a mentor, Noland said, it starts with reaching out. "I'd tell them that if you find someone who you're inspired by and they're willing to be a mentor—and talk with you, answer your questions, give you feedback from time to time—I'd say just reaching out is the first step. I actually opened up my website to have people contact me if they ever have any design questions, want a portfolio review, or want to pick my brain about anything. I think some people are open to that more than young creatives think. We just don't always have the time to just say, 'Hey, we're here if you want to talk to us.' But just reaching out is the first step. Don't feel discouraged if they don't get back—because they might just be busy."

Noland's story illustrates the fact that even if you don't succeed the first time, you shouldn't be discouraged. "I would say my biggest piece of advice—and it's something that I feel like always comes up—is, 'Don't accept that failure is the end of the road.' Sometimes you're just being turned in a different direction for the moment and there's probably something better up ahead than what you'd planned."

Sports Mascot

Ted Giannoulas,
The Famous Chicken

Job title: Mascot

Education/training: A good sense of humor

Key piece of advice: Deliver more than you promise.

For someone who attended journalism school at San Diego State in hopes of becoming a sportswriter, Ted Giannoulas never imagined he'd cultivate iconic status in the sports world as a mascot. But the San Diego Chicken, portrayed by Giannoulas since 1974, is arguably the most famous mascot in sports. It has inspired the spread of mascots worldwide and has even been featured in sets of Donruss baseball cards. Over the decades, the Chicken has performed not only at sporting venues—appearing at more than seven thousand sporting events along the way—but also for presidents and rock stars. The *Sporting News* editors even named Giannoulas one of the top one hundred most powerful people in sports of the twentieth century.

"I was really taken aback," Giannoulas said of being included on that list. "They put me right after Wayne Gretzky on that list. I guess they figured I'd really contributed to the landscape of sports in a unique way that made a difference."

It isn't hyperbole to state that Giannoulas invented his own industry within sports. He was originally hired by KGB-FM Radio in San Diego in the 1970s to wear a yellow chicken suit as part of a promotion to distribute Easter eggs at the local zoo. Shortly after, Giannoulas began appearing at Padres games—and the rest was sports mascot history. "What I tried to do was take my lifelong fascination [with] sports and merge it with my love of comedy to produce this unique act when I first started in 1974. It was a rock-and-roll radio station promotion, and it was supposed to be a one-week gimmick to draw attention to the station. The original concept of my assignment was to go to the zoo and give away candy Easter eggs. After a week of doing that, my job was pretty much done.

"But to take it a step further, I offered to go to Opening Night for the Padres and just be there in the grandstands as a walk-around billboard for the radio station. Management was okay with that. As I started doing that from game to game, I decided to implement some comedy bits, physical comedy stuff, just to draw more attention to myself. Fans started paying attention."

As a result, "the ratings for the station literally went from worst to first, in a matter of months, without any kind of format change. I was essentially a walk-around billboard in the community for the radio station and doing it in a way that was attracting attention, being entertaining, and becoming the talk of the town. That went from days and weeks to months, and eventually, to years.

"The whole concept was basically doing comedy by the seat of my pants. And all I was doing was just bringing my Canadian schoolboy sense of humor to bear in public in a chicken suit. And it resonated with fans—not only in California but across America and eventually around the world."

His advice on those wanting to follow in his footsteps? "Be original. Have a lot of energy for the audience. Keep it light because you're a walking cartoon. Consider yourself to be an ambassador of the team at all times. Enjoy what you do. Understand the game you're following and know it well."

Giannoulas elaborated further on some of these points. With as many as 250 appearances a year, it's not for the faint of heart. "For me, I didn't mind it, but it's challenging for a lot of people to do the traveling that I did. I'd literally do 250 games in a calendar year, and that required a lot of travel, night after night. I'd literally fly in the morning and perform in the evening—and do it all over again. Fly to the next town and perform again that night. Back-to-back! It was not uncommon for me to do fifty-nine games in sixty nights. For me, I enjoyed the travel, but it's not for everybody. I enjoyed doing these back-to-backs that it was second nature to me. It was living in the moment and enjoying it. It was work and a lot of effort, but it wasn't a 'job' for me."

For some, the costume would be uncomfortable. (I once put on a mascot suit at a baseball venue and felt uncomfortable because of the summer heat.) But Giannoulas said he's never had such an issue: "Growing up in Canada playing goalie, you wear a lot of gear and you sweat quite a bit, so that was a saving grace for me, that I could deal with that kind of sweat and heat. And I had a comfortable costume. It was lightweight for me and I could function in it. Some of the costumes might be a little more cumbersome for other mascots, so there's no telling. But it does take a different breed to have that stick-to-itiveness to hang in there and plug away [at] what you're doing. It brings pleasure to a lot of people. You need an extroverted personality to be involved in something like this."

With respect to the high energy level required to entertain the crowd, is this a skill that could be learned? Giannoulas weighed in with a succinct response: It depends on what you're inspired by. "I didn't know I would be inspired by this. I knew my inspiration was to one day be a comedian of some kind. But I fell into this and recognized that, okay, maybe I could achieve a few laughs with what I was doing. I wanted to be a sportswriter or a comedy writer, a standup comic or a comedy actor. I was going to college and doing this [being the San Diego Chicken] to begin with, part-time, when I started out. I fell into it, enjoyed it for the radio station, loved working at a rock-and-roll station, again, just dressed up in a chicken suit. I was never on the air. But I wanted to be. And I wanted other positions at the radio station. But ironically, I was such a good chicken that station management didn't want to take me out of that position because they knew they couldn't fill it with anybody else with a similar talent. It was a Catch-22 . . . : I was so good at what I was doing that I was never offered promotions to other positions at the station. So I kept on doing what I was doing—but still enjoyed it. By fate, it worked out in my favor, and I've been lucky for it ever since.

"So you have to draw yourself to what you're inspired by and make the best of that."

Because fans, young and old, ask for autographs and want to have pictures taken together (all with the costume still on, of course), a mascot can be incredibly popular. It's not uncommon to see mascots featured in the news or trending on social media. But you have to be an ambassador for your organization at all times—a responsibility Giannoulas always takes seriously—and not make the news for the wrong reasons. "If you're representing a team—or any organization—you've got to see yourself as an ambassador, albeit in an unconventional role," he said. "But you've got to look at yourself as being an ambassador. You've got to have the patience for posing for pictures. I love it myself. It might not be a cup of tea for somebody else. I've never turned down a single autograph request.

I've signed over a million autographs—easily—in my years. To this day, I still receive fan mail and sign all the baseball cards inside and send them back.

"Overall, you just have to work with the organization that you're with and try to achieve the goals that they're looking to achieve, especially visually, and garner awareness and attention. And anything you can add to that is always helpful."

Giannoulas offered a final bit of wisdom to young people who hope to launch a career in sports in some capacity: "If there's one commandment of what to do for success, it's simply this: Always deliver more than you promise. If you can do that and if that's in your heart, you pave your own road and, in fact, every door opens up for you. You can't do enough just to get by. You've got to want to do more on your own and do it sincerely on your own. If it's not in you, then find a line of work that *is* in you.

"But I know when I first started doing the Chicken, management was really surprised that I offered to do more after my one-week stint going to the zoo. I offered to go do sports events, which was unprecedented, unheard of, unconventional. Like, 'What? You're going to show up at a Major League Baseball game in a chicken suit?' I told them, 'If you sent me to the zoo to get attention, imagine what I could do at a ballgame with thirty thousand people, walking around with your call letters!' They looked at each other and said, 'Okay, makes sense to us!' There again, I brought ideas to the table for the cause. And that's what's involved here. Deliver more than you promise.

"It's one thing to say, 'Okay, I put in my hours.' And believe me, when I first started, those were difficult hours at the zoo in a hot papier-mâché suit. But I put in those hours. And not only did I put in those hours, it was no problem for me to stay an extra half-hour if need be, with these people still lining up for the candy Easter eggs that I was giving out and I still had an inventory to give out. I would just stay longer and continue giving them out. The simplest fundamental is you deliver more than you promise. It's easier to get ahead these days than ever before because if you've got that trait and that characteristic in you, you pave your own road."

International Baseball

Ryan Flynn, International Baseball Program CEO

Job title: Former CEO, Baseball New Zealand; CEO, Bhutan Baseball and Softball Association

Education/training: Bachelor's degree in English literature, minor in communications and writing (College of Saint Rose); college baseball playing career

Key piece of advice: Don't be afraid to cold-call people for an informational interview. If you think that someone out there can assist you, there's no harm in chasing anyone down in the world who you respect, who you've read about, who you think can make a difference in your life.

Ryan Flynn, whose love for travel has taken him around the globe over the past three decades, first made his mark in international baseball when he led Guam's national team to within three wins of the 2000 Olympic Games in Sydney after having played college ball in America. An astute marketer with a passion for sales, the former freelance writer has also made a career of fundraising in the sports business, raising upward of $1 million for the Guam national team.

After leaving the Guam national program, Flynn returned to his roots in the United States and spent the next eight years away from the world of sports. But a passion to get back into the game saw him return to international baseball in 2009 as he left the States to take on the challenge of growing "America's pastime" in New Zealand. During his nearly decadelong tenure running New Zealand's national program, he not only significantly increased the profile of baseball in the country but also got a professional team—the Auckland Tuatara—up and running for the 2018–2019 Australian Baseball League season.

In the spring of 2019, seeking a new challenge, Flynn stepped down as the CEO of Baseball New Zealand and began running the Palau Coffee Company in Palau. In May 2021, he was hired to be CEO of the Bhutan Baseball and Softball Association, with the task of building the South Asian country's baseball and softball program.

Flynn took some time out of his busy schedule in the fall of 2019 to chat by phone from his home in New Zealand, discuss his career in international baseball, and share some advice for students seeking a career in sports.

DON'T BE AFRAID TO COLD-CALL PEOPLE YOU RESPECT

For more than a decade in Flynn's professional life, former LA Dodgers general manager Fred Claire has served as one of his mentors. Since Flynn had never played or worked for the Dodgers organization, a fair question to ask is how he came to know Claire, who spent thirty years in various roles with that franchise.

"I basically cold-called Fred about fifteen years ago," Flynn explained, "just because I knew about him as a legend in the industry and heard wonderful things about him and he was so successful and well-spoken of among friends and everything I'd read. I called him as I was trying to get a company off the ground, and I'd always been a baseball guy."

For Flynn, it wasn't at all intimidating to simply pick up the phone and cold-call Claire. "As an American, I wasn't shy about calling people that I respected or had read about that I think I would respect. I called Fred and, really, from that first phone call, he's never left my side. We hit it off immediately, and he saw someone who was passionate and like himself, and we just really never stopped talking. And all of the big decisions in my life, I've relied on him in the fifteen years since, since my early to mid-thirties. I'm very fortunate to be one of the people that he gives time to in life."

Of course, not everybody has that type of confidence when it comes to simply picking up the phone and calling up a busy sports executive. As Flynn said, though, if the goal is to build a professional relationship and have that individual as a mentor, it's an action worth taking.

After all, as long as you articulate yourself in a professional manner and explain the purpose of your reaching out, what's the worst that can happen? "I don't see what the harm is—other than hearing rejection or just someone not picking up," he said. "I don't know why you wouldn't call anybody in the world that you want to call. I mean, what's the harm? If you think that someone out there can assist you—and you have a passion for something—there's no harm in chasing anyone down in the world who you respect, who you've read about, who you think can make a difference in your life. Just because you haven't been connected with them before doesn't mean you can't be connected with them in the future. That's simply a phone call or a well-written e-mail. Communication is so important in the world—[for example,] to know how to get a message across or write an effective e-mail laying out what you want to do in life.

"Again, that's what I've done, and that's helped me a great deal. I think some of that is the American in me, even though I've lived half of my life outside of America. But I think that [it's] really, really important to chase [whatever it is that you want]. If you chase the jobs you want, why wouldn't you chase the people that you want to meet?

"The only bad thing that can come out of that is a 'No,' and you've gotta put that past you immediately. I've been on both sides. I've worked for Anheuser-Busch, where I've given out money in sponsorship. I've been on the national body side—the international baseball side—where I'm basically a professional beggar, begging for money and resources to help small programs grow. I'm used to rejection. I really don't feel it at all. People need to just dust off immediately that one [rejection] phone call—[and then] two minutes later, jump on the next phone call. That's what it's about. You're gonna hit it eventually if you stay with it—and [if] you have a passion, you're gonna get it."

THE ART OF FUNDRAISING: HAVE PASSION WHEN YOU'RE SELLING

A major part of Flynn's responsibilities in sports involves fundraising, which, naturally, never intimidates him because of his outgoing personality. He added, too, that one has to exhibit a strong level of passion when communicating with the other side, whether the task is fundraising or doing sales. Having that passion is key and is something he would advise students to be aware of, especially if they wish to work in college athletics or any position in sports, as fundraising and/or sales tends to be a big part of the job.

"[It's important that] you find something that you enjoy—and it doesn't have to be the biggest passion, but you enjoy it," Flynn explained. "[Perhaps] you like working for a certain group of people—they're good family or you have a good boss—or you believe in the mission, [or] you believe in the institution you're selling.

"To me, that's what it's about. You find it. You have a passion for it. If you can speak about it as an authority on it, people feel when someone is passionate. Passion is what keeps you going when you have nothing. You have no money. You have no resources. It's what brings people on board to believe in your vision, and so you're gonna hook people. If you want to make people believe as much as you believe, that's selling. It's difficult for a lot of people to sell what they don't believe in, and people can see through that. So if you find something you love—even if you have to start [at an] entry level but if you believe in it and you know it—that should be a pretty simple thing. You just face rejection and just bounce back.

"I mean, it's difficult when you get to the doorstep and you work for months and months and months, and then you fail. But one out of one hundred, you're gonna hit. And when I arrived in New Zealand, there were about two hundred baseball players in the country and we had no staff—and just my wife and my family in 2009. They brought me out to be the CEO of the national baseball program and try to rival Australia and play on the world stage. It was a big gamble. There was nothing here. I had to build [everything] from scratch, and all the equipment in the country was in our little garage. We had, like, two bags of baseballs.

"Now, we've gotten already all the way to twenty-fifth in the world. We have two dozen kids playing college baseball. We've been in the Ripken World Series six times [and] the Little League World Series. We have eight kids who've been signed by Major League Baseball teams. We have eight thousand players. We've gone from three clubs to twenty-two clubs in the country. It's been a good run . . . [and it's] all based on early passion because I believed in what I was doing—which just was nonstop, just selling the program with the same messaging. And you're going to find people who believe in it if you believe in it. You just have to make them care. Make people care about what you care about. That's it."

OPPORTUNITIES ARE OUT THERE IF YOU'RE WILLING TO RELOCATE

Flynn firmly believes that opportunities are out there if you're willing to travel or relocate. Yet there are some who may not be willing or able to do so. Having experienced the thrill of traveling to multiple countries and seeing the world, Flynn offered some advice to those who might be hesitant in terms of relocating. "They would just cut their chances down," he said matter-of-factly. "If they have opportunities in their neighborhood and their state or in their country—and if they're not willing to travel—then that's their decision. But you certainly have [fewer] opportunities if you're not willing to move about [and] see what's out there. It's a great, big, wonderful world. And if you've got a few skills—everybody's got a few things they can do well—and if you look around, you might find the best opportunities are far, far away from home.

"It's not easy all the time leaving extended family, but sometimes the rewards are a lot greater when you succeed in other places—because you did it on your own and, to some degree, you toughed it out. And then you can always go home again. So, to me, I can't imagine another life other than seeing the world. There's so many good people, even with all the destruction and nastiness in the world, and so many opportunities out there around the world."

Flynn pointed to his own experience overseas as being extra meaningful in his life: "Who would've ever thought when I was a young kid playing college ball that I'd be in New Zealand building a baseball program that now is starting to make waves? I would never change any of that. It's made me exactly who I am, and it's intoxicating, traveling the world and meeting people who love what you love, and making allies around the world."

THE FUTURE OF INTERNATIONAL BASEBALL: OPPORTUNITIES ABOUND

Of course, Flynn first became involved with international baseball some time ago. He offered some advice for youngsters who have an interest in pursuing a career in the sport internationally.

"There's the World Baseball Classic. Even though baseball isn't in the Olympics in Paris in 2024, it'll probably be back in LA in 2028. A lot of countries are playing the game now at a very high level. You still have Major League Baseball as the 'big brother' that does a lot of the development programs and academies around the world. The World Baseball Softball Confederation based in Lausanne, Switzerland, is the international body for the sport of baseball. If they really have goals being in baseball, you've got all thirty major-league teams, you've got Minor League Baseball, you've got MLB in New York, [and] you've got independent baseball.

"And you've got international baseball, [where] the jobs aren't that plentiful unless you speak multiple languages and are willing to relocate and work for very little. But if you're a coach or a young administrator, there are some opportunities. And remember the Australian Baseball League? Well, we started a team in Auckland [in 2018]—the Auckland Tuatara—which we got off the ground after ten years. There are opportunities out there, but you have to call the national federations."

The Baseball Winter Meetings, added Flynn, are an event not to be overlooked. Anyone serious about seeking opportunities in the game, even internationally, should strongly consider attending the annual Winter Meetings, where valuable contacts can be made with the right people to point you in the right direction. "MLB always has internships, and you go to the Winter Meetings or the general manager meetings or the All-Star Game, and you'll see most people are there for those weekends, and those are good times to get your CV or résumé in front of folks. I've dealt with a lot of those people and I've given people internship opportunities all the way from Canada and America out here in New Zealand, to give them a head start. So there are people that will [give] them [that opportunity] if they're aggressive with their résumés."

LOVE THE GAME IF YOU WANT TO WORK IN IT

During his tenure in New Zealand, Flynn hired his fair share of employees. What would he say he looked for in a candidate or in somebody that he would potentially hire? "It depends on what I'm looking for," he said. "I've hired a bunch of people— coaches, administrators, marketing people, website designers—so it depends on what you're looking for. But basically, you look for the normal [traits]: a keen interest in baseball and strong references. I do think it pays to know the game a little bit when you're trying to get into the game. I know skills are transferable, but I do look for people that love and enjoy the game because you have to put in a lot of time in the sport for very little money to start out with. So if you do love the game and feel like you're contributing to the success of an organization, it's something that you love, that's important. Now, you can convert people to love the game, but that just takes a little bit longer. But then, the basics: the strong grades, a strong background, very diverse, willing to travel, open-minded . . . those are things I'd looked for in the past."

VALUABLE LESSONS LEARNED APPLICABLE TO A CAREER IN SPORTS

Having had his share of mentors along the way, Flynn was willing to share his experience and advice with others wanting to work in sports. In terms of lessons he's learned throughout his professional career, he believes there are several that are valuable for youngsters seeking a career in the sports world:

1. Realize you can carve out your own path—and pursue that path. "For me, you can tell I went my own way. I didn't go through MLB. I'm an American, but I didn't drive three hours to Yankee Stadium—even though I know [Yankees general manager] Brian Cashman—and try to get a job with the Yankees. I carved out my own path. I love to travel. You know, you've got to make yourself invaluable, right? You've got to carve out a niche that other people can't do or won't do—that you believe you can do better than anyone, right? So you've got to go out and carve out your own. I'd made jobs open up through my gift of gab—and my passion."

2. Take the initiative and show how you bring value to your organization. "I carved out gigs that I wanted to do and that I wanted to be a part of. And so that's really important. You're not gonna get hired if you're just another number, right? There are a lot of smart people in the world, and you've got to find a way to add value to an organization. And you'll hear this a million times, but you've got to show that you'll do what you'll bring to the table. And I turned this job from executive officer into CEO because I showed the organization what it needed. I wrote the proposal [outlining] where the organization should go. I didn't wait for someone to tell me where the organization should go. So I knew, from my experience—even though it wasn't a ton of experience—I felt like I knew where they needed to go, and they bought into it once they saw my proposal. So I didn't wait for their proposal. I told them. I think that's pretty important."

3. Have passion in what you do. Like many executives in sports, Flynn has his own personal mantra, one he has followed throughout his career. "I think the one big one that I'm known for in the baseball world—and wherever I'm known, because I get around a lot and I know a lot of people in the baseball and business worlds—is passion. I champion underdog stories. I love startups. I love getting something built. I'm not a maintainer. I don't want to sit and just maintain. I don't want to sit in a cubicle. I'm on the move and [that] fits my personality. And I do like to find jobs and opportunities and starts that fit my personality. But the biggest one is passion. I have to be doing what I love, or it's just not worth it. "Again, if you have a passion for something, you'll build a group of people who believe in the same thing—if you could effectively tell that story and bring that passion to other folks. So, for me, I have to have passion. I'm moving into coffee now. We're building a coffee plantation in Palau, on a small island. My wife is from Palau, and I love the island and I love the people and I love the product. So for me, it's another passion where I know that I'll have the energy and I know we'll be successful because

I enjoy everything about it. If I didn't, if I was selling vacuum cleaners door-to-door, I just wouldn't. So I'd rather take less money and enjoy what I do for the amount of time you have to put into it—than the opposite."

A FINAL PIECE OF ADVICE: AIM HIGH AND JUST GO FOR IT

When asked to provide a final piece of advice for students wanting a career in sports, Flynn offered the following suggestion: Know what you want and go for it—even if you have to travel outside of your comfort zone. "Pick out what area in sports you want to be in, because there's multiple areas. There's marketing, scouting, coaching . . . and then, scour the world. Start realistically where you want to be, where you think you can be, and aim high.

"If you fall back, you fall back in the middle somewhere. But aim as high as you can and go for what you love. And if it doesn't work, then fine. Everybody typically has more than one passion—or you can have more than one passion, right? I love baseball, but I also love the outdoors and I love my family. I love fishing. Find things in sport that you love the most, and don't be deterred. There are a lot of opportunities out there. You may have to travel a little further. You might have to do some jobs you don't dig right out of the gate. But at the end of the day, if you really want it, you'll get it. Just face rejection and go for it."

Conclusion

Parting Words of Wisdom

DARRYL DUNN, ROSE BOWL OPERATING COMPANY
CEO AND GENERAL MANAGER

Darryl Dunn has served as CEO and general manager for the Rose Bowl Operating Company (RBOC) in Pasadena, California, since 1999. The RBOC is the organization that manages the Rose Bowl, one of the most famous venues in sporting history. As CEO/GM, Dunn is responsible for managing all aspects of the Rose Bowl facility, including contract negotiations with prospective events, ongoing relationships with existing tenants, marketing, finance, operational needs for the stadium, tournament operations, and long-term strategic planning.

In a conversation with me, Dunn offered some leadership lessons that can be beneficial to anyone interested in a career in sports and sports management.

Lead by Example

"I think it's similar to being involved in athletics or competition," Dunn said. "It's inspiring others, leading by example. That's the number-one thing. If you expect people to work hard, you better work hard. You need to show that you care, that you're passionate about something, that you're very responsible. Also, show them personal support as well as professional support. Everybody has a life that they go home to. You need to respect that and support that."

Don't Take Things Personally When Dealing with Criticism

Being in top management positions, there's always criticism that comes along with the job. Dunn's advice on dealing with criticism: "I think you just try to not take it personal[ly]. It's hard sometimes. But also, if you can reflect on it and try to understand the other person's perspective, [that's a way to deal with it]. When I have been criticized, usually I'll try to go to that person who's critical of me and try to understand why. And also, I think people will know that you care, which does alleviate it.

"At the same time, [with] some criticisms, you just can't help it. At the end of day, you're going to look in the mirror and know that you've done the best that you possibly can do, and you can't take it personal[ly]."

Make Yourself Stand Out

"I've always said this: The hardest job in the world I've ever had was trying to get a job," said Dunn. "It's a full-time job, and it's a tough, tough, tough job. It's full of rejections, and it's so hard. But as long as you're willing to work hard, and go in and volunteer or intern, [you'll get that opportunity]. But you need to do something that makes yourself stand out. I notice [the hard workers in my organization, as do other managers in their own respective organizations]. I notice people who are here early and stay late. [Even though] I'm here early and I stay late—and I work a lot—I'm never the first one here, and I'm never the last one here, ever."

When Dunn sees his staffers willing to go that extra mile to get the job done, he knows those individuals do indeed possess the qualities needed to be strong leaders, whether that's within the organization or elsewhere down the road.

Develop Good People Skills

Because working in sports means dealing with people—whether they're customers, clients, coworkers, or management—knowing how to effectively interact with others is a skill that can't be overlooked. That includes, for instance, communicating using good body language and knowing how to make proper eye contact. "Having people skills [is certainly critical]: Just looking somebody in the eye and just being helpful, [for example]."

Keep Improving Yourself

Dunn provides his own example when discussing the importance of recognizing opportunities to improve upon one's own skill sets: "It's important [too] to realize that no matter where you are, there's always ways to improve and get better. When I was going for this job [with the Rose Bowl] and the opportunity was available, I knew part of this position involved public speaking, which I didn't enjoy very much. At first, I hired a personal coach to help me with it, and he told me to join Toastmasters. I did, and I was fortunate enough to realize that was going to be an important part of the job and I needed to improve and get better. So always look at yourself in the mirror and try to be honest with yourself, and ask yourself, 'What can you do to get better?' For me, it was public speaking, and I did something about it."

To sum up, Dunn went back to the key qualities for anyone looking for a career in sports: "So hard work, dedication, good people skills . . . there are a few [other qualities essential for a sports business professional], but those would be the biggest ones. I'm a huge believer in the idea that the cream usually rises to the top. But you have to put yourself in that position. You have to have the right attitude. You're going to have to work your tail off."

MATT BLANEY, CALIFORNIA LEAGUE DIRECTOR OF OPERATIONS/MARKETING

Matt Blaney, whose father Charlie spent thirty-two years working in the LA Dodgers organization, got his start in professional baseball as a pitcher in the minor leagues: one year with the Dodgers and two with the Red Sox. After realizing he wasn't going to reach the majors, he followed in his dad's footsteps by staying in the game via the front office route and even had the opportunity to work with him in what was then the California League. The younger Blaney spoke with me to give insights to students aspiring to work in the sports industry.

The first point Blaney made is the importance of staying in touch with people in the industry because you never know when an opportunity will come up. "When I got done playing," he said, "I kept in contact with a lot of other people in the two organizations that I'd played for. One of them moved on and was in scouting with the Cincinnati Reds, so I called him. I was living out in Baltimore at the time, and he said there was an opening as a scout out there, but I would need to go to scout school. So I went to scout school and worked for another scout in the area down in Baltimore, in the Delaware area, in Virginia, and a little bit into Pennsylvania."

Blaney soon realized, though, that his interest was more in player development, not scouting. "My father always said to look at scouting and player development as 'scouting hooks them and player development cooks them.' I prefer the player development side and statistical side and analytical side, as opposed to traveling just for the love of the game to see one player." After attending the Winter Meetings in 2004 to seek job opportunities, he landed a few interviews and ultimately received a one-year internship with the Vero Beach Dodgers in Florida. "That internship allowed me to do pretty much everything in baseball, from working for a minor-league team in ticket sales and sponsorships and everything that goes along with it to player development—because part of the internship was to run the Gulf Coast League [now known as the Florida Complex League] team, which is all player development. So that allowed me to gain some experience in that aspect of the game."

After stints with the Arizona Fall League in Peoria (in operations management) and with the Washington Nationals (as manager of Florida operations), Blaney joined his father in helping run the California League. "Being able to work side-by-side with my father has just been an amazing opportunity. He says that he learned this from people like Fred Claire and Peter O'Malley, where in baseball it's always better to work with 'good people' first as opposed to 'good baseball people.' The idea is to surround yourself with good, loyal, honest, hardworking people. And if they happen to know baseball, then that's even better, as opposed to going for maybe somebody who knows baseball but doesn't have some of those qualities I've just described."

An important lesson here for students wanting to get their foot in the door: Don't worry if you feel you don't know enough about the sport. From management's perspective, they always want to hire those "good people" first; then management can teach them what they need on the job. "It's tough to learn to be loyal, hardworking, and dedicated," Blaney said. "But learning stats and, on the player development side, learning the analytics, that's something that you can do. Or learning how to sell sponsorships or doing ticket sales if you work at the minor-league level. These are things that you can learn on the job."

In terms of what he has learned that he can pass on to students looking to work in sports, Blaney offered a few thoughts: "I've only ever worked in baseball, but I imagine some of this apply to most industries. One thing you need to be ready to do: Be ready and willing to go beyond your job responsibilities and help out another part of the organization. That's especially [important] when you're starting out, and it doesn't matter what your job title is, and whether your role is in player development, scouting, or ticket sales.

"When I was with the Nationals, even though I was technically a minor-league employee and working for player development, I often would field phone calls from scouts looking for help on their side, whether it's paperwork or whatever. So you've just gotta be willing to put on many different hats and help out however many people you need to, regardless if it's in your job description or not, because these professional teams often don't have a lot of staff or the budget for them. So you've gotta be willing to help out a scout with some report, and then maybe help out a minor-league coach who needs some help. I'd even throw batting practice or hit ground balls sometimes if they were down a coach—I'd change out of my office clothes and go out on the field and do it.

"And ask to do it. Don't just wait to do it. Just say, 'Hey, if you need some help, if you need someone to drive this player to the airport, yeah, I'll do it. If you need somebody to run this package over to the stadium, yeah, I'll leave the office and do it.' You just gotta be willing to help out as many people as you can in each department."

Also be willing to move anywhere at any time, said Blaney. "Most people that I know in the industry have moved away or have changed locations multiple times early on in their career. So if you're willing to move cities, move across the country, move an hour away, move five states away, whatever it is, to get that opportunity, then I think that you need to be willing to jump on that."

ROSS PORTER, BASEBALL BROADCASTER

Ross Porter, who earned a radio journalism degree at the University of Oklahoma, spent twenty-eight years as a play-by-play announcer for the LA Dodgers from 1977 to 2004. He also called NFL games and college basketball for NBC Sports in the 1970s.

Even in his eighties, Porter has continued to dedicate himself to the job, calling games for the Cal State Northridge Matadors baseball team as if he were at Dodger Stadium. For the online broadcast on GoMatadors.com, he studies statistics and background information for anecdotes. He also spends time with the coaches to find out interesting tidbits he can pass along to listeners.

To help students and youngsters aspiring to work as sports announcers someday, Porter offered the following advice.

The Dodger Days

"Preparation is very important when you're getting ready for a broadcast. You must learn all you can about the teams you'll be talking about on the air. When I was with the Dodgers for twenty-eight years, I kept separate files on each team that I would see. In each file, I would put newspaper articles or notes, magazine stories, or personal questions that needed to be answered. At the stadium, you'll be provided much information on each team by that team's publicity department before each game. I would take a yellow highlighter and mark the notes that would make for a better broadcast."

Establish Rapport with Your Sources

"Talking to the coaches, managers, or players before the game will also give you stories that will make you sound very informed. If someone gives you information and asks you not to quote him, always honor his wishes and not betray him. That trust can lead to a long-term working relationship with the other person."

Develop Your Own Style

"As far as being an announcer, practice calling games by sitting in front of a TV set, turning the volume off, and talking into a small tape recorder as you describe the action of the game you are watching. Then listen to your tape and review what you sounded like, what you thought was good and what you didn't like. Develop a style to your broadcasts. Do this over and over again."

Know the Rules and the Names

"Know the rules of the sport you are announcing. In baseball, what's the infield fly rule? In football, the fair catch rule; in basketball, the difference in a charge and a block. Very important is the pronunciation of the players' names. Go over every name. [Hopefully] there is a pronunciation guide in every team's publication. If not, ask someone to give you the names you're not sure about. Nothing is worse than mispronouncing a player's name because it shows you didn't do your homework. There will be people listening who will laugh at the way you missed a name."

Passion and Accuracy

"What personal skills are required? A passion for what you are doing that shows on the air, and a desire to be better today than you were yesterday. Accuracy is highly important. Get your facts right, work on making your comments shorter than longer—less is best—and don't be afraid to accept criticism after you ask a member of your family or a close friend to give you an honest answer on how they think you are doing. Continue to tape yourself, listen to the tape, and make adjustments."

Preparing for a Broadcasting Career

"What education or training is required? No parent wants to hear me say this, but it's true: Going to college may broaden your education and make you more intelligent, but it won't replace the needed experience you'll get working for a small radio station to begin your livelihood. Having a college degree, which I have, meant nothing in advancing my broadcasting career. In high school, my most important class was typewriting because it taught me how to put my thoughts on paper faster. Journalism classes introduced me to writing. That became essential as I wrote everything myself in preparing scripts for my broadcasts. No other person ever typed a word for me. I have never used a teleprompter even once."

JEFF PEARLMAN, SPORTSWRITER AND *NEW YORK TIMES* BEST-SELLING AUTHOR

Jeff Pearlman is the *New York Times* best-selling author of nine books, including *The Bad Guys Won* (a biography of the 1986 New York Mets, published in 2004), *Boys Will Be Boys* (a biography of the 1990s Dallas Cowboys, published in 2008), and *Showtime* (a biography of the 1980s LA Lakers, published in 2014). He has also written biographies of sports legends Barry Bonds (2006), Roger Clemens (2009), Walter Payton (2011), and Brett Favre (2016). His eighth book, *Football for a Buck: The Crazy Rise and Crazier Demise of the USFL*, was released in 2019 and his most recent book, as of the time of our interview, was *Three-Ring Circus: Kobe, Shaq, Phil, and the Crazy Years of the Lakers Dynasty*, released in 2020. His biography of Bo Jackson is expected to be released in 2022.

A former *Sports Illustrated* senior writer—as well as ESPN.com columnist and staff writer for *Newsday* and the (Nashville) *Tennessean*—Pearlman presently writes a weekly column for the *Athletic* while contributing to other sites and publications, ranging from *Bleacher Report* to the *Wall Street Journal* to *Sports Illustrated* to CNN.com. He also maintains a personal online blog, *The Quaz*, where he posts a regular Q&A series with athletes, politicians, actors, singers, and many others.

Pearlman took some time out of his schedule in the summer of 2019 to offer some advice to students seeking a career in sportswriting:

1. If you're a student wanting to become a sportswriter someday, start creating content now. Start now. There are so many outlets that didn't exist when I was coming up. So start a Facebook page that focuses only on lefty relief pitchers from Guam. Or kickers named Joe. Start a blog. Start a podcast. Tweet. There are just endless ways. And when I was a kid, you really only had the student newspaper and maybe [a] radio station. There are no excuses today.

2. If your dream is to write best-selling sports books, prove yourself first by writing articles and learn the writing profession. I was a baseball writer for *Sports Illustrated*, and an agent reached out to me. I'd never thought much about becoming an author, but we discussed the idea of the 1986 New York Mets—a team I appreciated hugely as a kid growing up in the Empire State. So I put together a proposal, shopped it, and had HarperCollins bid. And here I am. As for young people, I think I'd say—walk before you can run. A book done well is torture mixed with pleasure. But largely torture. You're alone with your thoughts, a laptop, and seventeen Coca-Colas. You love what you wrote, then hate it, then maybe like it. It's hard work that beats you down. So when I meet people with limited experience who say, "I wanna write a book!"—I think,

"Great. But first, write some articles. Learn the profession. Get acclimated. Then 100 percent go for it."

3. When approaching an interview subject whom you believe may be difficult and not want to answer your questions, start out by building a rapport with that person. I always carry a baseball bat in my trunk. Kidding. One of the oldest tricks in the book is saving your "hard" questions. Get the person talking first. Find commonalities: "Oh, you're from Boise? So's my aunt. What part?" Ask questions the subject is happy to answer. Nothing threatening. Then, once the relationship has softened, say, "Look, I know this is a hard question, but . . ." It generally works. Also, be authentic. Always be authentic. These are human beings.

BILL SHUMARD, SPORTS NONPROFIT PRESIDENT/CEO

Bill Shumard served as president/CEO of Special Olympics Southern California (SOSC) from June 2005 through 2020, helping the organization become recognized as one of Special Olympics' premier programs in the worldwide movement that serves nearly 5 million athletes in 180 countries.

What got Shumard interested in sports business was both his love for baseball and his passion for college sports. "I grew up in Southern California and actually was schooled a lot on baseball by listening to a young red-headed announcer by the name of Vin Scully," he said. "Listening to it a lot on the radio with Vinny, reading a lot in the newspaper, my passion really fueled my competence in the spoken word, the written word. So, because I could write about it [and] talk about it, I became a journalism major at Long Beach State. When I was there, I was in the Sports Information Department. They hired me in that job full-time when I graduated. I did that for three years before the Dodgers called and offered me a low-level, entry-level position."

Shumard began working for the Dodgers in 1975 and ended up staying for twelve years. During that time, he was promoted three times, ultimately becoming the club's director of community services and special events, a position he held for his last seven years with the team. "But my goal was to be a college athletic director, so I left the Dodgers [in 1988 and joined] the University of Southern California and their Athletic Department to learn athletic fundraising. I knew if I was going to be an athletic director, I needed to learn how to fundraise." While initially anxious about the idea, Shumard soon understood that fundraising actually wasn't as daunting if you believed in the product you were selling. "When I got to USC in a fundraising position, I said, 'This isn't any different than how we would market or sell the Dodgers!' It's just a different audience, and it's having an excellent product that you're passionate about that sells itself! Whether it's Dodger baseball or it's Special Olympics, they're unique products that create a lot of passion and have a lot of sellability to them."

In 1994, Shumard reached his "ultimate career goal" when he returned to his alma mater, Long Beach State, to serve as athletic director for ten years. Five years into his tenure, he became a volunteer member of the SOSC's Board of Directors when the SOSC's biggest competitive event of the year was moved to the LBSU campus. "After five years, the chairman of the board said, 'We've gone through about three CEOs in seven years. You need to come in here and take this job—and run it like a sports organization.' That was the spring of 2005—and it's the best job I've ever had."

What lessons can students looking to work in sports today learn from Shumard's successful career path? "When I give speeches in graduate-level business classes," he said, "I tell them that you gotta find that intersection, that sweet spot, where your competence meets your passion because that's where your significance will be in life. If that's sports, then where specifically, in what discipline, and at what level. In my early years with the Dodgers, I was just a little guy on the totem pole. I wasn't doing a whole lot that I was passionate about. I had to learn to be really competent so that I could set myself apart from other people and be trusted with bigger stuff."

Shumard also took the lessons he learned at Dodger Stadium to heart, applying those principles at each stop after leaving baseball. "In those days, the Dodgers were one of the top one hundred companies in America. *Forbes* and the *Wall Street Journal* would send business reporters to Dodger Stadium to interview Fred Claire. He'd tell them, 'We have this secret formula. Come to work early. Stay until the job is done. Return every call within sixty minutes. Return every piece of mail within twenty-four business hours. When you make a mistake, own it. Treat everybody from the switchboard operator to the owner of the club with the dignity and the respect they deserve.' Fred's message was this: 'When you get everybody in the organization executing to a level of excellence in these basic competence areas, you're going to have a great organization.' I remember Fred bought a pair of shoes at Nordstrom one time, and he was so impressed with how he was serviced, he called us all in. We got the lecture of how Nordstrom sold those shoes and the service they provided for him, and the message was we'd better be treating our clientele that way, too. I took those lessons with me wherever I've gone.

"[I'll also share this story from] four years ago [about] a guy on my board, a high-level grocery executive with a grocery chain down here. He got us a check-stand campaign fundraiser, which means that for an entire month in that market chain when you go to buy your groceries, they ask you when you pay your bill if you want to round up your bill and donate anything to Special Olympics. He said, 'We're going to give this to the Special Olympics in Southern California for the month of July. You'll make a million dollars on it!' He calls me three weeks into July and says, 'Congratulations, Bill! You went over the million-dollar mark today.' Then, he goes into the list of competence [areas], saying, 'We love you guys because you come to work early, you stay late, you return every call, you're responsible, you're trustworthy, you're thorough . . .' It's pretty exciting, and I said, 'Those things Fred and the Dodgers pounded into the head of a twenty-six-year-old kid, three decades earlier, just raised a million dollars to change a lot of lives.' It all came from what I call a twelve-year doctoral degree that I earned at Dodger Stadium."

A final piece of advice from Shumard, who also serves as chair of Long Beach State's Advisory Council for the Graduate Program in Sport Management: Be proactive, not passive. "One thing we try to teach at our [graduate] program [in Sport Management at Long Beach State], where every student has to do three internships in eighteen months, is to get the students out there early and often—and get past that passivity because you're not going to get ahead unless you're competent enough to lead yourself and sell yourself. And I'm talking about doing it with integrity, class, and dignity, and not overselling yourself. Just like with any career, sports is absolutely the same. If you're going to advance, you have to build the network. You have to ask the questions. You have to expose yourself to different things. One of my keys at the Dodgers: Since I was so low on the totem pole, I ended up taking on a lot of things that nobody else wanted. I built the whole department there in twelve years, and in the process learned a whole lot more than what I learned initially with a journalism degree. That prepared me better for going out and advancing my career. Talking to people that were farther along in their career that had been successful, asking for their advice, observing them, picking good mentors . . . all of that is part of the process."

CHARLES HARRIS, SPORTS MANAGEMENT IN BASEBALL AND HOCKEY
Charles Harris serves as an adjunct professor and internship coordinator for the Long Beach State sports management program while also running his own social media consulting group. A graduate of the University of California, Irvine, he has spent much of his career in sports management, having worked for the LA Dodgers, the team then known as the California Angels, and the Mighty Ducks of Anaheim. During his time with the Dodgers, Harris took the advice of play-by-play broadcaster Vin Scully and went to Israel in the mid-1990s. He wound up spending eight years there, learning to speak Hebrew and building a successful marketing and communications company.

"When students approach me for advice about their future sports manage-ment careers, there are a lot of things I tell them," Harris said. "First, they've gotta figure out what area they want to work in. At Long Beach State, it's an eighteen-month program where the students are required to have internships. So part of what I tell them is, get some practical experience but also learn as much as what you want to do as much as you don't want to do.

"The second thing is, you gotta get your foot in the door. The job opportuni-ties that you get aren't going to be your last. But start providing value. And, really, I learned the 'Dodger Way' of doing business. That starts from being first in and being last out, and always be willing to do jobs. When I talk to students all the time, it's, 'How do you build a thriving network of people that you know that you can exceed their expectations?'" You do that, Harris explained, so that people will trust you, and you'll trust them to help you in your career—simply because we all need a little help in the sports industry, to help push our careers forward.

Harris also elaborated on being exposed to the "Dodger Way." Working for the Dodgers, he explained, enabled him to learn important life lessons that can be applied to just about any field: "First, best business practices, work ethic, and how you treat your team starts from the top down. Leaders emulate their bosses and mentor. Peter O'Malley, the team owner, and Fred Claire, the general manager, set the right examples for all employees, all the time.

"Second, come early and stay late. Of course, working in baseball will never be known as a 9-to-5 job—it starts long before the first fans arrive and often ends after the sportswriters file their stories. When you're passionate about your job, the clock matters less.

"A third lesson comes from my former spring-training roommate and Dodgers executive Robert Schweppe, who's often spoken to my graduate sports manage-ment classes at Long Beach State. One of his key messages is this: Make yourself valuable. Find out what others aren't doing or won't do—and then start doing it. Volunteer for assignments outside of your comfort zone. When leaders saw him take the initiative, he became more and more valuable.

"Fourth, answer your phone. Return all messages. Answer your e-mails. Like everybody else, communication is nonstop these days. That said, Dodger execu-tives always knew to be available and return requests. This has always stayed with me."

The final piece of advice Harris had for students: Take advantage of opportu-nities that present themselves. This could entail working with other professors to achieve a long-term dream, transitioning an internship into a full-time position after graduation, or simply just getting a foot in the door of where you want to be.

"The following story is one of the latter," Harris said. "A very intelligent woman who graduated from the Long Beach State program was seeking a position in college athletics with a top-tier Division I program. One day, while walking on campus, she learned that the decision maker wanted to interview her in the next ten minutes. The problem was, the call came as a complete surprise and she wasn't prepared for the interview. She'd just completed a morning workout and was dressed in sweats and a T-shirt—not exactly what anyone wants to wear for a job interview."

Thinking quickly, the woman approached another student, a freshman whom she'd never met. The other woman appeared to be about the same size and weight and was wearing an outfit suited for an interview. "The grad student in the sports program had the nerve to approach this stranger and ask if she'd agree to briefly switch clothes so she could interview properly," Harris continued. "Surprisingly, the other student agreed. So they swapped garments in the bathroom and, as it turned out, the woman secured the job. But had she not taken the chance and approached the stranger, she may not have the great position she has today."

The lesson here: Take chances when given an opportunity. "For that former student of mine, it certainly paid off. And, to finish off the story, once in a while, she told me, she sees this stranger around. They smile, but it's an awkward smile, and then they each move on without saying a word."

KURT COLICCHIO, FORT COLLINS FOXES BASEBALL CLUB OWNER

A graduate of the USC Marshall School of Business Entrepreneur Program, Kurt Colicchio is an experienced entrepreneur who has been involved in sports for three decades. But he didn't start out in sports. Upon graduation, Colicchio started and operated a movie prop rental business in Hollywood, California, before selling it five years later. That's when he transitioned into baseball, becoming a part owner of the Yakima Bears, a minor-league affiliate of the Arizona Diamondbacks.

Since 2004, he's been the owner of the Fort Collins Foxes Baseball Club, a collegiate summer team in the Mountain Collegiate Baseball League.

For people unfamiliar with collegiate summer leagues, Colicchio offered an explanation. "There are teams like ours in summer leagues all over the country," he said, adding that Fort Collins, Colorado, is an hour north of Denver. "Some of the more famous leagues are the Cape Cod League and Northwoods League. What these leagues do is they provide college players a place to play during the summer when college baseball is done. We play in June and July, maybe creep into August a little bit. We offer players a chance to play in a league where we use wooden bats. Major-league scouts like that because they get to see college kids hit with wood or pitch to wood—because normally, in college baseball, they use aluminum bats. And scouts want to see guys use wood because that's what they'll be using if they go pro. We operate our team a lot like a Minor League Baseball team in that we do promotions and special events at every game, giveaways, between-inning contests for kids, and things like that."

What that means in terms of job opportunities for students looking to gain experience working in sports is that just like teams in MiLB, there are summer positions available in various areas with clubs in every collegiate summer league across North America. "Every year we hire a publicity intern," Colicchio explained, referring to his own franchise, "and that person writes our press releases after every game and handles any media relations. They update our Twitter and Facebook accounts also. That's a great position for students wanting to get into sports journalism—or any journalism, really—because it gives them hands-on opportunities to have relationships with people in the media.

"We also have a number of game operations internship positions available each summer for students. It's good for those interns because if you're going to go into a lot of sports jobs, you really need to have a bit of balance and experience in all facets of the operations. Doing game operations really does help students in terms of relations with fans and players, getting players on the team to cooperate with promotions and things like that."

The experience of working for a collegiate summer team gives students something to add to their résumés, added Colicchio. He makes a point of writing LinkedIn recommendations for his former interns, and he's especially excited when those determined to continue working their way up within the industry go on to achieve their dreams of working for big-league organizations. "I have one intern for me back in 2006 and she's now in ticket sales with the Texas Rangers. Another intern—who was actually a player at one time and then he got hurt and he interned for me the next season—is in charge of spring training operations with the Rangers. A couple of other interns who went into the sports field had limited success and then decided to do something else. Although not all of my interns stay in sports, they've done well in the careers that they've decided to do. They've all said the internship position with the Foxes help them a lot, because it gave them an understanding of customer service and pleasing your customers—pleasing the fans."

So what's the bottom line for students wanting to break into sports? "They should do a couple of internships, make some connections, and get some experience through those to build their résumés," said Colicchio. "Once you go on to look for a paying job in sports, you have to realize that you have to 'pay your dues.' Sports business is a lot like working in Hollywood or the recording industry. There's a lot of people that want to do that job and there's only so many jobs. They have to understand that they'll be working for a couple years for many hours for low pay, at the beginning, and that's like a waiting out process. If you stick with that for whatever [timeframe] you want to give yourself—let's say for a minimum of three years—then things start to get better in terms of job positions and pay. People need to realize they're not generally going to walk into a position that pays six figures right away. They're going to be working sixty hours a week plus and making enough to just get by. But if they can do that and understand they're going to have to do that for a few years, then opportunities along the way start really opening up more.

"Students or graduates need to know that's what they'll have to do. There'll be times where it's tough. I know people that have gone through this where it's tough to be working for low pay while your friends are making more money in a different career. But if you really want to stay in sports, stay with it and eventually 'the worm will turn.'"

Appendix: Useful Websites

There are thousands of websites related to careers in sports in North America. I am not attempting to provide a comprehensive list. What I do want to do is provide a list that some of the interview subjects in this book have recommended, as well as websites that may be of particular interest to readers. Note: These websites were accessible at the time this book was revised. I cannot guarantee that a site will be in operation at a later date.

Life in the Front Office   https://www.lifeinthefrontoffice.com/
    This podcast publishes regular interviews with sports industry leaders to provide insights for those interested in the world of sports business. The podcast features executive producer Jake Hirshman and cohosts Fred Claire, Andy Dolich, Pat Gallagher, and Rick Horrow, along with their guests.

Upwork   https://www.upwork.com/
    Upwork is a global freelancing platform where businesses and independent professionals can connect.

Baseball Winter Meetings   https://www.baseballwintermeetings.com/
    If you are looking for jobs in professional baseball, you can check out the website for the Baseball Winter Meetings.

Professional Baseball Employment Opportunities   https://www.pbeo.com/job_fair
.aspx
> The Professional Baseball Employment Opportunities website is the official
> employment service of Minor League Baseball, with most of the jobs available
> being internships and entry-level positions.

TeamWork Online   https://www.teamworkonline.com/
> TeamWork Online connects job seekers to careers in sports and live events,
> with the major professional leagues (MLB, NBA, NFL, NHL, and MLS) re-
> cruiting employees through its platform.

Street & Smith's *Sports Business Journal*   https://www.sportsbusinessdaily.com
/Journal.aspx
> Street & Smith's *Sports Business Journal* provides news and information sports
> industry leaders need to succeed in their professions.

Hashtag Sports   https://hashtagsports.com/
> Hashtag Sports is a website providing insights sports industry leaders need to
> succeed in their professions.

Black Dog Hockey   https://bdehockey.com/
> Black Dog Hockey is a livestreaming and video-on-demand website that
> provides streaming coverage of both major high school hockey leagues in
> Southern California (the Anaheim Ducks and Los Angeles Kings High School
> Hockey League), as well as other hockey leagues and events.

Inside the League   http://insidetheleague.com/
> Inside the League is a consultancy for people in the game of football (agents,
> financial planners, scouts, and others) with the goal to help people succeed in
> the business of football. The site provides information, newsletters, tools, ar-
> chives, one-on-one assistance, and other resources for people in the business.

Succeed in Football   https://succeedinfootball.com/
> *Succeed in Football*, a blog written by Inside the League founder Neil Stratton,
> is a site with the goal of helping people succeed in the business of football.

Each of these websites will lead you to many more. Take the time to explore
the various sites and make your own evaluations about their value to you.

Bibliography

BOOKS

Bender, Gary, with Michael L. Johnson. *Call of the Game: What Really Goes on in the Broadcast Booth*. Chicago: Bonus Books, 1994.

Hendrick, Tom. *The Art of Sportscasting: How to Build a Successful Career*. Lanham, MD: Diamond Communications, 2000.

Horrow, Rick, with Rick Burton and Myles Schrag. *The Sport Business Handbook: Insights from 100+ Leaders Who Shaped 50 Years of the Industry*. Champaign, IL: Human Kinetics, 2020.

Joyce, Gare. *Future Greats and Heartbreaks: A Year Undercover in the Secret World of NHL Scouts*. Toronto: Doubleday Canada, 2010.

Rosenthal, Harold. *Baseball Is Their Business*. New York: Random House, 1952.

Shapiro, Ronald M., with James Dale. *The Power of Nice: How to Negotiate So Everyone Wins—Especially You!* Hoboken, NJ: Wiley, 2015.

Stratton, Neil. *Moving the Chains: A Parent's Guide to the NFL Draft Process*. CreateSpace Independent Publishing Platform, 2018.

WEBSITES

Clifford, Catherine. "Tony Robbins: This Is the Secret to Happiness in One Word." CNBC, October 6, 2017. https://www.cnbc.com/2017/10/06/tony-robbins-this-is-the-secret-to-happiness-in-one-word.html.

Gandy, Mark. "LinkedIn Is for MLB Bat Boys and College Students Too." LinkedIn, March 16, 2017. https://www.linkedin.com/pulse/5-questions-bat-boy-san-diego -padres-mark-gandy?trk=portfolio_article-card_title.

Garcia, Ahiza. "So You Want to Be a Sports Agent? Here's What You Should Know." *CNNMoney Sport*, May 26, 2018. https://money.cnn.com/2018/05/26 /news/sports-agent-russell-westbrook-giancarlo-stanton/index.html.

Halberstam, David J. "Catching up with Vin Scully." *Sports Broadcast Journal*, August 27, 2018. http://www.sportsbroadcastjournal.com/catching-up-with -vin-scully-the-great-master-shares-tips-for-announcers-and-others/.

Seifert, Kevin. "XFL Cancels Regular-Season Games, 'Committed' to Playing in 2021." ESPN, March 12, 2020. https://www.espn.com/xfl/story/_/id/28894247 /xfl-cancels-regular-season-games-committed-playing-2021.

INTERVIEWS
Interviews are listed in chronological order.

J. P. Hoornstra. Telephone interview, January 28, 2019, and November 20, 2020.

Charlie Blaney. Telephone interview, January 30, 2019.

Chris King. Telephone interview, January 31, 2019.

Ari Kaplan. Telephone interview, April 5, 2019.

Rick White. Telephone interview, April 5, 2019.

Steve Brener. Telephone interview, April 8, 2019.

Ross Porter. E-mail correspondence, April 11, 2019.

Pat Gallagher. Telephone interview, April 15, 2019.

Jake Hirshman. Telephone interview, April 16, 2019.

Bill Shumard. Telephone interview, April 18, 2019.

Andy Dolich. Telephone interview, April 24, 2019.

Darryl Dunn. Telephone interview, May 8, 2019.

Charles Harris. Telephone interview, May 10, 2019.

Richard Kee. Telephone interview, May 14, 2019.

Jeff Fellenzer. Telephone interview, May 15, 2019.

Ronald Shapiro. Telephone interview, June 4, 2019.

Jeff Pearlman. E-mail correspondence, June 19, 2019.

Ben Hwang. Telephone interview, August 9, 2019.

Marsha Collier. Telephone interview, August 21, 2019.

Ryan Flynn. Telephone interview, October 9, 2019.

Barry Turbow. Telephone interview, October 14, 2019.

Matt Blaney. Telephone interview, October 16, 2019.

Peter Seidler. Telephone interview, October 28, 2019.

Ted Sobel. Telephone interview, October 29, 2019.

Ann Meyers Drysdale. Telephone interview, February 25, 2020.

Kurt Colicchio. Telephone interview, February 27, 2020.

Neil Stratton. E-mail correspondence, February 28–March 5, 2020.

Marshall Payne. E-mail correspondence, March 2020–March 2021.

Steve Granado. Telephone interview, March 5, 2020.

Mark Gandy. E-mail correspondence, April 25, 2020.

Cole DeVos. E-mail correspondence, April 26, 2020.

Debbie Antonelli. Telephone interview, August 25, 2020.

Jeff Levering. Zoom interview, January 15, 2021.

Kris Budden. E-mail correspondence, February 2021–May 2021.

Ted Giannoulas. Telephone interview, February 19, 2021.

Aggie Dent. Zoom interview, March 30, 2021.

Sydney Noland. Zoom interview, April 7, 2021.

Chelsea Heyward. Zoom interview, April 22, 2021.

Russell Robards. Zoom interview, June 15, 2021.

Mark Langill. Telephone interview, June 23, 2021.

Index

Page numbers in *italic* refer to figures.

About the Author

K. P. Wee is an educator based in Vancouver, Canada, with a passion for helping students and writing about sports. The author of multiple sports-related books—including *The 1988 Dodgers: Reliving the Championship Season* (2018), *Tom Candiotti: A Life of Knuckleballs* (2014), *The Case for Barry Bonds in the Hall of Fame* (2021), *The End of the Montreal Jinx: Boston's Short-Lived Glory in the Historic Bruins-Canadiens Rivalry, 1988–1994* (2015), and several other baseball and hockey books—Wee graduated from the University of British Columbia in Vancouver with a degree in commerce and business administration. He has worked for the local Vancouver Canadians (Minor League Baseball) and Greater Vancouver Canadians (Major Midget Hockey) on the media relations and broadcasting side, and hosts a podcast called *The K. P. Wee Podcast.*

CPSIA information can be obtained
at www.ICGtesting.com
Printed in the USA
LVHW090905240723
753027LV00079B/41